UPROOTING RACISM

How White People Can
Work for Racial Justice

Paul Kivel

New Society Publishers

Library of Congress Cataloging-in-Publication Data:
  Uprooting racism : how white people can work for racial justice / Paul Kivel.
      p.   cm.
  Includes bibliographical references.
  ISBN 0-86571-337-5 (hdc.) — ISBN 0-86571-338-3 (pbk.)
      1. United States—Race relations.   2. Racism—United States.   3. Race
  awareness—United States.   4. Whites—United States—Race identity.   I.
  Title.
  E184.A1K477 1995   305.8'00973—dc20   95-36948

ISBN Hardcover   USA 0-86571-337-5   CAN 1-55092-276-9
ISBN Paperback   USA 0-86571-338-3   CAN 1-55092-277-7

Cover design by Margie Politzer. Book design by Martin Kelley. Printed on partially-recycled paper using soy-based ink by Capital City Press of Montpelier, Vermont.

To order directly from the publisher, add $3.00 to the price for the first copy, and add $1.00 (and GST in Canada) for each additional copy. Send check or money order to:

New Society Publishers
PO Box 189
Gabriola Island, BC V0R 1X0

Table of Contents

Tables of Lists, Exercises and Assessments

Publisher's Note

IN THIS BOOK, Paul Kivel is taking on a lot. He's speaking to white people as a fellow white person about a hush-hush subject: racism. He's speaking with an honesty that allows for confusion and for admission of his own inner prejudices. In an era when many whites express pride of the advancements of civil rights movement, he asks why so much of our world is still racially-proscribed.

Our society has been built upon a foundation of racism for so long that it's become part of the landscape: always there, seldom acknowledged. In this book, Kivel acknowledges and he questions. He asks us where we came from, he asks us what we know. He's resisted the temptation to make this a manual of political correctness, and has instead allowed us to share our own prejudices with him as we read.

Kivel challenges us to look at our place in society. Just because we've begun to unlearn racism doesn't mean the person washing the dishes of a favorite restaurant isn't still African American. Or that the editor of a favorite magazine isn't still a white person. Or that the taxi driver we hail isn't still classified an illegal alien by a government restricting immigration from darker-skinned regions of the world.

Paul Kivel doesn't give us pat answers to these dilemmas. He knows there will be no point at which we can sit back and consider our job completed. We must continue to wrestle with these questions, and in the confusion find moments of connection and of clarity.

Uprooting racism is of course a large task, much larger than any one of us. But by working in our communities, and by engaging with our neighbors, workmates, and friends, we can make a difference. May this book inspire and confuse you!

Martin Kelley
for the New Society Publishers

Acknowledgements

WE HAVE A long and distingu... history on this continent of white people who have fought against racism and racial violence. This history begins in the days of Bartolomew de Las Casas, a Spanish priest who documented the atrocities that Columbus and other early conquistadores committed against the Native Americans in the West Indies. It continues today with white people fighting against hate crimes, police brutality, housing and job discrimination, and the recent attacks against immigrants and poor people of color. These efforts by white people have been inspired by the constant, unrelenting fight by people of color for survival, for justice, and for an end to the political, economic and cultural exploitation they have experienced in this country.

My deepest gratitude goes to the multitudes of people of color who have challenged racism in small and large ways over the centuries, and who have demonstrated by their lives that the lies of racism are untrue, inhumane and violate the integrity of each person who colludes with injustice.

I am also proud to be Jewish and to be able to contribute to the historic struggle of Jewish people to survive waves of anti-Semitism and create our lives anew in the framework of freedom and justice that Judaism provides. I want to acknowledge my Jewish foreparents and the many Jews who are still on the frontlines of the battle for racial justice because they understand the connections between anti-Semitism and racism.

There are many people who have inspired my work and writing, most of whom I have never met. I have read their words, heard their songs, seen their actions and hope to be true to their vision.

I want to specifically acknowledge those who I have learned from and who have supported my work in the last few years. They are Margot Adair, Martin Cano, Jim Coates, Hari Dillon, Steve Falk, Isoke Femi, Margot Gibney, Sonia

Jackson, David Landes, Lee Mun-Wah, Namane Mohlabane, Daphne Muse, Ayana Morse, and Kiran Rana, and to my mother Betty Jean Kivel.

I also thank my wonderful "Jews schmooze" group: Alina Evers, Chaya Gusfield, Julie Nesnansky, Adee Horn, Ariel Luckey, Aurora Levins-Morales, Ilana Schatz, Richard Shapiro, and Penny Rosenwasser.

Several people reviewed early drafts of the book and gave me support and feedback. Special thank you's to Robert Allen, Kostas Bagakis, Allan Creighton, Victor Lewis, Yeshi Neumann, Barry Shapiro, and Hugh Vasquez.

It has been my great pleasure and challenge over the years to work with Heru-Nefera Amen, Victor Lewis and Allan Creighton at the Oakland Men's Project. I have learned much from their passion for justice, their gentle caring, and their fierce dedication to freedom.

My partner, Micki, has been a loving support, insightful editor, wonderful co-parent, and shares my vision of a just world.

My appreciation also goes to the staff at New Society Publishers who, despite going through substantial internal change, have provided strong and consistent support to this project from their initial enthusiasm for the book, through the final editing and production. My thanks to Barbara Hirshkowitz and T. L. Hill at New Society Publishers and to Chel Avery for her copyediting, and Margie Politzer for her cover design. My special thanks to Martin Kelley who has guided it through the entire process with skill and dedication.

Dedication

To my family
  Micki, my love
  Ariel, Shandra, and Ryan, my inspiration

  and to all those fighting for justice

Preface

*B*EFORE I WROTE this book I accumulated a long list of reasons why it was an important project. Racism is pervasive, its effects devastating, the need to fight against it urgent. People of color are being blamed for our social problems and attacked on all fronts. Recent immigrants, African American women on welfare, youth of color, and affirmative action programs are just some of the current targets of white anger. It seems like gains we made in civil rights and social justice in the 1960s and 1970s are being rolled back in the 1980s and 1990s.

I could also see the huge impact racism had on my relationships with other people, on what my children learned in school, on how we dealt with economic issues at the state and federal level, and on what sports and music I paid attention to. Racism is everywhere, influencing us at every turn. There is no shortage of immediate reasons why writing a book like this one is a project that needed to be done.

In the workshops my co-workers and I were facilitating participants were eager to talk about these issues and anxious to become involved. Somehow, few of them were able to translate their understanding of the issues and their commitment to ending racism into concrete community action. When they asked me for resources there were no guides for critical thinking and social action I could point them to. What was available about racism or white people was theoretical—interesting but not practical.

With all this in mind, I sat down to write this book. I suddenly accumulated a long list of reasons why I couldn't do it. I wasn't qualified. The subject was too big. The issue was too important. How could I add anything new? The connections between racism, anti-Semitism, gender and economic issues were too complex. People of color have addressed all the issues much more powerfully than I could. I would make mistakes. I would leave important pieces out. People of color would be angry at me. Other white people would call me racist. Jews would say I didn't write enough about anti-Semitism. Gentiles would say I wrote too much. People would expect me to have all the answers. The entire task felt formidable, scary, fraught with problems, and I felt ill-equipped to carry it out successfully.

I procrastinated. I hoped someone else would do it. "There must be someone else who knows more, or writes better, or knows how to say it the right way." "There's certainly someone who could do it without making mistakes or looking foolish." These thoughts went through my mind as I waited for someone else to step forward.

Then one day I recognized these feelings. They were the same feelings that white people experience in our workshops—the same "reasons" they give for not doing more to stop racism. I knew that if I let these feelings stop me from taking the risk of writing this book I would be succumbing to the paralysis that often keeps white people from taking action against racial injustice. When confronting the reality of racism we become sad, angry, overwhelmed, confused, numb, lonely, tired, bored, anxious and passive. When faced with the need to intervene, speak up, or take action against racism, we become tentative and uncertain, filled with questions and concerns, waiting for someone more qualified to step up.

There is no one who can take our place or do our part. I realized it was crucial for me to write what I could, that was my responsibility. Yes, it's scary. Yes, I will make mistakes. I don't know all the answers; I won't be able to cover everything; some people might not like what I write. But a book like this needs to be written, and I'm in a position to write it.

Many white people have stood up against racism. They used their feelings to guide them to action, not to stop their involvement. I needed to call on their examples of risk taking, moral integrity, and strategic action to realize that what I do makes a difference.

I'm sure you will experience many feelings as you read this book. Let them guide you, but don't let them stop you. It is easy to become overwhelmed by our feelings, by how much there is to do, and by how confusing and risky it seems. We need to concentrate on what it is we can do, how we can make a difference.

Whenever I become overwhelmed thinking about how much there is to do, I remind myself of a saying by Rabbi Tarfon. I hope it will guide you as well.

It is not upon you to finish the work.
Neither are you free to desist from it.

Introduction

"Only Justice Can Put Out the Fire" [*]

THIS IS A book about racism for white people. It is not another book about how bad racism is, filled with facts and figures about inequality and injustice. In this book I want to talk to you personally about what it means to those of us who are white, and how we can make a difference in the struggle for racial justice.

There is fire raging across the United States—usually a series of brush fires erupting whenever conditions are right, sometimes a firestorm, always a smoldering cauldron. Whether it is major urban uprisings, intellectual debates, or everyday conflicts in our neighborhoods and schools, racism is burning us all. Some of us have third degree burns or have died from its effects, many others live in the charred wreckage. Most of us suffer first and second degree burns at some time in our lives. We all live with fear in the glow of the fire's menacing and distorted light.

As white people we do many things to survive the heat. We move to the suburbs, put bars on our windows, put locks on our hearts, and teach our children distrust for their own protection. We believe the enemy is "out there"—and we can be safe "in here." We never talk about what it means to be "in here" with other white people and why we are so afraid of people with darker skin colors "out there." Since we don't talk about our fears, we are precluded from doing anything effective to put out the fire.

Poll after poll shows that most white Americans are scared. We are scared about violence, we are scared about the economy, we are scared about the

---

[*] A line in a song by Romanovsky and Phillips.

1

safety, education and future of our children. Much of the time those fears are directed toward people of color—long-term residents or recent immigrants. It is easy for us to focus on them, and yet doing so is devastating to our ability to address the critical national issues of jobs, education, social infrastructure, family violence and economic development.

Since the uprising in South Central Los Angeles in 1992 white people are even more afraid than before. Once again the injustice of racism was brought to our national attention by people of color. We saw the fire flare up and again we were frightened. Many of us wanted to do something, to pick up a bucket and throw water on the flames, but the size of the blaze seemed to make our individual efforts useless. Besides, many of us thought that we were too far away from the cause of the fire to make a difference. People of color were defined as the problem and the inner cities as the site.

In fact, there are already flames in our (all too often predominately white) schools, churches, neighborhoods and work places. Poverty, family violence, crime, drugs, fear, suicide and despair are not limited to somewhere "out there" nor to "those people." Our houses are burning out from under us, and we need to pick up our buckets and start carrying water now. But just like the volunteer fire departments in rural communities and small towns, we need to be part of a fire line where everyone realizes that when the sparks are flying anything can catch on fire. We need to be a community which is alert for the signs of sparks and embers so they can be put out before a bigger blaze develops.

We don't need scare tactics. They just reinforce the fear and paralysis. We don't need numbers and statistics. They produce numbness and despair. We need to talk with each other, honestly, simply, caringly. We need to learn how to talk about racism without rhetoric, which fans the flames, without attack, fear or intimidation, which keep people off the lines. We need to share fire fighting suggestions, advice, exercises and approaches so that we can work together to fight the fire.

Racism is often described as a problem of prejudice. Prejudice is certainly one result of racism, and it fuels further acts of violence toward people of color. However the assumption of this book is that racism is the institutionalization of social injustice based on skin color, other physical characteristics, and cultural and religious difference. White racism is the uneven and unfair distribution of power, privilege, land and material goods favoring white people. Another way to state this is that white racism is a system in which people of color as a group are exploited and oppressed by white people as a group. Although we can and should all become more tolerant and understanding of each other, only justice can put out the fire of racism. We will certainly have to examine our fears and misconceptions to see why we stay home while the fire sweeps our nation. Our primary purpose in doing so will be so that we can get as many strong, able and committed bodies on the front lines as quickly as possible.

As we have witnessed many times in European and American history the fires of racism include the flames of anti-Semitism. Most of the Jews in the United States are of European background. Sometimes these Jews are considered white and sometimes not, just as Asian Americans are sometimes considered white or not, depending upon the complex responses of white people. Jewish people are vulnerable to the same kinds of violence, discrimination and harassment that most people of color have experienced. At the same time those Jews who are of European descent are buffered from racism's worst aspects by the benefits of being white, as are many people of Southern and Eastern European heritage. Because of this complex dynamic in American society, understanding and confronting anti-Semitism is a crucial link in the struggle to end racism. In this book Jews of European descent will be referred to as white *and* as targets of racism. Jews of color are always targets of racism from white people and even from Jews of European descent. They are also vulnerable to anti-Semitism from other people of color.

Anti-Semitism is similar to, different from, and intertwined with racism. Groups holding political power in Europe have exploited, controlled and violated other groups of people based on religion, race, culture and nationality (as well as gender, class and sexual orientation) for hundreds of years. There is tremendous overlap in the kinds of violence that have been directed at these groups and the kinds of justifications used to legitimize political, economic and cultural exploitation and dominance. Racism and anti-Semitism are two primary, closely related tools that groups in power have used to maintain their advantage. I will make connections between the two throughout the text. The section on Jews in Part Four will explore these complexities in more detail.*

When I wrote my book *Mens Work*† I quoted a statement from Alice Walker in the preface. The statement was about how the fear of not being perfect can inhibit committing oneself to public action about a particular issue. She was talking about speaking out against cruelty to animals even though she occasionally ate meat. I referred to writing about sexism even though I wasn't perfectly non-sexist.

---

* The inside/outside status of Jewish people is a result of the inconsistencies of racism and anti-Semitism and the complex interplay between the two. The complexity can be confusing to both Jews and non-Jews alike. These issues will be explored in more detail later in the book.

† *Men's Work: How to Stop the Violence that Tears Our Lives Apart* (Hazelden/Ballantine, Center City, Minnesota and New York, 1992.)

It is crucial that we speak up about issues of injustice, violence and inequality. It is true that our words have more moral credibility if we are leading the good, clean life and are totally consistent in what we say and what we do. We have to "walk the walk" not just "talk the talk."

However issues of social justice are not fundamentally about individual actions and beliefs. This book is about white racism, which is a social system. Although my personal attitudes and actions can either support or confront racism, racism is completely independent of me. In fact, even if most of us were completely non-racist in our attitudes, there are many ways that unequal wages, unequal treatment in the legal system and segregation in jobs, housing and education would continue.

Our beliefs and actions are important. We are responsible for how we treat the people around us and whether or not we are fighting against injustice or contributing to it. But as long as we focus only on individual actions and ignore community and organizational responses, we will leave the system of racism intact.

This book is about uprooting the system of racism. We need to re-examine our individual beliefs and actions in order to participate effectively in that uprooting. This book will help you look at how you have learned racism, what effects it has had on your life, what have been the costs and benefits to you, and how you have learned to pass it on. More importantly, this book will help you become a member of a network of people who are committed to eliminating racism. It offers you connections, strategies, perspectives and guidelines for becoming involved in the struggle.

Don't take it too personally. You did not create racism. You may have many feelings while reading this book. Confronting racism may trigger guilt, horror, embarrassment, defensiveness, anger, excitement, discovery, anxiety, inspiration, jealousy, competitiveness, loneliness, despair or confusion. Acknowledge the feelings, talk about them with others, get support, but don't get stuck in the feelings. If our feelings immobilize us we cannot strategically plan how to sabotage the system.

This book is not about unlearning racism.* It is fine for us to unlearn racism. But many of us live in highly segregated or highly stratified communities and have only limited opportunities to pass on racism in our daily encounters. Unlearning racism makes it easier for people of color to live and work with us but it doesn't necessarily challenge the system to change. Unlearning racism may or may not be a path to taking action to eliminate racism. In a society where individual growth is so often not only the starting

---

* Unlearning racism refers to workshops where participants can "unlearn" the lies, myths and stereotypes about people of color and white people that foster racial prejudice.

place but also the end point of discussion, strategies for unlearning racism often end in complacency and inaction.

Racism has existed in this hemisphere since Columbus and his crews invaded the shores of the West Indies and slaughtered, raped, enslaved and exploited the native peoples living there. Since his arrival there has been continuous active resistance from people of color. Throughout that time there has also been a strong and steady stream of white people who have supported that resistance and contributed to the struggle to end racism. This book is an invitation to join that tradition of white people. It offers you some guidance about how to be more effective in that struggle.

This book does not document the existence of racism. There are many books and thousands of studies showing the direct, devastating impact of racism on the daily lives of the tens of millions of people of color in this country. That there is inequality and injustice in our educational, political, legal, medical, housing and employment systems is amply documented and indisputable. I will present few statistics and little information proving racism exists.[*]

This book provides some suggestions and starting points based on the fact that racism exists, it is pervasive, and its effects are devastating. Because of this devastation we need to start doing everything possible to end racism. The first step is for us to talk together, as white people.

---

[*] There are some excellent resources listed in the bibliography which provide that kind of information.

PART I

What Color Is White?

Let's Talk

I AM TALKING to you as one white person to another. I am Jewish, and I will talk about that later in this book. You also have an ethnic identity you are probably proud of. You also have a religious background, a culture, a country of origin and a history. Whatever your other identities, you probably are not used to being addressed as white.

"Other" people are African American, Asian American, Native American, Latino/as or Arab Americans. "Other" people have countries of origin and primary languages which are not English. Rarely in this country do we identify ourselves or each other as white. It is an adjective which is seldom heard explicitly, but is everywhere implied. People are assumed white unless otherwise noted, much as people (and animals) are assumed to be male.

Read the following lines:

"He walked into the room and immediately noticed her."

"This new sitcom is about a middle-aged, middle-class couple and their three teenage children."

"The average American drinks two cups of coffee a day."

"Women today want to catch a man who is strong, but sensitive."

"She didn't know if she would get into the college of her choice."

"My grandmother lived on a farm all her life."

"I have a friend who has AIDS."

"He won a medal on the Special Olympics basketball team."

Are all these people white? Read the sentences again and imagine the people referred to are Chinese Americans. Does that change the meanings? Try making them Native American. How does that change the meaning? If you are of Christian background what happens when you make them Jewish?

In reality, we would have to specify they are Chinese American or Native American or Jewish because we would not automatically assume they were.

Similarly with you and me. We assume we are white. It can seem like we're stating the obvious. Yet there is something about stating the obvious that makes us feel uneasy, marked. Why notice? What's the point of saying I'm white?

We have been led to believe that racism is a question of particular acts of discrimination or violence. Calling someone a name, denying someone a job, excluding someone from a neighborhood—that is racism. These certainly are acts of racism. But what about living in a white suburb where people of color are excluded or harassed? What about working in an organization where people of color are paid less, have more menial work or fewer opportunities for advancement? Racism affects each and every aspect of our lives, *all the time*, whether people of color are present or not.

People of color know this intimately. They know that where they live, work and walk, who they talk with and how, what they read, listen to or watch on TV, their past experiences and future possibilities are all influenced by racism. As white people we also know this, but do not talk about it. We will discuss why we don't talk about it later. Because we don't talk about it, naming whiteness can seem scary, foolish, unnecessary, pointless or illegitimate.

Of course there are times when we talk with the unspoken assumption that we are white. When the subject is desegregation, or integration, or immigration, or affirmative action we are clear about being white and speaking about "them," i.e., people of color.

For the next few days notice how rarely you see or hear the words white, Caucasian, or Euro-American. Where is it implied but not stated specifically? Where is African American or Latino/a specified so you can infer who is white without it being named?

Carry your whiteness with you. During the day, in each new situation, remind yourself that you are white. What difference has it made/does it make? Who is around you, what are they doing, are they white or people of color? What difference do you notice that it makes? Write down what you notice. Discuss it with a friend.

Particularly notice whenever you are somewhere where there are only white people. How did it come to be that there are no people of color there? Are they really not there, or only invisible? Did they grow some of the food, originally own the land, build the buildings, or clean and maintain the place where you are?

"I'm Not White"

RECENTLY I WAS doing a workshop on racism and we wanted to divide the group into a caucus of people of color and a caucus of white people, so that each group could have more in-depth discussion. Immediately some of the white people said, "But I'm not white."

I was somewhat taken aback because although these people looked white they were clearly distressed about being labeled white. A white, Christian woman stood up and said, "I'm not really white because I'm not part of the white male power structure that perpetuates racism." Next a white gay man stood up and said, "You have to be straight to have the privileges of being white." A white, straight, working class man from a poor family then said, "I've got it just as hard as any person of color." Finally, a straight, white middle class man said, "I'm not white, I'm Italian."

My African-American co-worker turned to me and asked, "Where are all the white people who were here just a minute ago?" Of course I replied, "Don't ask me, I'm not white, I'm Jewish!"

Most of the time we don't notice or question our whiteness. However, when the subject is racism many of us don't want to be white, because it opens us to charges of being racist and brings up feelings of guilt, shame, embarrassment and hopelessness. There are others who proudly claim whiteness under any circumstances and simply deny or ignore the violence that white people have done to people of color.

Those of us who are middle class are more likely to assume we are white without having to emphasize the point, and to feel guilty when it is noticed or brought up. Those of us who are poor or working class are more likely to have had to assert our whiteness against the effects of economic discrimination and the presence of other racial groups. Although we share the benefits of being white, we don't share the economic privileges of being middle class and so we are more likely to feel angry and less likely to feel guilty than middle class counterparts.

Whatever our economic status, most of us become paralyzed with some measure of fear, guilt, anger, defensiveness or confusion if we are named as white when racism is being addressed.

In this country it has always been dangerous even to talk about racism. "Nigger lover," "Indian lover," and "race traitor" are labels which have carried severe consequences. You probably know the names of white civil rights workers who were killed for their actions against racism, such as Goodman, Schwerner, and Luizzo. Many of us have been isolated from friends or family because of disagreements over racism. A lot of us have been called "racist."

Saying "I am white" may make us feel either guilty of being racist, or traitorous toward other whites. We don't want to be labeled or stereotyped. Talking about racism has often occurred in the context of angry words, hostility, accusations and divisiveness. We also may have fears about people of color separating from us if we are clearly identified as white.

In any case, some of us are quick to disavow our whiteness, or to claim some other identity which will give us legitimate victim status. We certainly don't want to be seen as somehow responsible for or complicit with racism.

We must begin here—with this denial of our whiteness—because racism keeps people of color in the limelight and makes whiteness invisible. To change this we must take whiteness itself and hold it up to the light and see that it is a color too. Whiteness is a concept, an ideology which holds tremendous power over our lives and, in turn, over the lives of people of color.

Our challenge in this discussion will be to keep whiteness center stage. Every time our attention begins to wander off toward people of color or other issues, we will have to notice and refocus. We must notice when we try to slip into another identity and escape being white. We each have many other factors that influence our lives, such as our ethnicity, gender, sexual orientation, class, personality, mental and physical abilities. Even when we're talking about these elements of our lives we must keep whiteness on stage with us because it influences each of the other factors.

What parts of your identity does it feel like you lose when you say aloud the phrase "I'm white"?

Part of our discomfort may come from the complex relationship our own family's ethnic and class background had to whiteness. Was your ethnic or cultural group ever considered not white? When they arrived in the United States, what did members of your family have to do to be accepted as white? What did they have to give up?

How has pride in being white (or becoming American) sustained you or your family? Has that identification or pride ever allowed you or your family to tolerate poverty, economic exploitation or poor living conditions because "at least we're not colored"?

If, when you move down the streets of major U.S. cities, other people assume, based on skin color, dress, physical appearance or total impression, that you are white, then in American society that counts for being white. This is where we are going to start talking about what it means to say, "I am white." I realize that there are differences between the streets of New York and Minneapolis, and between different neighborhoods within each city. But in American society there is a broad and pervasive division between white people and people of color, and most of us know from a very early age which side we are on. If we are white we are told or learn in early childhood who to stay away from, who not to play with, who not to associate with, who isn't one of our kind.* This is true even if our parents are liberal or progressive. The training is too pervasive within our society for anyone to escape.

Whiteness is about more than skin color, although that is a major factor in this country. People of color and Jewish people are also marked as different by dress, food, the smells of cooking, religious ceremonies, celebratory rituals and mannerisms. These features are all labeled racial differences, even though they may be related to culture, religion, class or country of origin. I'm sure you know whether you are treated as "white" or as a person of color by most of the people you meet.

Say "I am white" to yourself a couple of times. What are the "but's" that immediately come to mind? Do you quickly add on another identity, perhaps one where you might claim a victim status such as female, poor, lesbian or gay, Jewish or Italian? Do you defend yourself with statements such as, "I have friends who are people of color," or "My family didn't own slaves"? Do you try to separate yourself from other white people? ("I don't feel white." "I'm not like other white people.") Do you try to minimize the importance of whiteness? ("We're all part of the human race.")

We are understandably uncomfortable with the label "white." We feel boxed in and want to escape, just as people of color want to escape from the confines of their racial categories. Being white is an arbitrary category which overrides our individual personalities, devalues us, deprives us of the richness of our other identities, stereotypes us and yet has no scientific basis. However, in our society being white is also just as real, and governs our day-to-day lives just as much as being a person of color. To acknowledge this reality is not to create it nor to perpetuate it. In fact, it is the first step to uprooting racism.

---

* Several studies have shown that young children between the ages of two and four notice differences of skin color, eye color, hair, dress and speech and the significance that adults give to those differences. See McGinnis, Oehlberg, and Derman-Sparks.

Whiteness *is* problematic. All the fear, anger, frustration, helplessness and confusion we experience about admitting that we are white is the result of racism. Many of these feelings are what keep us from recognizing and talking about the effects of racism in our own lives and the devastation that racism wreaks in our society.

We may claim that we aren't white because we simply don't (or refuse to) notice race. I sometimes like to think that I don't. But when I'm in an all white setting and a person of color walks in I notice. I am slightly surprised to see a person of color and I look again to confirm who they are and wonder to myself why they're there. I try to do this as naturally and smoothly as possible because I wouldn't want anyone to think that I wasn't tolerant. Actually what I'm surprised at is not that they are there, but that they are there as an equal. All of my opening explanations for their presence will assume they are not equal. "They must be a server or delivery person," I tell myself. It is usually not until another white person introduces me, or gives me an explanation, that my uneasiness is laid to rest. (And even then I may inwardly qualify my acceptance). We notice skin color all the time but we don't "notice" race unless our sense of the proper racial hierarchy is upset.

When I first meet someone, and I think this is true for most of us, I identify their gender (and get anxious when I can't), I identify as much about their class as I can figure out, and I identify what their racial identity is. I have two categories, white and other. I'm interested in the other. In fact, because of my assumptions about the commonness of whiteness, I often assume a person of color will be more interesting than another white person. But whether we value it positively or negatively, the difference counts and we notice it.

Since I've been taught to relate differently to people who are African American, or Latino/a, or Asian American, I may need more information than appearance gives me about what "kind" of person of color I am with. I have some standard questions to fish for more information, such as: "That's an interesting name. I've never heard it before. Where's it from?" "Your accent sounds familiar but I can't place it." "You don't look American, where are you from?"

Sometimes we ask these questions of white Americans who have unusual names or unfamiliar accents. Most often we use them to clarify who is white and who isn't, and secondarily, what kind of person of color we are dealing with.

Many of us were taught that it is not polite to notice racial difference. We may have learned that racial difference is an artificial basis used to discriminate against and exploit people of color, and therefore we may over-compensate by pretending to ignore it. White people often say, "I don't care whether a person is black, brown, orange or green." Human beings don't come in orange or green. Those whose skin color is darker are treated differently in general and we, in particular, respond differently to them. As part of growing up white and learning racial stereotypes, we have been trained to stiffen up, be more cautious, fearful and hesitant around people of color. These are physiological and psychological responses that we can notice in ourselves and see in other white people. These responses belie our verbal assurances that we don't notice racial differences.

There's absolutely nothing wrong with being white or with noticing the difference that color makes. We were born without choice into our families. We did not choose our skin color, native language or culture. We are not responsible for being white or for being raised in a white-dominated, racist society in which we have been trained to have particular responses to people of color. We are responsible for how we respond to racism (which is what this book is about) and we can only do that consciously and effectively if we start by realizing that it makes a crucial difference that we are white.

"I'm Not Racist"

WHETHER IT IS easy or difficult to say that we're white, the phrase we often want to say next is "...but I'm not racist." There are lots of ways that we have learned to phrase this denial.

I'm not racist.

I don't belong to the Klan.

I have friends who are people of color.

I don't see color, I'm color blind.

I do anti-racism work.

I went to an unlearning racism workshop.

This book is not about whether you are racist or not, or whether all white people are racist or not. We are not conducting a moral inventory of ourselves, nor creating a moral standard to divide other white people from us.

To avoid being called racist we may claim that we don't notice color and don't treat people differently based on color. However, we all notice color in just about every situation we're in. It's not useful or honest for any of us to claim that we don't. It is too pervasive a construct of our society to avoid. When we say things like, "I don't see color," we are trying to maintain a self-image of impartiality and fairness (and whiteness). Some of the motivation behind the claim that we are color neutral is to establish that we don't mistreat people or discriminate against them because of their race. Ultimately, this disclaimer prevents us from taking responsibility for challenging racism because we believe that people who see color are the problem.

The only way to treat people with dignity and justice is to recognize that racism has a profound negative effect upon our lives, and therefore noticing color helps to counteract that effect. Instead of being color neutral we need to notice much more acutely and insightfully exactly the difference that color makes in the way people are treated.

Just as it's not useful to label ourselves racist or not, it is not useful to label each other. White people, individually and collectively, have done and continue to do some very brutal things in the name of whiteness. We may want to separate ourselves from the white people who commit these acts by claiming that they are racist and we are not. But because racism operates institutionally, to the benefit of all white people, we are connected to the acts of other white people.

Of course we're not members of the Klan or other extremist groups. Of course we watch what we say and don't make rude racial comments. But dissociating from white people who do is not the answer. We need to dissociate from their actions and challenge their beliefs. We can't challenge them, or even speak to them if we have separated ourselves from them, creating some magical line with the racists on that side and ourselves over here. This division leads to an ineffective strategy of trying to pull as many people as possible over to our (non-racist and therefore superior) side. Other white people will listen to us better, and be more influenced by our actions when we identify with them. Then we can explore how to work from the inside out together.

Perhaps most importantly, the people who are more visibly saying or doing things that are racist are usually more scared, more confused and less powerful than we are. (Or they are trying to increase their own power by manipulating racial fears.) It is often amazing how, when we get scared, confused or powerless, we do and say the very same things. Since racism leads to scapegoating people of color for social and personal problems, we are all susceptible to resorting to racial scapegoating in times of trouble. Visible acts of racism are, at least in part, an indication of the lack of power that a white person or group of people have to camouflage their actions. More powerful and well off people can simply move to segregated neighborhoods, or make corporate decisions that are harder to see and analyze as contributing to racism. Since the racism of the wealthy is less visible to us, those of us who are middle class can inadvertently scapegoat poor and working class white people for being more overtly racist.

We do need to confront words and actions which are racist when we encounter them because they create an atmosphere of violence in which all of us are unsafe. We also need to understand that most white people are doing the best they can to survive. Overtly racist people are scared, and lack the information and skills to be more tolerant. We need to challenge their behavior, not their moral integrity. We also need to be careful that we don't end up carrying out an upper class agenda by blaming poor and working people for being racist when people with wealth control the media, the textbooks, the housing and job markets and the police. We need to stay focused on the institutions themselves.

What is Whiteness?

RACISM IS BASED on the concept of whiteness—a powerful fiction enforced by power and violence. Whiteness is a constantly shifting boundary separating those who are entitled to have certain privileges from those whose exploitation and vulnerability to violence is justified by their not being white.

Racism itself is a long standing characteristic of many human societies. Justifying exploitation and violence against other peoples because they are "inferior" or different has a long history within Greek, Roman and European Christian traditions.

In more recent historical times in western Europe those with English heritage were perceived to be pure white. The Irish, Russians and Spanish were considered darker races, sometimes black, and certainly non-white. The white category was slowly extended to include northern and middle European people but still even fifty years ago definitely excluded eastern or southern European peoples, such as Italians, Poles, Russians and Greeks. In the last few decades, although there is still prejudice against people from these geographical backgrounds, they have become generally accepted as white in the United States.*

The important distinction in the United States has always been binary—between those who counted as white and those who did not. Drawing on already established "popular" classifications, whiteness was delineated more clearly in the United States in the 18th Century as slavery was introduced and distinguished from various forms of shorter term servitude.

Although a racial hierarchy was in place from the time of the earliest European settlers, racism was only defined "scientifically" as a

---

* In some northern and western European countries there are still strong and abusive patterns of racism against southern and eastern Europeans.

biological/genetic characteristic about one hundred and fifty years ago with the publication of Darwin's theory of species modification and Linnaeus' system of classification. These ideas were combined by others into a pseudo-scientific theory, eventually called Social Darwinism, which attempted to classify the human population into distinct categories or races and put them on an evolutionary scale with whites on top.

The original classification consisted of three categories—Caucasoid, Negroid and Mongoloid. These were not based on genetic differences, but on differences that Europeans and European Americans perceived to be important. They were in fact based on stereotypes of cultural differences and (mis)measures of physiological characteristics such as skull size (Gould 1981).

From the beginning the attempt to classify people by race was fraught with contradictions. Latin Americans, Native Americans, and Jewish people did not fit easily into these categories so the categories were variously stretched, redefined or adapted to meet the agenda of the Europeans and Americans who were using them.

For example, in the last century Finns were doing most of the lowest paid, unsafe mining and lumbering work in the upper mid-west. Although logically they were white, in terms of political, cultural and economic "common sense" they were black because they were the poorest and least respected group in the area besides Native Americans. The courts consistently ruled that they were not white, despite their skin color, because of their cultural and economic standing.

On the west coast, during the Constitutional debates in California in 1848–9, there was discussion about the status of Mexicans and Chinese. There were still Mexicans who were wealthy landowners and business partners with whites, while the Chinese were exclusively heavily exploited railroad and agricultural workers. It was eventually decided that Mexicans would be considered white and Chinese would be considered the same as blacks and Indians. This decision established which group could become citizens, own land, marry whites and have other basic rights (Almaguer, pps. 9–10, 54).

Today people of Finnish background are considered white, Latino/as are considered not white and Chinese Americans are conditionally white at times, not white at others, but clearly different from Blacks and Native Americans.

There was a complex and dynamic interplay between the popular conception of race and the scientific categories, neither of which was grounded in physiological or biological reality, but both of which carried great emotional import to "white" people and devastating consequences to "people of color," regardless of how they were being defined.

Although a few scientists still try to prove the existence of races, most scientists have long ago abandoned the use of race as a valid category at all. Human variability is so large and so widely dispersed that no particular racial groupings or distinctions are useful or justified. There is tremendous genetic difference or variation within "racial" groupings and huge overlap between them, making the categories themselves useless (Harding, section 2 "Science Constructs Race").

Genetic differences among humans can be explained by the distribution of genetic variables and don't correspond with any useful category of race defined genetically, by skin color or any other physical characteristic. That hasn't stopped many people from believing that distinct races exist and from trying to use scientific language to buttress their arguments. (For cogent refutations see Gould, Lewin, et al., and Goldberg.)

There is likewise no scientific (i.e. biological or genetic) basis to the concept of whiteness. There is nothing scientifically distinctive about it except skin color, and that is highly variable. All common wisdom notwithstanding, the skin color of a person tells you nothing about their culture, country of origin, character or personal habits. Because there is nothing biological about whiteness, it ends up being defined by contrast to other groups, becoming confused with ideas of nationality, religion and ethnicity.

For example, Jewish people are not a "racial" grouping. Jewish people share cultural and religious beliefs and practices but come from every continent and many different cultural backgrounds. Jews range in skin color from "white" to dark brown. Because race was falsely assumed to be a scientific category, being Jewish has often been assumed to mean that a Jew is genetically different than non-Jewish people.

I grew up learning that racial categories were scientifically valid and gave us useful information about ourselves and other people. In other words, racism had a scientific stamp of approval. It is difficult for me to let go of the certainty I thought I had gained about what racial difference meant. And, of course, there are always new attempts to prove to us that race means something. (See Fraser, Lewontin, et al., and Gould.)

What residual doubts do you have that there may be something genetic or biological about racial differences? ("But, what about...?") How can you respond to people who say that there are specific differences between "races"?

I began to understand the artificial nature of racial categories more clearly when I examined how moral qualities were attached to racial differences. This confirmed my suspicion that there was a political, not a scientific agenda at work in these distinctions.

The lack of a physical difference attached to whiteness hasn't prevented many people from assuming that they know what whiteness is, or what it is different from. Although some of these associations have changed or have had different prominence over time, they have generally been linked to moral qualities. These moral qualities have, in turn, been used to justify various forms of exploitation.

From the old phrase referring to a good deed, "That's white of you," to the New Age practice of visualizing oneself surrounded by white light, white has signified honor, purity, cleanliness and Godliness in white western European and mainstream U.S. culture. Because concepts of whiteness and race were developed in Christian Europe, references to whiteness are imbued with Christian values. We have ended up with a set of opposing qualities or attributes which are said to define people either as white or as not white.

The tendency to see the world in sets of opposites, either/or categories, is itself a core pattern of thinking developed in elite settings in Western Europe and the United States. Many other cultures do not divide the world into opposing camps. The English phrase "black-and-white" reflects our desire to divide things into opposites even though everyday reality is rarely clearly defined or neatly categorized. Classical Greek either/or logic and a Christian theology of good versus evil were combined to impose a good/bad set of values based on selected categories of racial difference. Some of the most common pairings are listed below.

"Dark" Qualities	"White" Qualities
superstitious	scientific
subhuman	human
crazy	sane
immoral	moral
animalistic	god-like
tainted	pure
abnormal	normal
emotional/angry	calm
primitive/uncivilized/ barbaric/savage	civilized
prone to dishonesty	well intentioned/decent
subversive	upholder of tradition
satanic	angelic
pagan	Christian
malicious	loving
godless	god fearing, wholesome
rude	polite
evil	benign
low class	middle class
crude/brutish	refined
demanding	restrained
intellectually inferior	intelligent
impulsive	thoughtful
traitor	patriot
fanciful	level-headed

weak link	strong specimen
lacking self control	prudent
manipulative	sincere
irrational	rational
radical	conservative
undignified	respectable
sinful	innocent
out of control	in control
impure/contaminated	pure
tainted/poisonous	innocuous/harmless
dirty	clean
illegal	legal/law abiding
needing permission	authorized
soulless/damned	saved
fringe/marginal	center
subjective	objective, detached
wild	calm
sexual/wanton	chaste
colorful	bland
disorganized	orderly
inefficient	effective
rebellious	upholder of tradition
traditional	modern
impatient	patient
self-righteous	righteous
rhythmic	stiff
devious	straightforward
promiscuous	committed
cloudy	clear
disease carrying	healthy
present time oriented	future oriented
un-American	American
dark	fair, blond

Which words in each pair do you associate with white people? Which words on the left do you use to discount people of color's demands for fair and equal treatment ("they are too..."), or to blame them for how they are treated in our society ("If they weren't so...")?

Qualities not associated with whiteness have been given negative meanings. They have become associated not only with people of color but also with children, workers, lesbians, gays and bi-sexuals, Jews and heterosexual white women; just those groups excluded from the political and scientific institutions that defined what normal should be.

In reality, individual character traits don't have anything to do with skin color, cultural background, age, gender, class or sexual orientation. The personalities and character of members of any cultural group are highly variable. Each of these polarities, however, encodes part of the historical meaning of whiteness to white people. The confirmation of our moral superiority allows us to justify a racial hierarchy with white people on top.

Not all white people had an equal voice in defining racial differences. Those with most power—who had the most to gain or preserve—set the terms. White landowners, church leaders—the educated and successful—systematically, though not collusively, defined whiteness in ways that extolled and legitimized their actions and denigrated others'.

These meanings are now many hundreds of years old. Today, none of us escapes the traps, lies and emotional resonances of these dichotomies. They are passed on to us from parents, school, literature, TV and the movies. It is difficult for any of us, powerful or less powerful, to dissociate "positive" qualities from white people and "negative" ones from people of color no matter how "color blind" we would like to be.

White people who have challenged racism and the false dichotomies upon which it is based have been labeled in various ways to show that they don't really belong to the white group. Labels such as "nigger lover," "race traitor," "un-American," "feminist," "liberal," "Communist," "unchristian," "Jew," "fag," "lesbian," "crazy," "terrorist" and "thought police" have all been used to isolate and discredit people and to imply that they are somehow outside the territory of whiteness and therefore justifiably attacked. We can see from the moral virtues attached to whiteness that only those who are white will be able to speak with authority. A powerful way to discredit any critique of whiteness or racism is to discredit the speaker by showing that they are not really white. This is a neat, circular convention which stifles any serious discussion of what whiteness means and what effect it has on people.

This leaves most of us who are white on pretty shaky ground. If we even point attention to whiteness and racism we risk being labeled not really white or a traitor to our "race." These accusations discredit our testimony and potentially lose us some of the benefits of being white such as better jobs and police protection from violence. Behind the names lies the threat of physical and sexual violence such as ostracization, firing, silencing, condemnation to hell, institutionalization, incarceration, deportation, rape, lynching and other forms of mob violence that have been used to protect white power and privilege.

We could usefully spend some time exploring the history and meaning of any particular pair of words on the list above. I encourage you to do so. Each one reveals some vital aspect of whiteness and racism. Here I want to point out four concepts that many of these words cluster around: purity, Christian, American and gender.

Appeals to group solidarity, particularly in the last two hundred and fifty years during which political concepts of the nation-state have developed, have often focused on the "racial" purity of some particular group of people. In different European countries, in the United States, in Australia and South Africa, white people have attempted to claim a purity of racial stock and a genetic superiority which entitled them to control the land and other people around them in a particular geographical area. (Other groups of people have done the same thing; racism is by no means exclusive to white people.) They have then set up economic and psychological boundaries to participation in that society for people defined as "other." People of color, Jews, Romany (often misnamed Gypsies), people with physical or mental disabilities, homosexuals, Irish, southern Europeans, Slavic peoples, the poor—each group has been defined as outsiders who could contaminate white racial purity and the strength of the nation-state through corruption, contagion and disease, dirt and uncleanliness, and intermarriage. Segregation, anti-miscegenation laws, medical experimentation, concentration camps and extermination have all been used at times to "cleanse" and "protect" whiteness and national identity. White people have considered anyone with even 1 percent African-American, Native, or Latino/a "blood" to be impure, not white, alien. The Nazis considered people to be Jewish if they had even one great-grandparent who was Jewish. Many of our fears today about intermarriage and mixed heritage children stem from these old misconceptions about racial difference and racial purity.

Another cluster of concepts and practices of whiteness centers around Christianity. Whiteness has often been equated with being a Christian in juxtaposition to being a pagan, infidel, witch, heathen, Jew, Moslem, Native American, Buddhist or atheist. Racial violence has been justified by a stated need to protect Christian families and homes. Pogroms, crusades, holy wars and colonial conquests have been justified by the need to save the souls of "uncivilized" and "godless" peoples (often at the expense of their lives).

Jewish people have lived within Christian-dominated societies (when permitted to) for nearly two thousand years. There is substantial Christian teaching and belief that Jewish people are dangerous and evil. These beliefs have been sustained even during periods of hundreds of years when Jews were not living near Christians (Glassman). Jews, along with Moslems, have become symbols to many Christians of the infidel. This anti-Semitism, originally based on religious and cultural differences, has become racialized over the centuries, conjoining Christian values and whiteness. It has exposed Jews to the same harsh reality of Christian violence toward non-Christians that pagans, Romany, witches and Moslems have experienced.

In addition, anti-Semitism has been passed on to Christians of color through Christian teachings. Religious leaders of both Eastern Orthodox and Catholic branches of Christianity, including most Protestant denominations, have accused the Jews of killing Jesus, using the blood of Christian children for Passover ritual, refusing to recognize the divinity of Jesus and of consorting with the devil. As Christianity was spread by Western colonialism and missionary practice, these teachings were incorporated into the beliefs of many Christians of color, passing on anti-Semitism.

Christianity, particularly its Protestant versions, is variously equated with moral, virtuous, pure, hard-working, saved, civilized, decent, God-fearing, righteous and, of course, white people. Today the majority of Christians in the world are people of color, but racism continues to be justified in Christian terms. Whiteness and Christianity remain inextricably entwined, targeting both people of color and Jews for continued violence.

At the same time there are core Christian values of love, caring, justice and fellowship which have inspired some Christians to work against white racism. For example, many white abolitionists were Christians inspired by religious teachings and values to work against slavery.

Another cluster of meanings centers around the concept of American. In the United States the concept of who is an American is often conflated with who is white. In fact, "All-American" is often used as a thinly disguised code word for white. A third generation Swedish- or German-American child is considered an all-American kid in a way that a third generation Japanese- or Chinese-American child is not.

In the same way, the patriotism of anyone with darker skin color is routinely questioned. Non-European citizens are continually suspected of having dual allegiances. During World War II U.S. citizens of Japanese heritage were interned in concentration camps and U.S. citizens of German heritage were not. Even when they fought in the armed services in wartime the loyalty of Asian American, Latino/a, Native American, Arab American, and African American soldiers has been challenged.

For those of us who are white, immigrating to this country and giving up our native cultures and customs was equated with the process of becoming American. We were told that when we assimilated completely, whether it took two generations or five, we would have made it. As long as we held on to our cultures we were less American, un-American, perhaps even anti-American. On the one hand, the definition of who was white was broadened over time to include virtually all European Americans. At the same time, the boundaries keeping people of color out were firmly maintained. Immigration policies and quotas consistently favored Europeans and much of the time completely excluded people who were not considered white. Even when they have legally arrived here, non-Native American people of color are routinely asked where they came from, and told to go back home.

The final cluster of words centers on gender. Whiteness strongly leans toward "male" virtues and "male" values. While terms of whiteness apply to men and women, there are also significant differences in which qualities men and women are associated with.

Each of the particular virtues of whiteness also has a gender version for men and women. White women are held to higher standards of chasteness, cleanliness and restraint than white men. The basis of women's rationality, righteousness and authority is supposed to lie with white men.

White women are presumed to carry white authority over men and women of color. Their authority is derived from their association with white men whose backing they are assumed to have. White women hold onto whiteness by the authority and protection of white men, or by their willingness to adapt to male roles and exert authority in traditionally male spheres to protect their white privilege as employers, supervisors or teachers. They can also be cast out of the circle of white male "protection" by being rebellious or by violating racial or gender norms.

White women have been held to be the purest realization of white values. They have been locked up within this symbolism, and tremendous violence has been done in their name for their "protection" and the protection of white civilization. White women have both colluded with and resisted their role and the violence it has justified.

Whiteness is a many faceted phenomenon, slowly and constantly shifting its emphasis, all the time maintaining a racial hierarchy and protecting the power that accrues to white people. It is a powerful fiction with wide ranging effects on our lives and on the lives of people of color. Although there are no natural or essential qualities or characteristics of whiteness, or of white people, it is not an easy fiction to let go of.

Words and Pictures

WHITENESS HAS BEEN a defining part of our culture for hundreds of years. We have embedded white people as good, and people of color as bad and dangerous, into our everyday language. Most words containing "black" have negative meanings, and those with "white" have positive ones. Looking more deeply at our words and their current meanings, we can find hundreds which code people of color and people of different cultures and ethnicities as dangerous, threatening, manipulative, dishonest or immoral. In fact, anything foreign or alien has connotations of being not white, not pure, not American and not Christian. We reinforce racism every time we use such language.

Each of the following words has a derogatory racial meaning implied in its definition or derivation. Can you list an alternative, racially neutral word you could use in its place?

black deed	black hearted
blacklist	blackmail
black market	black sheep
white lie	white knight
white hope	black magic
dark (as in dark day)	yellow journalism
to gyp (from gypsy)	alien
yellow peril	red menace
to scalp	to Jew down
Jew's harp	yellow bellied
war paint (referring to women's makeup)	

What other words can you think of that are racially derogatory?

Racially demeaning usage also needs to be challenged in our visual images. When the good guys wear white hats and ride white horses and the bad guys wear black, the same racially tainted values are passed on. Advertisements, movies and TV images also rely on the development of images of darkness to convey danger and to provoke white fear. What films have you seen where the use of images of white and black, light and dark, or the racial casting of the heroes and villains was used to reinforce white=good and dark=bad?

If we pay attention to the images around us we can literally see the pervasive influence that racism has on our everyday lives. Racial difference and racial hierarchy, like gender hierarchy, is built into our spiritual values, our national identity, our language, our visual imagery and our sense of who we are. So far we have looked at whiteness as a general social construct. Before going into more detail about how whiteness works in our lives, we need to look at the benefits and costs that whiteness brings to us.

White Benefits,
Middle Class Privilege

*I*T IS NOT necessarily a privilege to be white*, but it certainly has its benefits. That's why so many of us gave up our unique histories, primary languages, accents, distinctive dress, family names and cultural expressions. It seemed like a small price to pay for acceptance in the circle of whiteness. Even with these sacrifices it wasn't easy to pass as white if we were Italian, Greek, Irish, Jewish, Spanish, Hungarian, or Polish. Sometimes it took generations before our families were fully accepted, and then usually because white society had an even greater fear of darker skinned people.

Privileges are the economic "extras" that those of us who are middle class and wealthy gain at the expense of poor and working class people of all races. Benefits, on the other hand, are the advantages that all white people gain at the expense of people of color regardless of economic position. Talk about racial benefits can ring false to many of us who don't have the economic privileges that we see many in this society enjoying. But just because we don't have the economic privileges of those with more money doesn't mean we haven't enjoyed some of the benefits of being white.

We can generally count on police protection rather than harassment. Depending on our financial situation, we can choose where we want to live

* I draw on important work on privilege done by Peggy McIntosh, "White Privilege and Male Privilege: A Personal Account of Coming to See Correspondences Through Work in Women's Studies," Center for Research on Women, Wellesley College, MA 02181 (1988), as well as material from *Helping Teens Stop Violence* Allan Creighton with Paul Kivel, Hunter House, Alameda CA (1992).

and choose neighborhoods that are safe and have decent schools. We are given more attention, respect and status in conversations than people of color. We see people who look like us in the media, history books, news and music in a positive light. (This is more true for men than for women, more true for the rich than the poor.) We have more recourse to and credibility within the legal system (again taking into account class and gender). Nothing that we do is qualified, limited, discredited or acclaimed simply because of our racial background. We don't have to represent our race, and nothing we do is judged as a credit to our race, or as confirmation of its shortcomings or inferiority. There are always mitigating factors, and some of us have these benefits more than others. All else being equal, it pays to be white. We will be accepted, acknowledged and given the benefit of the doubt. Since all else is not equal we each receive different benefits or different levels of the same benefits from being white.

These benefits start early. Most of them apply less to white girls than white boys, but they are still substantial. Others will have higher expectations for us as children, both at home and at school. We will have more money spent on our education, we will be called on more in school, we will be given more opportunity and resources to learn. We will see people like us in the textbooks, and if we get into trouble adults will expect us to be able to change and improve, and therefore will discipline or penalize us less or differently than children of color.

These benefits continue today and work to the direct economic advantage of every white person in the United States. First of all, we will earn more in our lifetime than a person of color of similar qualifications. We will be paid $1.00 for every $.60 that a person of color makes. We will advance faster and more reliably as well.

There are historically derived economic benefits too. All the land in this country was taken from Native Americans. Much of the infrastructure of this country was built by slave labor, incredibly low-paid labor, or by prison labor performed by men and women of color. Much of the housecleaning, childcare, cooking and maintenance of our society has been done by low wage earning women of color. Further property and material goods were appropriated by whites through the colonization of the West and Southwest throughout the 19th century, through the internment of Japanese Americans during World War II, through racial riots against people of color in the 18th, 19th and 20th centuries, and through an ongoing legacy of legal manipulation and exploitation. Today men and women and children of color still do the hardest, lowest paid, most dangerous work throughout the country. And we, white people, again depending on our relative economic circumstances, enjoy plentiful and inexpensive food, clothing and consumer goods because of that exploitation.

We have been taught history through a white-tinted lens which has minimized our exploitation of people of color and extolled the hardworking, courageous qualities of white people. For example, many of our foreparents gained a foothold in this country by finding work in such trades as railroads, streetcars, construction, shipbuilding, wagon and coach driving, house painting, tailoring, longshore work, brick laying, table waiting, working in the mills, furriering or dressmaking. These were all occupations that Blacks, who had begun entering many such skilled and unskilled jobs, were either excluded from or pushed out of in the nineteenth century. Exclusion and discrimination, coupled with immigrant mob violence against Blacks in many northern cities (such as the anti-black draft riots of 1863), meant that recent immigrants had economic opportunities that Blacks did not. These gains were consolidated by explicitly racist trade union practices and policies which kept Blacks in the most unskilled labor and lowest paid work.

It is not that white Americans have not worked hard and built much. We have. But we did not start out from scratch. We went to segregated schools and universities built with public money. We received school loans, V.A. loans, housing and auto loans when people of color were excluded or heavily discriminated against. We received federal jobs, military jobs and contracts when only whites were allowed. We were accepted into apprenticeships, training programs and unions when access for people of color was restricted or nonexistent.

Much of the rhetoric against more active policies for racial justice stem from the misconception that we are all given equal opportunities and start from a level playing field. We often don't even see the benefits we have received from racism. We claim that they are not there.

Think about your grandparents and parents and where they grew up and lived as adults. What work did they do? What are some of the benefits that have accrued to your family because they were white?

Look at the following benefits checklist. Put a check beside any benefit that you enjoy that a person of color of your age, gender and class probably does not. Think about what effect not having that benefit would have had on your life. (If you don't know the answer to any of these questions, research. Ask family members. Do what you can to discover the answers.)

*White Benefits Checklist**

☐ My ancestors were legal immigrants to this country during a period when immigrants from Asia, South and Central America or Africa were restricted.

---

* This checklist works well as a stand up exercise in a workshop or other group situation. As each item is read by a facilitator, everyone in the group to whom the item applies stands up silently for a moment, sits down, and then the next item is read. Discussion in pairs or as a whole group follows.

☐ My ancestors came to this country of their own free will and have never had to relocate unwillingly once here.

☐ I live on land that formerly belonged to Native Americans.

☑ My family received homesteading or landstaking claims from the federal government.

☐ I or my family or relatives receive or received federal farm subsidies, farm price supports, agricultural extension assistance or other federal benefits.

☐ I lived or live in a neighborhood that people of color were discriminated from living in.

☑ I lived or live in a city where red-lining discriminates against people of color getting housing or other loans.

☐ I or my parents went to racially segregated schools.

☐ I live in a school district or metropolitan area where more money is spent on the schools that white children go to than on those that children of color attend.

☑ I live in or went to a school district where children of color are more likely to be disciplined than white children, or more likely to be tracked into nonacademic programs.

☑ I live in or went to a school district where the textbooks and other classroom materials reflected my race as normal, heroes and builders of the United States, and there was little mention of the contributions of people of color to our society.

☑ I was encouraged to go on to college by teachers, parents or other advisors.

☑ I attended a publicly funded university, or a heavily endowed private university or college, and/or received student loans.

☐ I served in the military when it was still racially segregated, or achieved a rank where there were few people of color, or served in a combat situation where there were large numbers of people of color in dangerous combat positions.

☑ My ancestors were immigrants who took jobs in railroads, streetcars, construction, shipbuilding, wagon and coach driving, house painting, tailoring, longshore work, brick laying, table waiting, working in the mills, furriering, dressmaking or any other trade or occupation where people of color were driven out or excluded.

☑ I received job training in a program where there were few or no people of color

☑ I have received a job, job interview, job training or internship through personal connections of family or friends.

✗ ☑ I worked or work in a job where people of color made less for doing comparable work or did more menial jobs.

☐ I have worked in a job where people of color were hired last, or fired first.

☑ I work in a job, career or profession or in an agency or organization in which there are few people of color.

☐ I received small business loans or credits, government contracts or government assistance in my business.

☑ My parents were able to vote in any election they wanted without worrying about poll taxes, literacy requirements or other forms of discrimination.

☑ I can always vote for candidates who reflect my race.

☑ I live in a neighborhood that has better police protection, municipal services and is safer than that where people of color live.

☐ The hospital and medical services close to me or which I use are better than that of most people of color in the region in which I live.

☑ I have never had to worry that clearly labeled public facilities, such as swimming pools, restrooms, restaurants and nightspots were in fact not open to me because of my skin color.

☑ I see white people in a wide variety of roles on television and in movies.

☑ My race needn't be a factor in where I choose to live.

☑ My race needn't be a factor in where I send my children to school.

☐ I don't need to think about race and racism everyday. I can choose when and where I want to respond to racism.

What feelings come up for you when you think about the benefits that white people gain from racism? Do you feel angry or resentful? Guilty or uncomfortable? Do you want to say "Yes, but..."?

Again, the purpose of this checklist is not to discount what we, our families and foreparents have achieved. But we do need to question any assumptions we retain that everyone started out with equal opportunity.

You may be thinking at this point, "If I'm doing so well how come I'm barely making it?" Some of the benefits listed above are money in the bank for each and every one of us. Some of us have bigger bank accounts—much bigger. According to 1989 figures, 1 percent of the population controls about 40 percent of the wealth of this country (*New York Times*, April 17, 1995 "Gap in Wealth in United States called Widest in West"). In 1992, women generally made about 66 cents for every dollar that men made (Women's Action Coalition p. 59).

Benefits from racism are amplified or diminished by our relative privilege. People with disabilities, people with less formal education, and people who are lesbian, gay or bi-sexual are generally discriminated against in major ways. All of us benefit in some ways from whiteness, but some of us have cornered the market on significant benefits from being white to the exclusion of the rest of us.

The opposite of a benefit is a disadvantage. People of color face distinct disadvantages many of which have to do with discrimination and violence. If we were to talk about running a race for achievement and success in this country, and white people and people of color lined up side by side as a group, then every white benefit would be steps ahead of the starting line and every disadvantage would be steps backwards from the starting line before the race even began.

The disadvantages of being a person of color in the United States today include personal insults, harassment, discrimination, economic and cultural exploitation, stereotypes and invisibility, as well as threats, intimidation and violence. Not every person of color has experienced all the disadvantages described below, but they each have experienced some of them, and they each experience the vulnerability to violence that being a person of color in this country entails.

Institutional racism is discussed in detail in parts four, five, and six. But the personal acts of harassment and discrimination experienced directly from individual white people can also take a devastating toll. People of color never know when they will be called names, ridiculed or have comments made to them or about them by white people they don't know. They don't know when they might hear that they should leave the country, go home or go back to where they came from. Often these comments are made in situations where it isn't safe to confront the person who made the remark.

People of color also have to be ready to respond to teachers, employers or supervisors who have stereotypes, prejudices or lowered expectations about them. Many have been discouraged or prevented from pursuing academic or work goals or have been placed in lower vocational levels because of their racial identity. They have to be prepared for receiving less respect, attention or response from a doctor, police officer, court official, city official or other professional. They are not unlikely to be mistrusted or accused of stealing, cheating or lying, or to be stopped by the police because of their racial identity. They may also experience employment or housing discrimination or know someone who has.

There are cultural costs as well. People of color see themselves portrayed in degrading, stereotypical and fear-inducing ways on television and in the movies. They may have important religious or cultural holidays which are not recognized where they work or go to school. They have seen their religious practices, music, art, mannerisms, dress and other customs distorted, "borrowed," ridiculed, exploited or otherwise degraded by white people.

If they protest they may be verbally attacked by whites for being too sensitive, too emotional or too angry. Or they may be told they are different from other people of their racial group. Much of what people of color do, or say, or how they act in racially mixed company is judged as representative of their race.

On top of all this they have to live with the threat of physical violence. Some are the survivors of racial violence or have had close friends or family who are. People of color experience the daily toll of having to plan out how they are going to respond to racist comments and racial discrimination whenever it might occur.

In the foot race referred to above for jobs, educational opportunities or housing, each of these disadvantages would represent a step backward from the starting line *before the race even started*.

Although all people of color have experienced some of the disadvantages mentioned above, other factors make a difference in how vulnerable a person of color is to the effects of racism. Economic resources help buffer some of the more egregious effects of racism. Depending upon where one lives, women and men from different racial identities are treated differently. Discrimination varies in form and ranges from mild to severe depending on one's skin color, ethnicity, level of education, location, gender, sexual orientation, physical ability, age and how these are responded to by white people and white-run institutions.

Is it hard for you to accept that this kind of pervasive discrimination still occurs in this country? Which of the above statements is particularly hard to accept?

There is ample documentation for each of the effects of racism on people of color listed above. In many workshops we do a stand up exercise using a list of disadvantages for people of color to respond to. Those of us who are white are often surprised and disturbed about how many people of color stand when asked if they have experienced these things.

Most of us would like to think that today we have turned the tide and people of color have caught up with white people. We would like to believe (and are often told by other white people) that they enjoy the same opportunities as the rest of us. If we honestly add up the benefits of whiteness and the disadvantages of being a person of color, we can see that existing affirmative action programs don't go very far toward leveling the playing field.

The benefits of being white should be enjoyed by every person in this country. No one should have to endure the disadvantages that people of color experience. In leveling the playing field we don't want to hold anyone back. We want to push everyone forward so that we all share the benefits.

When we talk about the unequal distribution of benefits and disadvantages, we may feel uncomfortable about being white. We did not choose our skin color. Nor are we guilty for the fact that racism exists and that we have benefitted from it. We are responsible for acknowledging the reality of racism and for the daily choices we make about how to live in a racist society. We are only responsible for our own part, and we each have a part.

Sometimes, to avoid accepting our part, we want to shoot the bearer of bad news. Whether the bearer is white or a person of color, we become angry at whoever points out a comment or action that is hurtful, ignorant or abusive. We may accuse the person of being racist. This evasive reaction creates a debate about who is racist, or correct, or good, or well-intentioned, not about what to do about racism. It is probably inevitable that, when faced with the reality of the benefits and the harm of racism, we will feel defensive, guilty, ashamed, angry, powerless, frustrated or sad. These feelings are healthy and need to be acknowledged. Because they are uncomfortable we are liable to become angry at whoever brought up the subject.

Acknowledge your feelings and any resistance you have to the information presented above. Keep reading through this book and doing the exercises. Yes, it is hard and sometimes discouraging. For too long we have ignored or denied the realities of racism. In order to make any changes, we have to start by facing where we are and making a commitment to persevere and overcome the injustices we face.

We can support each other through the feelings. We need a safe place to talk about how it feels to be white and know about racism. It is important that we turn to other white people for this support. Who are white people you can talk with about racism?

When people say, "We all have it hard," or "Everyone has an equal opportunity," or "People of color just want special privileges," how can you use the information in this book to respond? What might be difficult about doing so? What additional information or resources will you need to be able to do this with confidence? How might you find those resources?

The Costs of Racism
to White People

WE TEND TO think of racism as a problem for people of color and something we should be concerned about for their sake. It is true that racism is devastating to them, and if we believe in justice, equality and equal opportunity for all then we should be trying to end it. Racism does produce material benefits for white people. However, the costs of racism to white people are devastating, especially to those of us without the money and power to buffer their effects. They are not the same costs as the day-to-day violence, discrimination and harassment that people of color have to deal with. Nevertheless, they are significant costs that we have been trained to ignore, deny or rationalize away. They are costs that other white people, particularly those with wealth, make us pay in our daily lives. It is sobering for us as white people to talk together about what it really costs to maintain such a system of division and exploitation in our society. We may even find it difficult to recognize some of the core costs of being white in our society.

For example, one of the costs of assimilating into white mainstream culture is that we are asked to leave behind the languages, foods, music, games, rituals and expressions that our parents and/or grandparents used. We lose our own "white" cultures and histories. Sometimes this loss leads us to romanticize the richness of other cultures.

We have been given a distorted and inaccurate picture of history and politics because the truth about racism has been excluded, the contributions of people of color left out and the role of white people cleaned up and modified. We also lose the presence and contributions of people of color to

36

our neighborhoods, schools and relationships. We are given a false sense of superiority that we should be in control and in authority, and that people of color should be maids, servants, gardeners and do the less valued work of our society. Our experiences are distorted, limited and less rich the more they are exclusively or dominately white.

There are many ways that racism affects our interpersonal relationships. We may have lost relationships with friends, family members and co-workers to disagreements, fights and tension over racism. At the same time we may have lost relationships with people of color because the tensions of racism make those relationships difficult to sustain.

Racism distorts our sense of danger and safety. We are taught to live in fear of people of color. We are exploited economically by the upper class and unable to fight or even see this exploitation because we are taught to scapegoat people of color. On a more personal level, many of us are brutalized by family violence and sexual assault, unable to resist it effectively, because we have been taught that people of color are the real danger, never the white men we live with.

There are also spiritual costs. Many of us have lost a connection to our own spiritual traditions as we have romanticized those of other cultures, such as Buddhism, or Native American beliefs. Our moral integrity is damaged as we witness situations of discrimination and harassment and do not intervene.

Our feelings of guilt, shame, embarrassment or inadequacy about racism and about our responses to it lower our self-esteem. Because racism makes a mockery of our ideals of democracy, justice and equality, it leads us to be cynical and pessimistic about human integrity and about our future, producing apathy, blame, despair, self-destructive behavior and acts of violence, especially among our young people.

It can be hard for us to be honest with ourselves about the costs of racism in our own lives. The following is a checklist to evaluate the costs of racism to white people. Put a check after each of the items that applies to you.

*Costs of Racism for White People: Checklist**

(Check each that applies)

☐ I don't know exactly what my European American heritage is, my great-grandparents' names, or what regions or cities my ancestors are from.

---

* From *Helping Teens Stop Violence*, © Oakland Men's Project, 1990 by Allan Creighton with Paul Kivel (Hunter House, 1992). Reprinted with permission.

☐ I grew up, lived, or live in a neighborhood, or went to school or a camp, which, as far as I knew, was exclusively white.

☐ I grew up with people of color who were servants, maids, gardeners or babysitters in my house.

☐ I did not meet people of color in person, or socially, before I was well into my teens.

☐ I grew up in a household where I heard derogatory racial terms or racial jokes.

☐ I grew up in a family or heard as a child that people of color were to blame for violence, lack of jobs or other problems.

☐ (For this category check all that apply.) I have seen or heard images or depictions, in magazines, on TV or radio, on cassettes, CDs or in movies of:

　　• Mexicans depicted as drunk, lazy or illiterate

　　• Asians depicted as exotic, cruel or mysterious

　　• Asian Indians depicted as excitable or "silly"

　　• Arabs depicted as swarthy, ravishing or "crazed"

　　• African Americans depicted as violent or criminal

　　• Pacific Islanders depicted as fun-loving, lazy

　　• American Indians depicted as drunk, savage or "noble"

　　• Any character-roles from nonwhite cultures depicted by white actors

☐ I was told not to play with children of particular other ethnicities when I was a child.

☐ I have sometimes felt that "white" culture was "wonderbread"* culture—empty and boring, or that another racial group had more rhythm, more athletic ability, was better at math and technology, or had more musical or artistic creativity than mine.

☐ I have felt that people of another racial group were more spiritual than white people.

☐ I have been nervous, fearful or found myself stiffening up when encountering people of color in a neutral public situation (for example, in an elevator, on the street).

☐ I have been sexually attracted to a person from another racial group because it seemed exotic, exciting or a challenge.

---

* I borrow this word from Margo Adair and Sharon Howell in "The Subjective Side of Politics."

- ☐ I was in a close friendship or relationship with a person of color, where the relationship was affected, stressed or endangered by racism between us or from others.
- ☐ I am not in a close significant relationship with any people of color in my life right now.
- ☐ I have been in a close friendship or relationship with another white person where that relationship was damaged or lost because of a disagreement about racism.
- ☐ I have felt embarrassed by, separate from, superior to, or more tolerant than other white people.
- ☐ I have worked in a job where people of color held more menial jobs, were paid less, or were otherwise harassed or discriminated against.
- ☐ I have been in an organization, workgroup, meeting or event which people of color protested as racist or which I knew to be racist.
- ☐ I have had degrading jokes, comments, or put-downs about people of color made in my presence and did not protest or challenge them.
- ☐ I have felt racial tension or noticed racism in a situation and was afraid to say or do anything about it.
- ☐ I have seen a person of color being attacked verbally or physically and did not intervene.
- ☐ I have felt angry, frustrated, tired or weary about dealing with racism and hearing about racial affairs.
- ☐ I live in a community where, for whatever reason, no people of color are present, so that some of these questions don't apply.

When we use this list for a stand up exercise with groups of white people, we see that we have all paid some of the costs of racism. Realizing what those costs are, we can easily become angry. If we are not careful, we can turn that anger toward people of color, blaming them for the problems of white racism. Sometimes we say things like, "If they weren't here we would not have these problems." Racism is caused by white people, by our attitudes, behaviors, practices and institutions. How do white people justify retaining the benefits of being white without taking responsibility for perpetuating racism?

Retaining Benefits— Avoiding Responsibility

*W*E HAVE SEEN how people of color experience acts of violence such as rape, battery, economic discrimination, lack of police protection/police brutality and poor health care. There is no time that a person of color is immune to harassment, discrimination or the possibility that she or he will be attacked. Money and other accoutrements of power afford some protection, but not completely, and not always.

During the first few years that I worked with men who are violent I was continually perplexed by their inability to see the effects of their actions and by their ability to deny the violence they had done to their partners or children. I only slowly became aware of the complex set of tactics that men use to make violence against women invisible and to avoid taking responsibility for their actions. These tactics are listed below in the rough order that men employ them.

Tactic	Typical Statement
Denial	"I didn't hit her."
Minimization	"It was only a slap."
Blame	"She asked for it."
Redefinition	"It was mutual combat."
Unintentionality	"Things got out of hand."
It's over now	"I'll never do it again."
It's only a few men	"Most men wouldn't hurt a woman."
Counterattack	"She controls everything."
Competing victimization	"Everybody is against men."

These tactics are part of a cycle in which these claims, particularly those of blame, counterattack, and competing victimization, lead to a justification of further violence.

As the battered women's movement tried to bring the prevalence and destructiveness of male violence to national attention it became clear that these tactics were used not only by individual men, but were also in general use in our society to avoid naming and responding to male violence.

As more of us began to interconnect issues of gender, race, class and sexual orientation, we could see how these tactics are used, consciously and unconsciously, by those in power to cover over the violence that is directed toward groups of people with less power. These are not gender specific tactics. They are the tactics of those who seek to retain their power and the privileges they have accrued.

Although these tactics follow a logical progression from outright denial to competing victimization, they are often used in combinations that make them confusing to argue against. It is important to remember that, although they appear as logical reasoning, all of the tactics are part of a strategy for explaining or justifying *already existing* injustice and violence.

We can learn to recognize and counter these tactics. I am going to use the history of the relationship between white Europeans and Native Americans to illustrate how these tactics have been (and still are) used to cover up the violence that white people commit toward people of color. There is more detailed information about that history in Part IV in the section on Native Americans. A brief summary here will have to suffice.

Denial

Denial is usually the first tactic employed and works very simply. The batterer says, "I didn't hit her."

European Americans say that Columbus was just looking for a trade route, the Pilgrims found a vast wilderness, and that the early colonists befriended the Indians and exchanged presents with them. At this level there is absolute denial that violence occurred and therefore of any responsibility for it.

Today we are using the tactic of denial when we say, "It's a level playing field," "Discrimination is a thing of the past," or "This is a land of equal opportunity."

Minimization

If the denial doesn't hold up because of the evidence—she has a broken arm—then the violence is minimized. The batterer says, "I didn't hit her, well, it was only a slap."

Native Americans were killed and their land taken. In response we say, "A few Indians died because they didn't have immunity to European diseases." We try to minimize the presence of the 12–15 million Native Americans in North America prior to 1492 and to minimize the violence we committed toward them.

Today we continue to minimize racism by saying, "Personal achievement mostly depends on personal ability," "Racism isn't prevalent anymore," or (about slavery) "There were a lot of kind slaveowners."

Blame

If the minimization doesn't hold up because the victim is in the hospital, then the batterer's effort shifts to a combination of justifying the violence and blaming the victim. "She asked for it." "She should have known not to say that to me." If the discussion is more general then men might make statements like, "Women are too emotional/manipulative/backstabbing."

Similarly, we know that millions of Native Americans died, not only from intentional transmission of diseases, but from being shot, tortured and enslaved. Since the blame has to fall on entire societies, we make statements like, "Indians were primitive." "They had not developed the technology to compete." "They were not physically able to resist the diseases, hold up under slavery [they didn't make good slaves!], they were naive, simple, heathens."

These justifications rely on a series of biological and psychological justifications for the abuse. Historically there have been continual attempts to "explain" away white violence against people of color as the inevitable result of genetic, biological, chemical, physiological or psychological differences. These differences often do not exist. Where they do, they are seldom related to real differences in behavior. In any case they never justify injustice and violence. What they do is shift the focus from the perpetrators of violence to the victims, subtly blaming them for being inferior or vulnerable to violence.

When we describe what happened in terms of the agency of the person or people with power the uses of these explanations becomes clearer. He hit her. He broke her arm. He put her in the hospital. Columbus invaded, killed, enslaved and tortured the Taino/Arawak peoples. The U.S. Army at Fort Clark deliberately distributed small pox infected blankets to the Mandan in order to kill them (Churchill 1994 p. 35).

Today we blame people of color for racism by saying, "Look at the way they act." "If they weren't so angry..." Or, "They are immoral, lazy, dumb or unambitious."

Redefinition

We want to hold adults responsible for what they do. Therefore we must carefully and accurately investigate what happened so that we can stop violence. If we don't look at the overall context and take differentials of power into account, we can be susceptible to the tactic of redefinition. For example, he says, "It was mutual combat." "She hit me first." "It takes two to fight."

If we can no longer claim that Columbus simply and innocently discovered America, we try to redefine that event too. The 1992 Quincentennial museum exhibit in New York was called "Encounter," a word implying some level of mutuality, equality and neutrality. In the same vein we say, "The settlers had to protect themselves from Indian attacks."

Today we redefine racism as a mutual problem by saying, "This country is just a big melting pot." "Anybody can be prejudiced." Or, "People of color attack white people too."

It Was Unintentional

At this point in the battle the group or individual with more power, who has clearly done something that resulted in some kind of devastation, might claim that the damage was unintentional and therefore their responsibility was minimal. The batterer says things such as, "I didn't intend to hit her." "I didn't mean to hit her so hard." "Things got out of hand."

First of all, claims of innocence by someone who has hurt you are always suspect. Adults are responsible for their actions and for the results of those actions. "I didn't mean to" is not an acceptable legal or moral excuse for being violent toward another person. Secondly, actual intent is often discernible from the pattern of action of the perpetrators of violence. When a man systematically tries to control a woman and then says, "I didn't mean to hit her," he is saying that he hoped to control her by non-physical means. When all else failed he resorted to hitting. The issue is power and control. Intent is clearly evident in the entire pattern of behavior.

We have said that the near-eradication of Native Americans and their food supplies, hunting areas and natural resources was the unintended result of European immigration. We know that the complete elimination of Native Americans from the United States was government policy as well as part of the general, everyday discourse of white Americans (see Section IV for details). It was stated government policy to kill Indians. Smallpox-infected blankets were intentionally distributed to Indians by government representatives.

Today we continue to claim racism is unintentional by saying, "Discrimination may happen, but most people are well intentioned." "She probably didn't mean it like that." Or, "It was only a joke."

It's All Over Now

Another way to defuse responsibility is by claiming that the violence happened in the past and is no longer an issue. The batterer says, "It's over with," or "I'll never do it again." He may finally claim responsibility (often indirectly), but he asserts that things have changed. Part of his claim is that the effects of the violence are similarly in the past and shouldn't influence us anymore. The trauma, pain, mistrust, fear, disrespect and vulnerability should just be forgotten. This discounts the seriousness of the violence, blames the survivor for not being able to let go of it and move on, and focuses on the perpetrator's words, not his actions. All we have is his promise that it won't happen again.

White people often claim that genocide, land grabbing and exploitation are things of the past. Most of our images of Indians reinforce that belief by focusing on Native Americans who lived one to three hundred years ago. The reality is that the effects of colonial violence are still readily apparent today. The small number of remaining Native Americans, the poor economic conditions, the alcoholism, the shattered traditions and devastated communities are the direct result of five hundred years of systematic oppression.

Furthermore, the same policies are in play today as they were hundreds of years ago. The violence did not magically stop at some point. White civilization did not back off and allow the Native nations to heal and recover. Across the country, land is still being taken, treaties are still being broken, Native culture, religion and artifacts are still being stolen and/or exploited, Native American nations are still denied sovereignty, Native Americans are still being killed by whites with some degree of impunity, and their land is still being exploited and laid to waste on a massive scale. Some of the violence takes different forms than it did a hundred years ago. It is important that we not use those differences to claim that we are not responsible for the violence that occurs today, or to blame Native Americans for the results of violence that white people committed in the past and continue to commit today. When we are dealing with structural violence, the proof of change is structural change, not claims of innocence.

Today we claim racism is all over by saying, "Slavery was over a long time ago." "The days of land grabbing are long gone." "That was before the Civil Rights Era." Or, "There aren't any Indians left."

It's Only a Few People

If we are unable to maintain that the violence was all in the past, we may switch to another tactic to make a current situation seem isolated. We might say that it's really only a few people who are like that—it is not systemic or institutionalized. In the case of domestic violence we contend that only a few men are batterers, most men treat women well. However, if 25–33 percent of all heterosexual relationships have an incident of the man hitting the woman—three to five million such incidents a year—then we are clearly talking about a social issue, not the isolated anger of a few men (Women's Action Coalition, pps 55–57).

Similarly, it wasn't just rogue officers like Custer disobeying orders, or cruel, greedy men like Columbus, or a few cowboys who killed Native Americans. Slavery, genocide and racism were built into the structure of all the institutions of our society and were everyday occurrences. We have inherited, perpetuated and benefitted from these actions. All of us are implicated.

Today we continue to use this tactic when we say, "Housing and job discrimination are the result of a few bigoted people." "The Far Right is behind the scapegoating of immigrants." "It's only neo-Nazis and Skinheads who do that sort of thing."

Counterattack and Competing Victimization

When all else fails and responsibility for the violence is inexorably falling on the shoulders of those who committed the acts themselves, there is a counterattack, an attempt to claim a reversal of the power relationships. This approach is usually combined with the final tactic, competing victimization. An individual batterer might say, "She really has all the power in our family." "If I didn't hit her she would run all over me." On a national level there are more and more claims that men are battered by women too, that women win custody and men don't, and that there is too much male-bashing.

To counter this tactic we must go back to what happened, who has power, and what violence is being done. Who ended up in the hospital, and who remained in control of the family resources? In the claims above we find that in about 95 percent of domestic violence cases the woman is the victim of a pattern of abuse, and in 5 percent of the cases the man is the victim (Women's

Action Coalition, pps 55–57). In 80 percent of custody cases the man does not even contest custody. In the remaining 20 percent, where the man wants custody, men get custody 63 percent of the time (*The Divorce Revolution: The Unexpected Social and Economic Consequences for Women and Children in America*, L. J. Weitzman, Free Press, New York 1985). The reality is not what the men would claim, nor what media reporting would have us believe.

We now have a national debate about multiculturalism which claims that people of color and women have so much power that American society itself is threatened. We are told that Native Americans and other people of color are a danger and a threat to our national unity and to our "American" way of life. White people are filing a competing claim of victimization, claiming to be the victims of multiculturalism.

We need to ask ourselves who was killed and who ended up with the land base of this country? Today, who has the jobs, who gets into the universities, who earns more pay, and who gets more media attention for their concerns, white people or people of color?

White people are counterattacking today by saying, "Political correctness rules the universities." "We just want our rights too." "They want special status." "They're taking away our jobs." Some of the ways we claim to be victims include saying, "White males have rights too." "I have it just as bad as anybody." And, "White people are under attack."

Those with power have many resources for having their view of reality prevail, and they have a lot at stake in maintaining the status quo. They will employ the above tactics to defend their interests. We must be aware of these tactics and able to counter them. When unchallenged, they can be used to justify further inequality and violence. If we keep our eyes clearly on the power and the violence we can see that these tactics are transparent for what they are, attempts to prevent placing responsibility on those who commit and benefit from acts of injustice. Our strongest tools are a critical analysis of who has power and an understanding of the patterns and consequences of present actions and policies.

Who Is a Victim?

S*OME OF US* believe that there is a certain glamour to being a victim. We may think victims get more attention, more respect, more care or simply have some inherently virtuous quality. We may even believe that some people would prefer to be victims, may even take active steps to achieve victim status. And sometimes, those of us with more power or privilege or less vulnerability to violence may think that the way to redirect attention, resources or virtue back to ourselves is to claim that we are victims too.

Men are doing this in custody cases, counter harassment and discrimination suits, and in charges of reverse discrimination. White people do this routinely in protesting affirmative action and special programs for people of color.

There is nothing, absolutely nothing, good about being a victim. Being a victim means you were not powerful enough to protect yourself from someone else's abuse. It means your life, livelihood or family was threatened and possibly taken away. Those of us who have been raped, robbed, battered, harassed, or discriminated against know how painful and longlasting the effects can be. Nor is it necessarily safe to step forward and describe one's victimization. Survivors of abuse are routinely not believed, blamed and revictimized.

Claiming to be victimized is not the same as being victimized. Who is the victim and who is the perpetrator of abuse in any particular situation depend on what actually happened and who has the power. In order to understand clearly who was victimized, we must ask the questions, "Who has the power?" and "Who did what to whom?"

Actual claims of reverse discrimination are rare, and many of them lack merit. A 1995 Labor Department draft report reviewing opinions by U.S. District Courts and Courts of Appeal found that between 1990 and 1994, of

47

the 3,000 discrimination cases brought forward, only 100 were charges of reverse discrimination. Of the 100, only six were found to have merit. Relief was provided in those six cases (*Oakland Tribune*, March 31, 1995, page A–9).

What is going on when white people claim reverse racism or claim to be victimized by people of color? Often we are being victimize, but not by people of color. We are economically exploited by white-owned corporations which move jobs overseas leaving our communities stranded and some of us unemployed. Then we are incited to blame people of color, Jews, and recent immigrants and we are deceived about the true cause of our exploitation.

An individual white person can be abused by a person of color. This is unfair and needs to be stopped and addressed. Any person can decide to hurt other people. We have seen in the sections on white benefits and the costs of racism that whites are not victims of people of color in any way similar to how people of color are hurt by racism everyday, in every aspect of their lives. Charges of reverse racism are usually part of a white strategy to deny white racism and to counterattack against attempts to promote racial justice.

So far we have been looking at the broad picture of whiteness and racism. In the next section we will look at some of the misunderstandings that prevent us from challenging racism effectively.

PART II

The Dynamics of Racism

The Enemy Within

ONE OF THE primary purposes and effects of racism and anti-Semitism is to keep people of color and Jewish people at the center of attention while keeping white people in general and white Christians in particular at the center of power. The majority of Americans have been abused, economically exploited, harassed and discriminated against. We experience tremendous physical, economic and emotional loss from social inequity and personal abuse. Like the proverbial thief who points off in the distance to get you to look away and then deftly picks your pocket, racism and anti-Semitism divert our attention from those who have the power to rob and hurt us. In our pain and anger, we often rely on traditional scapegoats and blame anyone around who is less powerful than we are. There are two primary ways this works.

People of color and Jewish people have long been portrayed as economic threats to white Americans. We have heard and perhaps used phrases like, "They will do anything." "They work for less." "They take away our jobs." "They are a drain on our economic system, eating up benefits." "They drive wages down and unemployment up." Or about Jewish people, "They control everything." "They are unscrupulous." "They rob us blind."

In fact, people of color and Jewish people don't make most of the economic decisions that affect our jobs and livelihoods. Closing factories and moving them to "cheaper" parts of the country or abroad, busting unions, blocking increases in the minimum wage, decreasing health care and other benefits—these are all intentional attempts by the wealthy, who are also predominantely white and Christian, to increase profits and personal gain. Corporate leaders lower wages, increase prices, increase their salaries and corporate profits with impunity. This results in real decreases in our standard of living. Keeping our attention on people of color, Jewish people and immigrants diverts our attention from the people who have been getting richer while we have been getting poorer.

There has been a vast redistribution of income toward the rich in the last fifteen years in this country, while the standards of living of the rest of us have decreased. Simultaneously, our national infrastructure has deteriorated, decent health care is beyond the reach of millions, our retirement funds have eroded and our schools are falling apart. We are right to be wary of any leader who says we need to tighten our belts and sacrifice. We don't have anything to spare. The wealthy do. They should be taxed at least to the level they were in 1970 to rebuild our country. We are not doing this for people of color, we are doing it for ourselves. We are being ripped off, not by welfare mothers earning four thousand dollars a year, but by corporate executives earning four hundred thousand dollars a year. Blaming immigrants, illegal workers, welfare mothers or other poor or less powerful groups diverts our attention from the people who own the power and wealth. We hurt ourselves and make it impossible to solve our economic problems when we don't understand the nature of racism. And the rich keep getting richer.

Economic Assessment

1. In your community, which corporations are the largest employers?

2. What decisions has this group made in the last few years which have affected employment levels and wages (e.g., opening or closing offices or plants, downsizing, moving production abroad, etc.)?

3. Which companies were taken over or bought out? Who took over, what happened to jobs, wages and working conditions after the takeover?

4. How would you describe the people who own these companies? Are they mostly or exclusively white? Are they primarily Christian? Are they men? (The fact that those who gain most are well off Christian white men does not mean that most Christian white men benefit from these actions.)

5. Which particular racial groups are being blamed for these decisions in your local area? In your state?

6. How much money have businesses put into promoting this scapegoating through political contributions, lobbying, political ads or public campaigns?

7. How do you benefit and what do you lose from those actions?

The second way racism turns our attention away from real exploitation and danger is by creating myths about family violence and sexual assault. We are taught that men of color and men from other cultures are dangerous. We have stereotypes about rapists being dark (i.e., black) strangers in alleys, about Asian men being devious and dishonest, about Latinos being physically and sexually dangerous. Racism has produced myths about every group of non-white, non-mainstream men being dangerous to white women and children.

The reality is that approximately 80 percent of sexual violence is committed within the same racial group by heterosexual men who know their victim ("Sexual Violence Facts and Statistics" Illinois coalition Against Sexual Assault 1993). We and our children are more likely to be beat up, sexually assaulted or abused by heterosexual white men.

Despite this reality, we continue to believe that we need to protect ourselves from men who are different. We justify public policies which disproportionately lock up men of color, primarily Latino and African American men, but these changes do not make it appreciably safer for us. Because we are led to believe that we need "our" men to protect us from men "out there," we are slow to recognize the violence of men in our family and dating relationships.

Racism makes us vulnerable to economic exploitation and violence from other white people. The relationships between these issues is complex, and I have only sketched the briefest outline here. Even so, it should be clear that effective action against racism makes the white community stronger, safer and more effective in fighting for economic justice and safety for all. It also allows us to join as allies with people of color in the struggle for economic justice and democracy. Most white people have as much to gain as people of color from the struggle to redistribute wealth to poor, working and middle class people. Most white people have as much to gain as people of color from making our families and communities safer. Rather than letting racism divide us, we need to work together to address these issues.

Fear and Danger

M*ANY OF US* in the United States today are afraid. We worry about crime, drugs, our children's future and our own security. Our fear is a result of many economic, social, political and personal factors. It is also linked to violence in news media, TV and the movies.

In a society where we are constantly presented with tales of danger and violence and told how vulnerable we are, it is not surprising that most of us are fearful. Racism produces a fear based society in which no one feels safe. However *being afraid is not the same as being in danger.*

For example, white people often fear people of color, and most people of color fear white people. White people are not usually in danger from people of color. People of color are in danger from individual acts of discrimination, hate crimes and police brutality from white people, as well as institutional practices which kill people through lack of health care, lack of police protection and unequal legal prosecution. White people are rarely killed, harassed or discriminated against by people of color.

To understand whiteness we need to look at how fear of people of color is manufactured and used to justify repression and exploitation of communities of color.

Have you ever been in your car when a person of color drove past, and you reached over to lock your car door? Have you ever had a man of color walk by and you touched your wallet or purse or held it tighter? Have you ever seen a person of color in your neighborhood and you closed a window, pulled a blind or locked a door? Have you ever had an adult or young person of color in your house and wondered, ever so briefly, if valuables were out? Have you ever seen a person of color with quality clothes, an expensive car or other item and wondered how they got the money?

I have done all of these things. I was taught to fear people of color. I was told that they were dangerous and that they would steal, cheat or otherwise grab whatever I had.

Many of these motions were practically involuntary. My hand was on my wallet before I realized it. Of course, I tried to turn the gesture into a casual motion so it wouldn't be apparent what I had done. For many years I did not realize I was doing this. Then I listened to people of color, particularly African American men (who we have been trained to fear the most), describe how white people were always afraid of them. I began to notice my own and other people's gestures—the tensing, the guardedness, the suspicion, the watchfulness.

White fear is primarily fear of men of color. (We also have fears about women of color, but they are not as visceral or pervasive.) For example, I grew up playing cowboys and Indians, always wanting to be the brave cowboy who protected the innocent homesteaders and settlers from the vicious (male) Indians ready to sweep down and destroy white outposts. I was learning that as a man I would have to protect (white) womanhood and (white) civilization.

Growing up in Los Angeles in the 1950s and early 1960s, I heard repeated stories about the masses of Mexican and Central American people pushing against our borders, pressing to get in, to overwhelm us. I remember a discussion with my parents in which I said I didn't think I ever wanted to have children because there were already so many people in the world. My parents tried to convince me that it was important that I have children because I was smart and educated and we needed more of our kind. I understood "our kind" to be white.* Again I was getting the message that we had to defend ourselves, reproduce ourselves, protect what was ours because we were under attack.

Many of the racial images that we hear today such as "illegal alien," "border patrol," "drug wars," and "the invasion of Japanese capital" are based on images of protection, defense, borders and danger. Many of us feel besieged. We talk as if we are under attack in many areas of our lives where we use to feel safe. We complain that we can't say what we want with impunity, we can't go where we want. We notice that people of color in the United States and abroad are demanding a more equitable distribution of the world's wealth. To counter these attacks on white power and to divert attention from the benefits we have accrued, we have created a fear of potential, retaliatory violence from people of color.

This pattern has a long history. Individual white settlers who took Native American lands feared retaliation. But many white people lived in cities and were not worried about Indian attack. White settlers, in conjunction with the

---

* Because we were Jewish and this was after the Holocaust, I also received messages about the importance of having children so that Hitler will not have succeeded in eliminating us.

U.S. government which wanted to "open up" Native American land, had to convince the public that Native Americans were dangerous and needed to be exterminated. A campaign, using books, pictures and the media, created images of Indians as primitive, cruel savages who wanted to kill white men and rape white women. This campaign made it easier to justify the appropriation of Native American lands, and the death and removal of Native Americans themselves. In the process, generations of us learned to fear Indians. Many children growing up today still do, even though there are only about three million Native Americans in all of the United States and Canada.* They are the ones who have suffered the effects of racial violence.

Over the course of 240 years of slavery, white slaveowners created the illusion of danger from African Americans to justify the harshness of their treatment, and to scare other white people into supporting their subjugation. White people feared African Americans even though they were so thoroughly dominated and brutalized as to offer little threat to whites. Slaves were brutalized publicly and routinely. Some fought back, but most were more interested in escaping than in retaliation.

This pattern of white fear and violence continues today. We are still presented with selected news coverage conveying African American men as the embodiment of danger itself. It is difficult for any white American not to have an immediate feeling of fear in the presence of an African American male. This fear, in turn, has justified massive and continuous control of the African American community through the schools, police, legal system, jails, prisons and the military. This control starts in pre-school or elementary school. It limits educational opportunities, jobs, skills and access to health care. It is enforced by police brutality and various forms of discrimination. These conditions produce stress, despair and desperation for African American young men, leading to their killing each other and themselves at high rates, living six years less than white men on the average. White violence leads to fear which is used to justify further white violence. African American men, not white people, are the victims of this cycle of violence.

Many times we use stories to justify the fear that we feel toward people of color. We might introduce them by such phrases as "I was attacked once by..." "I don't want to sound prejudiced, but I know someone who had a bad experience with..." or "It's unfortunate, but my one negative experience was..." We then use these single examples to reinforce a stereotype about a whole category of people and to prove the legitimacy of our fear of them.

---

* This number is from government figures. Racially motivated governmental policies exclude Hispanics and African Americans with Native American ancestry from current estimates. All current demographic figures are highly contested.

Is there a story that you use to justify your fears of people of color? What are stories that you've heard other white people use?

These shared stories can be a way to strengthen white solidarity by implying that we share a common danger. They reinforce our desire to be with white people and to avoid people of color. They also raise the stakes if we challenge racism because to do so seems to threaten our own security. How can we challenge other whites when we may need them in case of an attack?

Sometimes, when I realize the extent of the stereotypes I have learned and act from, I want to disavow the fear altogether and convince myself that there is nothing to be afraid of. Or, to counter the stereotype, I try to assume that all men of color are safe and all white men are dangerous. Yet I know that I am foolish if I simply reverse the stereotypes. In a society in which many people are dangerous and violence is a threat, we need to evaluate the danger from each person we're with. Any preconceived notions of danger or safety based on skin color are dysfunctional—they can actually increase our danger and make us less able to protect ourselves. For example, even as white women have moved to the suburbs, put locks on their doors and windows, and avoided urban streets at night, they have remained vulnerable to robbery and assault from white male friends, lovers, neighbors and co-workers.

Was there ever a time when you heard about violence that a white man committed and you said to yourself, "I never would have imagined that so-and-so could have done something like that"? We are often awarded a presumption of innocence if we are white. This works to our benefit when we are stopped by the police, shopping in a store, walking down the street, or renting equipment such as cars, tools or movies. Other white people assume we are safe until we are proven dangerous.

Have you ever been surprised that an African American or Latino man could commit a particular act of violence? We expect men of color to be dangerous. When Susan Smith killed her two children, she claimed that an African American man had kidnapped them. When Charles Stuart killed his pregnant wife in New York City, he stabbed himself and claimed an African American man had attacked them. When the federal building in Oklahoma City was bombed, most people immediately suspected Arab men as the culprits. Many of us accepted these statements without question because they fit with our expectations. In each situation search for the guilty white person was temporarily diverted toward men of color.

We fear people of color in great disproportion to any danger they may have for us. We trust white men in spite of the danger some of them pose. These fears become expectations which influence who we trust and how we evaluate danger. Even our personal vigilance is often increased when people of color are present and relaxed when only white people are around.

These expectations translate into feeling uneasy whenever there are significant numbers of people of color around us. It has been found that whites are most comfortable in interracial situations where people of color constitute a small percentage of the population. When the percentage rises to 15–20, white people often begin to feel that "they" are dominating or are unfairly represented. When people of color constitute 20–25 percent of the population, white people begin to describe people of color as the majority, or as having taken over.

As white people we must start by acknowledging the violence we have done to people of color throughout our history. We must understand how we have demonized them to justify that violence. Our fear of violence to ourselves is related to the violence we have done and continue to do to people of color. Therefore one way to lower our fear is to acknowledge and reduce our violence.

Jewish people have likewise been portrayed as dangerous—economically dangerous. Stereotypes that Jews own the banks and are crafty, unscrupulous and untrustworthy contribute to such anti-Semitic fears. Age-old Christian teachings that Jews killed Christ, and false documents like the "Protocols of the Elders of Zion,"* are additional currents in this river of fear.

Jewish people in the United States have been subject to verbal and physical attack, bombings, desecration of cemeteries, intimidation and murder by white Christians. Christians have not been attacked by Jews for being Christian. Again we can see that although the fear is mutual, Jewish people are in some danger from Christians whereas Christians are in no danger from being attacked by Jews.

Economically, most banks, major corporations and other institutions that make the financial decisions about jobs, pensions and health care are owned by Christians. They make the decisions to rob our Savings & Loans, steal from the government, move jobs overseas, create unsafe working conditions and bust unions. Christian fear works, like all racial fear, to divert people from the source of danger—people inside the mainstream who hold political, economic and social power. Jews are blamed for economic problems for which they are not responsible, and become the targets of further anti-Semitic violence.

All Jews experience the stereotypes and fear that white Christians and other non-Jews have of them. Jewish people know what it's like to be attacked because others have been trained to fear you. Jews who are white are feared

---

* The "Protocols" is a forged document purporting to be a plan by Jews to control the world. It was first published in Russia by Tsarist officials in the beginning of this century to direct Russian peasant's wrath for harsh economic conditions onto Jews. It was widely distributed by Henry Ford and other industrialists in the United States during the Depression and still circulates throughout the world.

and are taught to fear people of color. Many white Jewish concerns about violence focus on danger from African Americans, even though most anti-Semitic violence is committed by white Christians. Anti-Semitism should be challenged wherever it occurs, but primary energy should always go to defend against those with most power to do harm. Meanwhile, Jews of color* are attacked from all sides, by white Christians and Jews, and by Christian people of color.

The focus by white Jews on external danger from people of color also helps conceal the significant levels of domestic violence, sexual assault and child abuse within the Jewish community. When Jewish family violence is denied and minimized, and Jewish family values are held up as better than African Americans,' then racism is perpetuated. This racism justifies violence against African Americans while obscuring violence against Jewish women and children.

All of us who are white need to recognize just how deeply we have been trained to fear and distrust people of color and how much that fear guides our behavior, because that fear is easily manipulated by politicians, the media or corporate leaders. Christians need to acknowledge their fear and distrust of Jews for the same reasons. Our fear often leads us to misconstrue our own best political interests because our racial fear overrides our best thinking.

Our fear of African Americans is such that a single person can come to represent the danger we feel from an entire community. Many different individuals have been held up by politicians and the media to represent the "danger" of African Americans to white people in the last few decades since the beginning of the Civil Rights Movement. Such people as Malcolm X, Huey Newton, Eldridge Cleaver, Martin Luther King, Jr., Angela Davis, "Willie" Horton, Ice Cube, Jesse Jackson and Sister Souljah have all been used to symbolize danger and to manipulate white people's fears. As our fears of people of color increase we are more easily deceived by white leaders who have an aura of trustworthiness simply because they are white.

---

* A distinction between Jews who are white and Jews of color is only useful within the framework of a discussion of racism.

The Geography of Fear

THERE IS ALSO a geography of fear. We fear being in certain places and certain kinds of spaces. The geography of fear is built on perceptions of race, class and gender. For example we are all taught to fear violence in the inner city. Here "inner city" is a code word for "where African Americans and Latino/as live."

There is certainly more street crime in low income neighborhoods. There is not necessarily more family violence, drugs or economic crime. In any case, most of the crime and violence in low income neighborhoods is not racially motivated. People of color are the most common targets of crime by people of color, and white people are the most common targets of crime by white people. We tend to think that we are particularly vulnerable in inner city neighborhoods because of the racism of people of color. There is no evidence that this is so.

There are many areas in which straight white males feel fairly safe. They can roam the countryside and the suburbs and generally are not worried they'll be attacked. They can be alone in the woods, at the beach, or in the hills and not worry about being assaulted. White women alone are much less safe than white men alone, but white women with other women or with a man are not usually attacked. Lesbians and gay men are less safe than heterosexual white.

In what areas do you routinely feel safe? Why? How safe do you think people of color feel in those areas *you* feel safest in? Except in neighborhoods that are predominately people of their own ethnic group,* people of color are not safe alone or in groups. They are verbally attacked, harassed by police, "mistaken" for gardeners, servants or delivery people, and shunned or

---

* Even there they are vulnerable to higher levels of street crime *and* the threat of police brutality.

followed by shopkeepers. They are questioned and mistrusted by whites when they aren't in their own neighborhoods, which are assumed to be inner city ghettos. This is true even for people of color who live in suburban or rural areas. Women of color cannot assume they are safe and free from harassment and violence anywhere.

To sum up, there is nowhere that men and women of color are safe from crime, violence or white racism. Whites, on the other hand, are seldom vulnerable to violence from people of color, and can generally avoid high crime areas unless forced by economic circumstances to live or work in one. As white people we have been trained to see danger in the very presence of people of color. This will not change until we alter the negative images and portrayals of people of color in our society and learn to positively value their presence and participation.

Exotic and Erotic

*H*AVE YOU EVER imagined it was exotic, erotic or exciting to have sexual relations with a person of color or with a Jewish person? Have you ever been in a dating or longer-term relationship with a person of color or Jewish person where these elements were present?

Another way that racism and anti-Semitism overlap is in the eroticization of difference. White people's images of people of color and of Jewish people make them seem not only dangerous, but also exotic and erotic. Men of color, including Irish men and men from Southern and Eastern Europe at times when they were not considered to be white, and Jewish men, have been portrayed as wild, bestial, aggressive sexual beings with little or no restraint and insatiable appetites for white (Christian) women. White men have been trained to see men of color and Jewish men as sexual rivals, and are supposed to protect white women from them.

Similarly, women of color and Jewish women are portrayed as more passionate and sensual than white women. Through economic systems of exploitation, women of color and sometimes Jewish women have been available to white men as slaves, domestic help, factory workers, childcare workers, prostitutes and sex industry workers. White men have been able to sexually exploit women and then justify their abuse by citing the sexual nature of their victims. In fact, sexual exploitation of women who are vulnerable says more about the sexual nature of white men than of anyone else.

Traditional Christian sexuality permits only a narrow range of sexual behavior within a heterosexual marriage relationship focused on childbearing. Christian concepts of virtue and sin, good and evil are heavily intertwined with those limitations. White European society proscribed all practices that were not sanctioned by the church, labeled them as bad, and projected them first onto Jews and later onto people of color. Everything that was unwanted—

such as lust, passion, non-procreative sex, female assertion, sensuality and pleasure, titillation and non-marital sex—was labeled sinful, evil and not truly white. White Christian sexuality was portrayed as pure, chaste, procreative and restrained, at least in its ideal form.

White people experience all the varieties of sexual desire that any other group does. Whenever there has been dissent or rebellion within the white community, one way those with most power try to maintain control is to impose white, Christian sexual standards on those who are too independent. White women and poor and working class people, as well as lesbian, gay and bisexual whites, have always been persecuted for sexual trespass even when, as is usually the case, the real issue is independence and challenge to authority.

White people have eroticized African Americans more than any other group. Black has been seen as the opposite of white, and therefore the sexuality of Black people has been perceived as directly opposite the "chaste and controlled" sexuality of white people. In addition, African American slaves were seen as sexual commodities, particularly after the slave trade was declared illegal. Their ability to reproduce and increase the slaveowner's capital was nearly as important as their ability to work. They came to be defined by the sexual role that they were forced to play in the plantation economy. White people have since used these sexual projections to justify violence—most prominately, but certainly not exclusively—in lynchings, castrations and rape.

Training in white, primarily male, violence toward people of color starts early. Even young white men commit acts of violence toward people of color, Jews, and lesbians and gays of all colors because they fear the greater violence that their white peers will do to them if they don't.

In most discussions of masculinity we underestimate the role that racism plays. Many young men are challenged by other white men to prove they are real (white) men by participating in physical, sexual or verbal abuse of men of color and Jewish men. White male bonding at work, at school or in the extended family includes significant levels of racism toward men of color ranging from sitting around joking about men of color, to bonding as a team against an opposing team of color, to participating in an attack upon a specific person of color, to joining an explicit white supremacist group. Not participating in such "rites of passage" makes men vulnerable to physical and sexual aggression from others. Those who challenge racist (or sexist or homophobic) jokes or comments risk derision, attack and exclusion. Members of some sports teams, gangs, hate groups and clubs have even beat up members who threaten group solidarity.

White men also bond with others and "prove" their heterosexuality by verbally and sexually assaulting women of color and Jewish women. Having sex with a woman of color or a Jewish woman is often seen as the mark of the most (hetero)sexually experienced white men because these women are stereotyped as the most erotic, wild and dangerous women available. (There are other, less sexual stereotypes of women of color and Jewish women as well.) The ability not to be undermined or entrapped by "exotic" and "dangerous" women is a sign of success and reaffirms that a man is in control, is one of the (white Christian) boys, and that he knows the sexual and racial order.

When a young man is pushed by white male peers to assault or harass women or men of color, a lot is riding on the line—and he knows it. It is hard for most young men to avoid such pressure because the threat of violence from other white men is real and immediate. We can help young men refuse to participate by giving them tools for resisting male gender role training and for creating different options. These options can make the entire community safer. (See Creighton and Krivel 1992 and 1995).

The eroticization of people of color has been used to justify the control of entire communities. After the Civil War, when African Americans were no longer protected or valued as slaves, lynching became one form of repression against the African-American community. Before that time, there were almost no reports of African American men raping white women. During the first years that lynching was prevalent, rape was not a frequent justification. Lynching was used as a method to control an unruly, potentially dangerous ex-slave population, a way to terrorize them into not using their newly won freedom.

After the Reconstruction period, African Americans were no longer a credible threat to white people because of the dismantling of post-Civil War rights and the beginning of Jim Crow segregation. Lynching began to be justified by appeals to white people's fear of sexual aggression by African American men. Even then, rape of white women was only alleged in about a third of the situations where men were lynched. It was only after many more years that lynching became almost exclusively justified by claims of African American men's sexual aggression toward white women (Davis 1981, pps. 184–187; Pleck). Throughout all those years, and the thousands of lynchings which took place, white people committed eroticized violence against African American men by castrating, mutilating and lynching them in public, to the entertainment of the white community.

The disproportionate criminalization and punishment of African American men for violence against women continues today. It is evident in media images of African American men as sexual predators and in the disproportionate arrest, sentencing and incarceration of African American men for sexual offenses. These patterns are directly tied to attacks on the sexual explicitness of African-American musical lyrics, when similarly sexist language from white groups goes unnoticed.

White women don't have the same social, political or economic power as white men. They haven't been as influential in setting up people of color as either dangerous or erotic. Nonetheless, they have participated in the benefits of racism and have colluded in maintaining these stereotypes. White women have also been vocal critics of them, at least partly because of their negative effect on the power and position of white women themselves.

White women are taught that men of color are highly sexual beings whose very gaze will assault them. Therefore they "need" white men who are strong, aggressive and armed to protect them from this menace. These beliefs have directed the attention of white women to danger outside of their families diminishing their ability to defend themselves against rape, domestic violence, incest and murder from white men closer to home.

White women are also taught to regard women of color as competitors—temptresses and seducers of white men. This training adds to the general images of danger associated with people of color and makes it difficult for white women to regard women of color as allies. The solidarity between women needed in the struggle against sexism is undermined by racial violence and by white women's fear and mistrust.

At times, white women's groups have supported attacks against the African-American community in the name of women's safety. In the late nineteenth century the National American Woman's Suffrage Association refused to take a stand against lynching and mob violence and asked its staunch supporter Frederick Douglass not to come to meetings in the South. It did not support the organizing of chapters by Black women because it did not want to jeopardize white southern support for women's right to vote. Eventually the arguments within the organization became more explicitly racist. White women argued that if they could vote, it would buttress the supremacy of the white race against the demands of Black people, Indians and newly colonized Spanish-speaking people (Davis 1981, pps. 110–126).

More recently, in the 1970s and 1980s, the rape prevention and domestic violence prevention movements have called for stronger police and criminal justice response to violence against women. However, of the 455 men executed between 1930 and 1967 on the basis of rape convictions, 405 were Black (Davis 1981, p. 172). At times these movements have inadvertently contributed to the targeting of African American men insofar as they have not taken into account the racial bias in the legal system and the uses of rape and assault charges against men of color as a means of social control (Davis 1981; hooks 1981).

At other times white women's groups have been strong, if belated, allies to African American women and men in the fight against lynching, mob violence and false accusations of rape. The Association of Southern Women for the Prevention of Lynching did important and effective work through petition drives, letters and demonstrations. It was formed in 1930, after decades of pioneering work by Black women organizers such as Ida B. Wells, Mary Church Terrell and Mary Talbert (Davis 1981, p. 195).

Similarly, more women* in the rape prevention and domestic violence prevention movements have been paying attention to racism in the 1980s and 1990s, supporting women of color in leadership positions, reexamining police and criminal justice responses to violence against women, and developing an analysis that includes an understanding of race and gender.

The issues of race and gender intersect in African American women's lives. This crucial perspective has given them the ability to challenge the limited focus of much political work in this country. For example, in the mid-nineteenth century, Sojourner Truth challenged the suffrage movement to take racism and racial violence seriously with statements such as "if you bait the suffrage-hook with a woman, you will certainly catch a black man" (Davis 1981, p. 83). Ida B. Wells continued that tradition in conversations with Susan B. Anthony and statements to suffrage organizations at the end of the century.

African American women have long provided challenges to men and white women in political leadership to sort out the myths and the realities of race- and gender-based violence. Sojourner Truth, Ida B. Wells, Josephine St. Pierre Ruffin, Mary Church Terrell, Lucy Parsons, Claudia Jones, and Frances E. W. Harper were some of the African American women leaders in the abolition, anti-lynching and women's suffrage movements who understood the connections between gender and racial violence and provided constant challenges to the exclusive focus of each of these three movements.

Today some of the most nuanced analyses of the intersections of race, gender and class issues are in the writings of women such as Angela Davis, Paula Giddings, Patricia Hill Collins, and bell hooks.

We would do well to support the leadership of African American women. The dictates of racism and sexism devalue the experience of African American women and give them little credibility. We need to support their leadership and draw on their experience and insight so that our tactics in fighting against one "ism" don't lose us the war against another.

The previous section on fear and danger and this section on sexuality are even more intertwined than I have discussed so far. Because of the merging of sex and violence with racism in our society, images of people of color, which are seen as dangerous, are also seen as erotic. Because of prohibitions about sexual expression, erotic projections onto people of color make them seem more dangerous. This added danger then makes them seem more erotic.

---

* There have always been some strong and vocal white women in these movements working for complete inclusion of women of color and their needs. See "Disloyal to Civilization: Feminism, Racism, Gynephobia" in Rich 1979; and Braden "A Second Open Letter to Southern White Women" in "Southern Exposure" v. IV, no. 4, Winter 1977.

One way that people can challenge the authority of a society is to violate its sexual taboos. For young white people the taboos against interracial or interfaith sexual relationships, coupled with the eroticized stereotypes of people of color and Jews, makes having such relationships a gesture of rebellion against white norms. A sexual relationship with a person outside the norm becomes attractive—both arousing and dangerous—because of the characteristics projected onto people of color. Given the stereotypes and symbolism involved, any person of color or Jewish person—male or female, lesbian, gay or heterosexual—will provide some risk. Because white people have characterized blacks as the most dangerous and sexually "other," they represent the most risk.

Not all interracial relationships are based on projections, stereotypes and symbolic value. But these facets are part of all white people's conceptual baggage and do affect our actual relationships with people of color. Some white people have used people of color to make their sexual lives more exotic, erotic or thrilling, or to defy white (and parental) standards. There are residues of these erotic elements in our relationships with people of color even when we are not sexually involved with them. These residues interfere with our ability to treat them as valued and respected people.

This sense of the erotic and dangerous nature of people of color gets attached not only to their bodies, but also to their music, art and other elements of their culture. Music like rock-n-roll and rap have been sources of intergenerational conflict in white families, connected with issues of sexuality. National discussion about gender and family issues such as rape, domestic violence, teenage sexuality, sexual harassment, marital infidelity, interracial dating and miscegenation often have explicit and implicit racial references built into them.

I have used our beliefs about African Americans as examples in this section. Asian Americans, Latino/as, Native Americans, and Jews are each eroticized somewhat differently. Despite the tremendous differences in other cultures, there are remarkable similarities in white sexual beliefs and stereotypes about them because the hidden but central focus is whiteness and white sexuality, much of it derived from Christian teachings.

The sexuality we project onto people of color tells us a great deal about white concepts of virtue and immorality, good and evil, but little about white practice, and nothing at all about people of color. As long as we don't examine the sexual ideology of (Christian) whiteness, we will continue to be directed by our sexual fears and fantasies, leading us to commit injustice in the name of virtue.

The Myth of the
Happy Family

*B*ESIDES OUR UNDERSTANDING of sexuality, we have certain understandings of what a family is and what family relationships should be like. These too are affected by racism.

What did you learn as a child about what a family was? What did your parents convey? What did you learn from TV and movies?

The word "family" probably brings up images of people caring about each other, doing their part to make the whole group work well for everyone. Even when our own family was violent or otherwise dysfunctional, we may have felt that everyone else's was close to the norm. We talk about the human family, our extended family, a network of people or friends who feel like family, and our biological/created family.

The word family conveys good feelings, although we know that many families lack these qualities. It is perhaps easier today than in the past to acknowledge the existence of incest, domestic violence, marital rape, alcohol or other drug abuse and neglect. But it remains hard to see that some families "work" because they provide caring, support and nurturing for some members at the expense of others.

We are not equally privileged or equally safe within our families because of violence and unequal power. Those of us who are safe, cared for and thriving, or at least are not vulnerable to physical or sexual violence (often men and/or adults), can pretend that everything is all right because it is all right for us. It could be better, but from our perspective it certainly could be worse. Other people may tell us that it looks good from the outside as well, reinforcing our sense of the rightness of things. All too often what is working for us is not working for someone else. We have a sense of being part of a happy family, but some of the family is being abused.

The myth of the happy family is common in our culture. Many slaveowners in the South shared this myth. Men in families where there is incest and domestic violence often share this myth. Communities where there are people who are poor or homeless share this myth. White people share this myth.

The myth allows us to attack anyone who speaks out. When someone says, "This arrangement is not working for me because I am being abused, discriminated against, having my land taken away, being denied my freedom," we immediately respond by saying, "You are creating a problem with your complaints. Everything was okay until you brought this up. After all, we're really one big happy family and we care about each other."

The idea of family usually implies that if everyone plays their part then the whole unit works. Each person has a role, with a set of responsibilities and privileges within the family. For most of us this means a hierarchy where some people—such as parents, men, or elders—have more power and authority than others, such as children, women and younger people. The saying "Father knows best," from an old TV show, probably best captures this feeling. People don't know best for themselves, so the story goes, so they should defer to father/authority. Many of us assume that father will take into consideration everyone's needs and interests and benevolently make decisions that are good for all.

People who say they are unhappy in the family or who reject this hierarchy are labeled homewreckers who are breaking up the family, creating divisions, and disrupting the smooth functioning of the organization. They are called names such as rabblerouser, complainer, whiner, rebel or teenager, and are described as too shrill, harsh, angry, loud and aggressive. The presumption is that everything was okay until this person started complaining. In the 1970s and 1980s men used these terms to silence or discount women who were challenging incest, domestic violence and inequality in the family.

Racial relations in this country are often described as if we were all a big family. If people of color point out racism in our neighborhoods, offices, schools or churches, white people generally react with one of two responses. The first is to defend the family and cast out the troublemaking person of color. "Things were just fine before you got here and made it into a problem. You can just go back to where you came from if you don't like it." (This response also makes it seem like those who are dissatisfied are the ones with no right to be here).

The second response is to reassert white people's role as the benevolent fathers of the family who know what's best for everyone involved. People of color are seen as rebellious or ungrateful children. Our perspective is the overview, the dispassionate consideration of everyone's interests. If the children weren't so angry and rebellious and would just leave decisions to us, we would work it out and take care of their needs too.

A more useful assumption is that complaints mark issues that need changing. Rather than labeling people complainers, we need to take what they say seriously. Most people do not speak up easily in the face of authority or power. We have all been mistreated by people in authority, and few people joyously or enthusiastically create problems where none exist. When people object to what is happening, it is because someone is being exploited or abused or placed in an unsafe situation. Some kind of injustice is occurring.

People and groups bring up problems in different ways. The less powerful and less listened to need to be more forceful when bringing up the fact that the family system is not working for them. (In the extreme case where it is completely unsafe, then the violence is turned inward in self-destructive behavior—it is acted out. This is true for both individuals and communities.) The more forcefully people act up or act out in response to violence, the more loudly, forcefully and repressively we respond by saying that they are the problem.

White people, especially those with at least middle class incomes or financial security, have always said that the system works. It's a democracy, there is equal opportunity, hard work is rewarded and there are no special privileges.

Just as child assault, incest, domestic violence and marital rape are denied and covered over by the myth of the happy nuclear family, so too racism, poverty and discrimination are covered over by the myth of the happy social community. Our "families" will always look happy to those with more power, privilege or prestige, and will always be dangerous for those of us with less. A happy family can only exist when justice prevails, and when everyone in the family has an equal and adequate amount of power, safety, participation and autonomy.

We must reject any notion of a family which has a (white) father at the top making benevolent decisions for everyone else. This is not a realistic or democratic image of human relations.

Have you ever been in a situation which was formerly all white and subsequently integrated? Did the person (or people) of color raise issues of racism? How were they responded to? Did the racism they identified exist before they arrived?

I worked at a small non-profit community agency at a time when all the staff were white. After some discussions about racism we decided that the next person we hired would be a person of color.

We subsequently hired a Latina (I'll call her Sylvia) to join our staff and felt very satisfied with what we had done. After all, we felt we were taking a risk in order to do the right thing.

After working with us for a while, Sylvia began to bring to our attention various ways that we were discounting her experience and excluding her from decision making. In addition, she pointed out how we were not serving Latino/a clients well.

Some of us became very upset and felt attacked and discounted. It seemed like we had more racism now that Sylvia was on staff. It was easier before she came because we didn't have to watch what we said or did as much. She was labeled a troublemaker by some and called ungrateful by others. But neither she nor the problems would go away. We were eventually forced to take Sylvia's complaints seriously and decide what to do about them. Even then, we did not include her or other Latino/as in that process.

All of our responses had elements of the happy family syndrome in them. The racism Sylvia identified existed before she arrived, but we blamed her. We felt she was unappreciative of all we had done for her. When we acknowledged racial problems we still felt that we, the white people, should decide how best to fix things. We were the parents and she was the child, and the parents knew what was best.

Sylvia didn't stay long with this organization. We did learn some lessons about how our expectations about her and about our roles prevented us from acting effectively to identify and solve racial problems.

Many of us will be in all white situations which are subsequently integrated racially. What can you do to support people of color if they are attacked for pointing out racism?

Beyond Black and White

I GREW UP in a house in which an African American woman came once a week to clean. She was the only person of color that I knew personally as a child. Later, when I was in high school, a single African American student transferred to my apparently all-white high school. He was the object of tremendous attention and comment, much of it negative. For years we had talked about the prowess of the African American football and basketball teams in South Central Los Angeles, and now we had a black person among us.

These years were the 1950s and early 1960s, and the civil rights struggle was often in the news. African American athletes were integrating sports, and students were integrating schools, lunch counters, department stores and recreational facilities.

When I became an adult and looked back on my childhood, I thought that these public events and personal experiences defined my exposure to racism. Racism meant Black-White relations. When I began to read about racism, I came across books about the civil rights struggle, slavery and the black power movement. Even today the books I can most easily find about racism have titles like *Black Lives, White Lives: Three Decades of Race Relations in America, Black Children, White Dreams,* and *Race: How Blacks and Whites Think and Feel about the American Obsession* (Blauner, Cottle, and Terkel).

In the United States we tend to identify racism with the relationship between African Americans and whites. Even within the Jewish community,

Black-Jewish discussion groups and questions about Black-Jewish relations are the primary racial focus.

There are important reasons why the African-American struggle for justice and equality is at the forefront of our consciousness. The existence of slavery and Jim Crow segregation, and the struggles for justice led by African Americans have been defining historical forces in our development as a nation. African Americans have powerfully and unrelentingly challenged the myths of American democracy and economic opportunity.

The world is not just black and white. It is simple to say we shouldn't forget Spanish-speaking, Native American, Asian American and Arab American peoples when we discuss race. In reality, it takes more than tacking on the names of each group to adequately address the issues that a multiracial society raises. We can not build for a stable multicultural society on only two legs. Using the African American experience as the model for all communities of color in the United States distorts the history of the African American struggle for justice and full participation and renders invisible the identities and issues of other communities.

When anything is divided into black and white it makes it seem as if there is a clear dividing line between the two groups— no gray, no fuzziness, no gradations. Many people in this society are bicultural. Many people of color and white people are of racially mixed heritage. Some people of color are so light that they can pass as white.

The black-white division makes it seem as if white people are homogeneous. On the contrary, what counts as white has been contested throughout our country's history. At times the Irish were not white; Spanish, Italians and Greeks were not white; Russians and Poles were not white. There is tremendous complexity, intermingling, struggle for inclusion and resistance to incorporation within our European heritages and histories. At times, for example, Jewish people have been considered white and at other times as clearly not-white.

Nor has African-American culture been homogeneous. Some African-American people have been free for hundreds of years; others remained virtual slaves until just a generation ago. African Americans came from complex and very different African cultures and retained some of those differences for long periods in this country. Ethnic differences, regional differences, and class differences have made most generalizations about African American tenuous at best. Many African Americans have intermarried with Native Americans or with members of other ethnic groups.

The division of racial discussion into black and white is misleading in other ways. It obscures the long and devastating struggle of Native Americans for survival, cultural autonomy and sovereignty. Their struggle is largely misunderstood because it is so different from the African-American struggle.

The struggle of Spanish-speaking peoples, which is heavily intertwined with Native American struggles since both include resistance to colonization, is ignored and trivialized.

In a similar way, the presence, diversity, achievements and defeats of the many different Asian, Pacific Islander and Asian-American communities are lumped together as one and are oversimplified. Asian Americans are invisible in much of white-American culture and are excluded from political representation and social power.

Another result of black-white thinking is that we are unable to understand and develop truly multicultural environments. Many of us claim our communities are all white if there are no African Americans visible. This can make it seem like racism is a problem "over there," in urban, inner-city areas.

Racism is not only an issue for large metropolitan urban areas. Most communities in the United States, including those in the Midwest, Northwest and Southwest, are multiracial. There are often Native American, Spanish-speaking, Asian American, and Arab American people in our communities where no African Americans are present.

Which communities of color are routinely ignored or not seen by white people you know? What groups are habitually left out in your thinking?

Conversely, we believe we have integrated an event, neighborhood or workplace if there are African Americans present, even though other groups are absent. This belief creates an opportunism in which we choose to deal with the African-American community and ignore other communities, or choose other communities and ignore African Americans at our convenience. On the one hand, we claim that if we are addressing African-American concerns we are speaking about the concerns of all people of color. On the other hand, we sometimes avoid dealing with the harsh effects of racism on the African-American community by pointing to examples of the integration or progress of other non-white groups such as Asian Americans.

There are other negative results of perceiving racism as a problem of black and white. We maintain the illusion that whites are the majority and therefore deserve a disproportionate share of the national resources. Conversely, we fear that "people of color" are becoming the majority and that a monolithic group of darker-skinned people will take over. In addition, racial tension, economic divisions and hate crimes between different communities of color are misunderstood and ignored because white people are unable to distinguish the complex relationships between these groups.

We must delve into the complexity: we cannot be satisfied with what has been achieved. We have to keep asking the questions, "Who is still excluded?" "Who remains unseen?" "Who is still being exploited?" When new groups of immigrants arrive, we cannot conveniently forget that long-established communities of color still face racism every day.

Nor can we say that there is more of a certain group so we should put our attention there. Racist actions and policies in the past have determined the numbers of people in particular communities of color living today in the United States. The breeding of slaves, the killing of Native Americans, the restrictions on Asian immigration—all determined how many people of color are currently in this country. Human dignity and opportunity are not measured in quantities of people. Relatively small population groups such as Native Americans often deserve large amounts of retribution.

Complexity also exists within the categories we use. "People of color," "Asian American," or even "Korean American" are examples of categories which can confuse and mislead us more than they can help. We need to be talking about inclusion within particular communities. If we are talking about the Korean-American community, or the Lakota community, or the Salvadoran community, we need to ask, "Are the women of that community included? Are the young people included? Are the elders included? Are the poor included? Are the lesbians and gays and bisexuals included? Are the physically challenged included?"

Democracy means the inclusion of all people in the process of making decisions which affect their lives. Our society is undemocratic to the extent that anyone is excluded from the decision-making process. Racism is fundamentally undemocratic and makes a travesty of our democratic ideals. Fighting racism means extending democracy to include all people of color and moving beyond a black-white, or even a simple white-people of color focus.

What's in a Name?

THE WORDS WE use to describe groups of people have developed within the system of racism as it has changed historically. These words have changed, and continue to change, partly in response to the struggle to end racism, and partly in the resistance to and backlash against that struggle. All of our vocabulary is inadequate and frustrating. There is much to learn from attempts to use accurate and respectful language. We need to pay attention to the words we use because language itself is used to maintain racism.

The phrase "people of color," which I use in this book, is one such problematic term. Every human being is a person of color. The word "white," which has been used to describe European Americans, does not reflect anyone's skin color so much as a concept of racial purity which has never existed. I use the phrases "people of color" and "communities of color" to suggest the multitude of peoples and cultures which have been exploited by European-American society for the last five hundred years.

Other troublesome words used to refer to people of color include "minority" (people of color are a majority of the world's population and a majority in some of our communities); "third world" (it implies they come from somewhere else and don't belong in our communities; third also implies less worth than first or second); and "non-white" (this term equates white as the norm or standard and everything else as different or "non," i.e., negative).

The phrase "people of color" itself covers over so much complexity and diversity that it's sometimes more useful to state explicitly the group of people being referred to such as African American, Asian American, Arab American, Native American, or Latino/a. These terms as well are vast abstractions covering over the specific lives of tens of millions of people.

More specific referents like Japanese American, Hopi, or Lebanese are still generalizations which often cover over significant differences while giving a false appearance of inclusiveness. The male bias of our society gives most racial terms a male identification. I keep the masculine/feminine form of Latino/a precisely to remind us that women and men are included in each of these categories.

Who else is excluded from these categories? Does the word "African American" connote "poor" to white people? Does "Latino" mean "heterosexual"? Does "Asian American" assume "able-bodied"? Racial referents are coded for specific meanings relating to class, sexual orientation and physical ability, reflecting broad patterns of inequality within our society.

Language is important not because it should or can be "correct," but because it should convey respect and dignity to the people referred to. Everyone should have the choice to name themselves. Sometimes there is not agreement within a community about what people want to be called, often because there is really no coherent community in the first place. Nonetheless, there is always a clear difference between respectful terms and disrespectful ones.

Within the African-American community there are differences over whether to retain use of the word black, or to use African American. Neither term is without problems, although both terms are respectful.* These discussions reflect concerns about cultural pride, historical roots, the meaning of multiculturalism, and strategies for resisting racism. We can learn a lot about the concerns of people of color by listening to their discussions of the issues raised by different terms of self-identity. It is more important that we support those concerns than that we use the most correct words.

How have different communities of color renamed or redefined themselves during your lifetime?

It can be hard for white people to accept new terms because they represent challenges to long standing social relationships. Different words call forth different behavior. We may feel less secure that we know the racial rules—what to say and how to act. This alone can cause anxiety for many middle class Americans for whom knowing and following the rules is important.

Some of our resistance to new words reflects our desire to control racial boundaries and maintain power. We may even use changing terminology to try to discredit people of color. Focusing on the terminology is a way to divert attention away from the underlying challenge to white power and control that the changing vocabulary represents.

In the United States we have always been concerned about politeness and good breeding. Upper class and successful middle class people have long prided themselves on using correct language and being well behaved and

---

* Similarly, in the Native-American community there is disagreement over whether Native American or American Indian is the better term.

respectful. The use of correct racial terminology has been a signifier of class or breeding and has been used to disparage poor and working class people. In the South respectable whites, deriving great advantage from segregation, referred to African Americans as "Negroes" and looked down on people who used words like "nigger." Being overtly polite or respectful in language or personal encounters made these whites no less complicit in white racism.

When we criticize other white people today for not using the right language we may be showing our good breeding, masking our complicity with racism and using our own educational or class advantages to put down those with less opportunity. Language which is obviously derogatory or abusive should be challenged. But we need to be concerned with much more than language in fighting racism.

Some of us wonder why people of color want to be called African American, Chinese American or Mexican American. Why can't they just be Americans? Are they holding something back? Do they owe allegiance to another country or continent?

Sometimes people of color use these names as a response to the lack of acceptance and inclusion that they have experienced from white people in this country. At other times, people use them to indicate cultural and social connections that they feel to the countries or continents that their foreparents emigrated from. These names can indicate feelings of connection to distinct cultural communities, especially in response to the strong pressure in this country to give up one's culture in order to be accepted. Such naming can also be a call to a collective political identity. None of these practices have anything to do with one's loyalty to the United States.

We have adopted the word American for people who are citizens of the United States. (Literally, anyone born in North, Central or South America is an American.) It is not an ethnicity or culture. There are many different kinds of Americans, and our country encompasses thousands of distinct cultures and communities. Being an American doesn't mean denying one's culture, ethnicity or community. There is no single, national culture that defines what it means to be an American, however much some of us wish there were.

Being able to acknowledge and value one's cultural background is vital to personal and community health. This is even more necessary in a society that devalues most forms of popular cultural expression and minimizes historical roots and cultural development as ours does.

Part of the American myth, the frontier myth, was that we could create ourselves anew here. We portrayed the United States as a virgin territory where people could come and discover or create new selves. We conveniently "forget" that we had to kill off Native Americans to make that frontier empty. We had to chop down the vegetation to make it tillable. We had to deny our own cultural histories, practices and customs to fit in. Some of our families did deny or cover up their cultural practices. The traditions of others were lost over time. Today many of us can hardly identify with any specific ethnic identity or culture.

Many of our foreparents resisted assimilation and carried on strong and proud Italian, Greek, Irish, Swedish, German, Russian or Portuguese traditions. But most of us grew to believe that this was a land of newness, separated from the old tired traditions of other, primarily European countries. This mythology makes it very difficult to acknowledge the strengths and contributions of people from various cultures, particularly non-European ones, to our American mix.

American culture has come to mean white European-American norms, values, beliefs and traditions. Patriotism has become overlaid with a national chauvinism which reinforces white racism. We have used our national borders, immigration policies, literary canons and patriotic homilies to maintain the dominance of white norms. It is ironic that in this time of a global economy, international trade, world sports competitions and global cultural communication, our appeals to nationalism and protectionism have increased.

We face a challenge that is even larger than incorporating all Americans into our national identity. We must fundamentally question why we give so much credence and importance to our national identity. Whose interests does it serve? Nationalism in many countries has led to protectionism, aggression, xenophobia, internal repression and war. Who has benefitted from these patterns?

There is no reason we can't be proud of being American and of the positive achievements of our fellow citizens. And we can be proud of being New Yorkers, or Texans or from the Northwest. We can take pride in our cultural, religious, ethnic and other identities. However, when that pride fosters feelings of superiority, arrogance, competition or the denigration of others who are not part of our group, we are breeding intolerance and violence. Further, when we use "American" as a code for who we, white people, consider good, or rich, or smart, or successful enough to be part of "our" country, we are maintaining racism in disguise. When we blame our problems on non-Americans, whether they are immigrants without papers, Japanese capitalists, Arab oil producers or South American drug cartels, we are again refusing to look at our own complicity in these situations and are failing to take responsibility for our own problems. It then becomes easy for our economic and political leaders to stir up fear and anger against "foreigners," which fuels more racial violence.

Nationalism can be used to reinforce racism in the opposite direction as well. If we try to pretend that we have all assimilated into one large melting pot and that differences of culture, tradition and community no longer exist we can maintain white norms and white racism by pretending to have transcended them. Saying "We're all just Americans and therefore nobody should claim to be Asian American" can be a way to deny the inequality and injustice that still operate in this country. This false inclusion is just as strong a support to racism as exclusionism is. In both cases we are using nationalism to speak about and reinforce white dominance.

There is no natural or homogeneous national community in this country. Nation states are complex. Ours was created over centuries and includes diverse peoples and communities. Any attempt to define or create a single national culture will inevitably disenfranchise and oppress many of us. It can only be done with power, control and violence, to the benefit of some and the detriment of others.

Discussion of racism inevitably focuses on boundaries and divisions. Who is on "our" side and who is not? Making our boundaries more inclusive doesn't eliminate this competitive and exclusive kind of thinking. Our national borders are arbitrary constructions of historical circumstance influenced by wars, colonization patterns, trade, treaties and resistance struggles. We have seen countries throughout the world break up, consolidate and change borders and redefine "national" identity. These transitions have generally fueled nationalism, racism and religious fanaticism.

Nationalism in the United States has been used not only to exclude some people from our national identity, but to control all those who live within the national boundary, and to persecute for disloyalty those who are labeled traitors or "un-American." Our challenge is to accept and embrace the full diversity of who we are and strive for inclusion without expecting people to think or act like we do.

People will always make choices about what traditions to keep or discard, and what to name themselves. They deserve respect for the choices they make. Many Americans have cultural or social ties to other countries—some Italians to Italy, some Irish to Ireland, some Jews to Israel, some Vietnamese to Vietnam, some Bolivians to Bolivia, some African Americans to Ghana, Benin, South Africa or Egypt. We each live within complex webs of international culture and communication, and no U.S. border stops or limits these kinds of cultural connections. Connecting to traditions and cultures which reach beyond U.S. borders is a source of strength, inspiration, creativity and support for many Americans. We need to encourage those connections, not use them to persecute people for having "divided" loyalties.

One of the purposes of maintaining whiteness is to construct a normative set of values which defines who is entitled to certain resources and privileges. In response, people of color come together to juxtapose their numbers and their social and political influence against that entitlement. They define themselves as people of color against the ultimate dividing line that white racism creates. In small groups in which white people are dominant, people of color may band together for similar reasons.

At a different level, because the binary discussion of race relations puts everything in a black-white framework, Asian Americans, Arab Americans, Latino/as, and Native Americans have formed broad coalitions to strengthen their political bargaining power for the distribution of resources, services and political representation. In earlier historical periods there were no Asian Americans, there were only Japanese Americans, Chinese Americans, Korean Americans; these groups have come together, downplaying their differences, for strategic reasons to claim resources and representation against white or African-American claims.

At the same time as they work in coalition as Asian Americans, particular ethnic and national groups are reasserting the uniqueness of their experiences and the importance of their needs for resources, recognition and political representation as Korean Americans, Filipino/as, or South Asians. This is a strategic response because white culture denies the importance of cultural identity on the one hand, and on the other hand tends to see all people of color as "other," without recognizing their specificity.

Finally, many people from particular ethnic groups want simply to be "American." The force of racism in this society makes it nearly impossible for a Latino/a or Asian American to be "just American." White Americans regularly perceive them to be Latino/a or Asian and therefore not completely, 100 percent loyal Americans.

Each of these levels of self-definition and coalition is an important and valid strategic response to the realities of whiteness in U.S. society. Each tells us something about whiteness as it is currently understood and perceived.

There is nothing "essential" about any of these forms of identity. They are each historical responses to the politics of white society. That doesn't mean these identities are not real. They are real, important, serious and significant in the struggle to end racism. They will not go away when racism is eliminated, although they might look very different at that time. As white people, we need to respect the ability of people of color to name themselves. We also need to support the forms their struggles against racism take and learn about the resistance of white racism to change.

We cannot forget that communities of color are trying to survive in a white-controlled society. They have to constantly redefine their strategies for survival and resistance. Many of their words are bought out, coopted, commercialized or lose their meaning over time. The slogan "Black is beautiful," originally coined to strengthen pride and self-esteem in the African-American community, is now being used by advertisers to market shampoo, skin cream, alcohol and clothes. We can learn much about ourselves and about tactics of resistance to cultural domination by listening to the language of resistance of people of color.

Resistance to white racism can seem to end up recreating clearly delineated, separable groups. The terms "people of color," "African American," "Korean American," "Latino/a"—all self-chosen labels in reaction to white racism—can seem to create or reflect real, stable cultural or political entities. They demarcate broad currents within certain groups which are part of the dynamic of the resistance to racism.

Individual responses to the fluctuating dynamics of resistance are varied. Particular people of color may herald new forms of resistance, hold on to traditional patterns, or emphasize or de-emphasize racial identity at different points in their lives. There is much debate within communities of color about tactics of resistance, including naming practices. And these communities themselves are vast and complex without the clearly defined boundaries which we, white people, want to ascribe to them.

Finally, to add one last complicating but crucial factor: race/ethnicity is only one of the factors in the makeup of our identities. At times other factors such as geographical origin, gender, sexual orientation, parental or work role, may supersede ethnicity as a primary focus. It is important to respect the choices individual people of color make about when and how much to identify with their "racial" identity, and how to understand it, knowing that our society gives a distorted and overemphasized meaning to racial identity.

Separatism

M*ANY WHITE PEOPLE* become upset when people of color get together without us. In our workshops my colleagues and I sometimes separate people into racial groups. There are always white people who protest by saying, "I want to know what they have to say." "How can we deal with racism without people of color?" "How come they get their own group?" "I think their group will be more fun." "This is reverse racism."

Racism is divisive. Each of these responses reflects some of the pain and confusion of that divisiveness. Although our lives are heavily influenced by our being white, with all the privileges and benefits, costs, limits and opportunities that entails, it is difficult for us to admit that we are white. It is difficult to look around and identify other white people and to recognize that we are in this together. We can learn from each other. We *need* to learn from each other.

It is particularly hypocritical for us to complain about people of color being separatist; for the last five hundred years it is white people who have excluded people of color from our homes, "our" schools, "our" workplaces, "our" neighborhoods and from "our" country. Even today people of color are routinely excluded or harassed or told to leave and go home by white people in all kinds of circumstances. Most of us don't want to be excluded, but we are not so great at inclusion either. It is only in the last thirty-five years that people of color have been able to meet in and control their own space without the threat of intrusion by white people of authority and even that privilege is commonly violated because of our fears of people of color "banding together."

People of color have been controlled and segregated throughout U.S. history. There are strategic reasons why they might want to meet together without white people. They may want to be in a safe environment, to enjoy each other's company, to talk about racism, to congregate with people who share certain things, not to have to focus attention on white people and white culture. Some of these are the reasons that any group of people with shared interests or concerns get together. Others are particular to the needs of a minority group in a larger social setting.

Physical and emotional safety is a crucial concern. Women know they aren't necessarily safe with men just because they say, "I'm liberated," or "I'm a feminist." For the same reasons, people of color know that they aren't necessarily safe when white people say similar things. At least in terms of racial abuse, it is generally safer for people of color when white people are not around. It is also safer for them to talk about difficult issues, to be vulnerable and to acknowledge conflicts and disagreements within their community without the danger that the things they say will be used against them by white people.

Congregating in a group without white people is also less distracting for people of color. Rarely do we whites sit back and listen to people of color without interrupting, without being defensive, without trying to regain attention to ourselves, without criticizing or judging. People of color can't talk with and listen to each other with the same amount of attention and respect when white people are present.

People of color spend a tremendous amount of time and energy taking care of white people. This has been true historically as people of various ethnic groups cared for our children, took care of our homes, cooked our food and made our clothes. It has also been true emotionally. People of color have often counseled us, nurtured us in our old age, been our teachers, assuaged our guilt about racism, covered over their pain and anger to protect us, assured us that we were okay even though we were white, and out of economic necessity, put aside the needs of their families and communities to take care of ours. One of the assumptions of whiteness, particularly for people of middle class economic status or higher, is that people of color will put our needs first. They have been dependent on jobs and goodwill from white people for so long that many have learned how to do it well. It occurs so commonly and routinely that few of us notice it going on.

In separated groups people of color don't have to take care of white people and therefore can take care of themselves and each other. They can talk about their experiences of racism, they can talk about white people and white society, without worrying about or having to respond to the questions, insecurities, misinformation and defensiveness of white people.

There are many reasons people congregate. Safety, shared interests, and mutual support are primary ones. These are the same reasons white people congregate. If you look around a school cafeteria you might see white students, Latino/a students and Asian American students sitting in separate groups. If you looked closer and knew more about the groups, you might discover that most of the social groupings had to do with shared interests, experiences and concerns. Yet many of us who are white might say that the people of color are cliquish or separatist, and we might feel offended.

Since so many public spaces in our society are white in tone, structure and atmosphere, people of different ethnic groups need space to enjoy their own cultural uniqueness, strengths and styles. They are not necessarily rejecting individual white people, or plotting revenge or revolution. White society has controlled communities of color while all the time fearing that they would rebel. Anytime we see many of them together, we become afraid. This fear reflects our own understanding and guilt about the inequalities of the past, as well as the fears we have been taught about people who are different.

Our fear of separation can also lead us to ignore our responsibility for most of the separation. People of color are still routinely and persistently denied access to much public and most private space in this country. There is tremendous and undeniable segregation in housing, schools, jobs and recreational facilities. People of color do not choose to live in barrios, ghettos and reservations any more than white people do. Those that do, do so out of lack of choice. This lack of choice has been created by white-controlled institutions and individual discrimination. We segregate communities of color and rarely notice or challenge it. But when a group voluntarily congregates we oppose their right to do so.

It is to our advantage when people of color congregate voluntarily without whites. None of us wants to be racist or to see racism perpetuated. But most of us are not very adept at noticing racism when it occurs, or responding vigorously to it. When people of color come together for discussion and support, they become more able to point out and challenge racism.

We can also benefit from the opportunity to talk with other white people. Seldom do we consciously get together with other whites and talk about racism, about being white and about working for racial justice. We need this time together.

All too often we let people of color take responsibility for or challenging racism. We describe it as their issue. We fail to see how seriously and continuously it affects us. In an all white group we have a chance to explore our questions, concerns and fears about racism. We have an opportunity to gently challenge other white people about it. We have an opportunity to develop plans for confronting racism and becoming better allies for people of color. Let's take advantage of it!

How could you bring together white people you know to think about some of the issues raised in this book? Who are some white people who can help you do this?

Intervening with other white people about racism is an important way that we become allies for people of color. The next part of the book looks in detail at the ways we can be strong, effective allies in stopping racism.

PART III

Being Allies

What Does an Ally Do?

BEING ALLIES TO people of color in the struggle to end racism is one of the most important things that white people can do. There is no one correct way to be an ally. Each of us is different. We have different relationships to social organizations, political processes and economic structures. We are more or less powerful because of such factors as our gender, class, work situation, family and community participation. Being an ally to people of color is an ongoing strategic process in which we look at our personal and social resources, evaluate the environment we have helped to create and decide what needs to be done.

This book is filled with things to do and ways to get involved. These suggestions are not prioritized because they cannot be. Times change and circumstances vary. What is a priority today may not be tomorrow. What is effective or strategic right now may not be next year. We need to be thinking with others and noticing what is going on around us so we will know how to put our attention, energy, time and money toward strategic priorities in the struggle to end racism and other injustices.

This includes listening to people of color so that we can support the actions they take, the risks they bear in defending their lives and challenging white hegemony. It includes watching the struggle of white people to maintain dominance and the struggle of people of color to gain equal opportunity, justice, safety and respect.

We don't need to believe or accept as true everything people of color say. There is no one voice in any community, much less in the complex and diverse communities of color spanning our country. We do need to listen carefully to the voices of people of color so that we understand and give credence to their experience. We can then evaluate the content of what they are saying by what we know about how racism works and by our own critical thinking and progressive political analysis.

It is important to emphasize this point because often we become paralyzed when people of color talk about racism. We are afraid to challenge what they say. We will be ineffective as allies if we give up our ability to analyze and think critically, if we simply accept everything that a person of color states as truth.

Listening to people of color and giving critical credence to their experience is not easy for us because of the training we have received. Nevertheless, it is an important first step. When we hear statements that make us want to react defensively, we can instead keep some specific things in mind as we try to understand what is happening and determine how best to be allies.

We have seen how racism is a pervasive part of our culture. Therefore we should always assume that racism is at least part of the picture. In light of this assumption, we should look for the patterns involved rather than treating most events as isolated occurrences.

Since we know that racism is involved, we know our whiteness is also a factor. We should look for ways we are acting from assumptions of white power or privilege. This will help us acknowledge any fear or confusion we may feel. It will allow us to see our tendencies to defend ourselves or our tendencies to assume we should be in control. Then we will be able to talk with other white people so these tendencies don't get in the way of our being effective allies.

We have many opportunities to practice these critical listening and thinking skills because we are all involved in a complex web of interpersonal and institutional relationships. Every day we are presented with opportunities to analyze what is going on around us and to practice taking direct action as allies to people of color.

People of color will always be on the front lines fighting racism because their lives are at stake. How do we act and support them effectively, both when they are in the room with us, and when they are not?

It can be difficult for those of us who are white to know how to be strong allies for people of color when discrimination occurs. In the following interaction, imagine that Roberto is a young Latino student just coming out of a job interview with a white recruiter from a computer company. Let's see how one white person might respond.

Roberto is angry, not sure what to do next. He walks down the hall and meets a white teacher who wants to help.*

---

* Adapted from *Men's Work: How to Stop the Violence that Tears Our Lives Apart* (Hazelden/Ballantine, 1992).

R=Roberto, T=teacher

T: Hey, Roberto, how's it going?

R: That son of a bitch! He wasn't going to give me no job. That was really messed up.

T: Hold on there, don't be so angry. It was probably a mistake or something.

R: There was no mistake. The racist bastard. He wants to keep me from getting a good job, rather have us all on welfare or doing maintenance work.

T: Calm down now or you'll get yourself in more trouble. Don't go digging a hole for yourself. Maybe I could help you if you weren't so angry.

R: That's easy for you to say. This man was discriminating against me. White folks are all the same. They talk about equal opportunity, but it's the same old shit.

T: Wait a minute, I didn't have anything to do with this. Don't blame me, I'm not responsible. If you wouldn't be so angry maybe I could help you. You probably took what he said the wrong way. Maybe you were too sensitive.

R: I could tell. He was racist. That's all. (He storms off.)

What did you notice about this scene? On the one hand the teacher is concerned and is trying to help. On the other hand his intervention is not very effective. He immediately downplays the incident, discounting Roberto's feelings and underestimating the possibility of racism. He seems to be saying that racism is unlikely—it was probably just a misunderstanding, or Roberto was being too sensitive.

The teacher is clearly uncomfortable with Roberto's anger. He begins to defend himself, the job recruiter and white people. He ends up feeling attacked for being white. Rather than talking about what happened, he focuses on Roberto's anger and his generalizations about white people. By the end of the interaction he is threatening to get Roberto in trouble himself if he doesn't calm down. As he walks away he may be thinking it's no wonder Roberto didn't get hired for the job.

You probably recognize some of the tactics described in Part I. The teacher denies or minimizes the likelihood of racism, blames Roberto, and eventually counterattacks, claiming to be a victim of Roberto's anger and racial generalizations.

This interaction illustrates some of our common feelings that get in the way of intervening effectively where discrimination is occurring. First is the feeling that we are being personally attacked. It is difficult to hear the phrase "all white people," or "you white people." We want to defend ourselves and other whites. We don't want to believe that white people could intentionally hurt others. Or we may want to say, "Not me, I'm different."

There are some things we should remember when we feel attacked. First, this is a question of injustice. We need to focus on what happened and what we can do about it, not on our feelings of being attacked.

Second, someone who has been the victim of injustice is legitimately angry and they may or may not express that anger in ways we like. Criticizing the way people express their anger deflects attention and action away from the injustice that was committed. After the injustice has been dealt with, if you still think it's worthwhile and not an attempt to control the situation yourself, you can go back and discuss ways of expressing anger.

Often, because we are frequently complacent about injustice that doesn't affect us directly, it takes a lot of anger and aggressive action to bring attention to a problem. If we were more pro-active in identifying and intervening in situations of injustice, people would not have to be so "loud" to get our attention in the first place.

Finally, part of the harm that racism does is that it forces people of color to be wary and mistrustful of all white people, just as sexism forces women to mistrust all men. People of color face racism every day, often from unexpected quarters. They never know when a white friend, co-worker, teacher, police officer, doctor or passer-by may discriminate, act hostile or say something offensive. They have to be wary of *all* white people, even though they know that not all white people will mistreat them. They have likely been hurt in the past by white people they thought they could trust, and therefore they may make statements about all white people. We must remember that although we want to be trustworthy, trust is not the issue. We are not fighting racism so that people of color will trust us. Trust builds over time through our visible efforts to be allies and fight racism. Rather than trying to be safe and trustworthy, we need to be more active, less defensive, and put issues of trust aside.

When people are discriminated against they may feel unseen, stereotyped, attacked or as if a door has been slammed in their face. They may feel confused, frustrated, helpless or angry. They are probably reminded of other similar experiences. They may want to hurt someone in return, or hide their pain, or simply forget about the whole experience. Whatever the response, the experience is deeply wounding and painful. It is an act of emotional violence.

It's also an act of economic violence to be denied access to a job, housing, educational program, pay raise or promotion that one deserves. It is a practice which keeps economic resources in the hands of one group and denies them to another.

When a person is discriminated against it is a serious event and we need to treat it seriously. It is also a common event. For instance, the government estimates that there are over two million acts of race-based housing discrimination every year—twenty million every decade (Ezorsky, p.13). We know that during their lifetimes people of color have to face many such discriminatory experiences in school, work, housing and community settings.

People of color do not protest discrimination lightly. They know that when they do white people routinely deny or minimize it, blame them for causing trouble and then counterattack. This is the "happy family" syndrome described earlier.

People of color are experts in discrimination resulting from racism. Most experience it regularly and see its effects on their communities. Not every complaint of discrimination is valid, but most have some truth in them. It would be a tremendous step forward if we assumed that there was some truth in every complaint of racial discrimination even when other factors may also be involved. At least then we would take it seriously enough to fully investigate.

How could the teacher in the above scenario be a better ally to Roberto? We can go back to the guidelines suggested earlier for help. First, he needs to listen much more carefully to what Roberto is saying. He should assume that Roberto is intelligent, and if he says there was racism involved then there there probably was. The teacher should be aware of his own power and position, his tendency to be defensive and his desire to defend other white people or presume their innocence. It would also be worthwhile to look for similar occurrences because racism is usually not an isolated instance, but a pattern within an organization or institution.

Let's see how these suggestions might operate in a replay of this scene.

T: Hey, Roberto, what's happening?

R: That son of a bitch! He wasn't going to give me no job. He was messin' with me.

T: You're really upset, tell me what happened.

R: He was discriminating against me. Wasn't going to hire me cause I'm Latino. White folks are all alike. Always playing games.

T: This is serious. Why don't you come into my office and tell me exactly what happened.

R: Okay. This company is advertising for computer programmers and I'm qualified for the job. But this man tells me there aren't any computer jobs, and then he tries to steer me toward a janitor job. He was a racist bastard.

T: That's tough. I know you would be good in that job. This sounds like a case of job discrimination. Let's write down exactly what happened, and then you can decide what you want to do about it.

R: I want to get that job.

T: If you want to challenge it, I'll help you. Maybe there's something we can do.

This time the teacher was being a strong, supportive ally to Roberto.

"Thank You for Being Angry"

A *PERSON OF* color who is angry about of discrimination or harassment is doing us a service. That person is pointing out something wrong, something that contradicts the ideals of equality set forth in our Declaration of Independence and Bill of Rights. That person is bringing our attention to a problem that needs solving, a wrong that needs righting. We could convey our appreciation by saying, "Thank you, your anger has helped me see what's not right here." What keeps us from responding in this way?

Anger is a scary emotion in our society. In mainstream white culture we are taught to be polite, never to raise our voices, to be reasonable and to keep calm. People who are demonstrative of their feelings are discounted and ridiculed. We are told by parents just to obey "because I said so." We are told by bosses, religious leaders and professional authorities not to challenge what they say, "or else" (or else you'll be fired, go to hell, be treated as "crazy"). When we do get angry we learn to stuff it, mutter under our breath and go away. We are taught to turn our anger inward in self-destructive behaviors. If we are men we are taught to take out our frustrations on someone weaker and smaller than we are.

When we have seen someone expressing anger, it has often been a person with power who was abusing us or someone else physically, verbally or emotionally. We were hurt, scared or possibly confused. Most of us can remember a time from our youth when a parent, teacher, coach, boss or other adult was yelling at us abusively. It made us afraid when those around us become angry. It made us afraid of our own anger.

A similar response is triggered when a person of color gets angry at us about racism. We become scared, guilty, embarrassed, confused and we fear everything is falling apart and we might get hurt. If the angry person would just calm down, or go away, we could get back to the big, happy family feeling.

Relationships between people of color and whites often begin as friendly and polite. We may be pleased that we know and like a person from another cultural group. We may be pleased that they like us. We are encouraged because despite our fears, it seems that it may be possible for people from different cultures to get along together. The friendships may confirm our feelings that we are different from other white people.

But then the person of color get angry. Perhaps they are angry about something we do or say. Perhaps they are angry about a comment or action by someone else, or about racism in general. We may back off in response, fearing that the relationship is falling apart. We aren't liked anymore. We've been found out to be racist. For a person of color, this may be a time of hope that the relationship can become more intimate and honest. The anger may be an attempt to test the depths and possibilities of the friendship. They may be open about their feelings, to see how safe we are, hoping that we will not desert them. Or the anger may be a more assertive attempt to break through our complacency to address some core assumptions, beliefs or actions.

Many white people have been taught to see anger and conflict as a sign of failure. They may instead be signs that we're becoming more honest, dealing with the real differences and problems in our lives. If it is not safe enough to argue, disagree, express anger and struggle with each other what kind of relationship can it be?

We could say, "Thank you for pointing out the racism because I want to know whenever it is occurring." Or, "I appreciate your honesty. Let's see what we can do about this situation." More likely we get scared and disappear, or become defensive and counterattack. In any case, we don't focus on the root of the problem, and the racism goes unattended.

When people of color are angry about racism it is legitimate anger. It is not their oversensitivity, but our lack of sensitivity, that causes this communication gap. They are vulnerable to the abuse of racism everyday. They are experts on it. White society, and most of us individually, rarely notice racism.

It is the anger and actions of people of color that call our attention to the injustice of racism. Sometimes that anger is from an individual person of color who is talking to us. At other times it is the rage of an entire community protesting, bringing legal action or burning down buildings. Such anger and action is almost always a last resort, a desperate attempt to get our attention when all else fails.

It is tremendously draining, costly and personally devastating for people of color to have to rage about racism. They often end up losing their friends, their livelihoods, even their lives. Rather than attacking them for their anger, we need to ask ourselves how many layers of complacency, ignorance, collusion, privilege and misinformation have we put into place for it to take so much outrage to get our attention?

The 1965 riots in Watts, as never before, brought our attention to the ravages of racism on the African-American population living there. In 1968 a national report by the Kerner Commission warned us of the dangers of not addressing racial problems. Yet in 1992, when there were new uprisings in Los Angeles, we focused again on the anger of African Americans, on containing that anger, protecting property and controlling the community, rather than on solving the problems that cause poverty, unemployment, crime and high drop-out rates. As soon as the anger was contained, we turned our attention elsewhere and left the underlying problems unaddressed. The only way to break this cycle of rage is for us to seriously address the sources of the anger, the causes of the problems. And in order to do that, we need to talk about racism directly with each other.

It's Good to Talk
about Racism

*R*ACISM IS AN everyday influence on our lives which has great power partly because we don't talk about it. Talking about racism lessens its power, breaks the awful, uncomfortable silence we live within. Talking about it makes it less scary.

Talking about racism is an opportunity to learn about people of color and to reclaim our lives and true histories. We can ask questions, learn and grow in exciting ways that have been denied us.

Racism is a gross injustice which kills people of color, damages democracy and is linked to many of our social problems. Talking about it helps make our society safer for people of color and safer for us as well. Talking about racism keeps us from passing it on to our children. Talking about racism allows us to do something about it. Because it seems scary or confusing to talk about racism, we can forget that there are lots of good sound reasons for doing so. You can probably think of reasons I haven't mentioned. It is a useful group exercise to brainstorm the reasons it is good to talk about racism.

We actually talk about race all the time, but we do it in code. Much of our discussions about economics, military issues, neighborhood affairs, public safety and welfare, education, sports and movies is about race. Some of the code words we use are "underclass," "welfare mothers," "inner city," "illegal aliens," "terrorist," "politically correct" and "invasion."

These color-coded words allow white people to speak about race or about people of color, whether in the United States or abroad, without having to admit to doing so. We don't have to risk being accused of racism; we don't have to worry about being accountable for what we say. We can count on a mutual (white) understanding of the implications of the words without having to specify that this comment is about race. In order to be allies of people of color, we need to break the code of silence and subterfuge between white people in our talk about racism. Dealing with racism, then, is not just talking about it, but talking about it openly, intentionally, with the goal of ending it. It calls for us to demystify and analyze our coded interactions.

I want to look briefly at the seven words and phrases mentioned above to decipher the meanings they contain, including the ways that class perceptions are intertwined with racial ones. This analysis should help us challenge other white people when they fall back on racial code words.

"Underclass" generally stands for African Americans who are poor. It suggests they are a separate group from other poor people, a class by themselves which is "below" the rest of us. It connotes hopelessness, desperation and violence, and implies that this group lives by values which are different from ours and is therefore immune to efforts to change their economic circumstances.

This word operates, like most racially coded words, by labeling a particular group as a group of color and then creating or exaggerating their characteristics so that we feel completely separate from them. The negative qualities attributed to this group then become justifications for our treatment of "them."

African Americans have no monopoly on poverty in this country. There are over twice as many poor whites as poor blacks (chideya, p.18). Nor is there a special "culture of poverty" (another racially coded phrase). There are certainly significant negative effects of poverty, but well-paying jobs, access to decent housing and schooling would mitigate most of these effects very quickly.

"Welfare mothers" is another phrase which seems to have a clear definition but actually has several layers of racial meaning. For most white people the word represents African American women and teens who have children without being married. Our image is of a woman with several children who lives rather well for long periods of time on welfare to avoid working for a living. In turn, the expense of providing for welfare mothers is said to be draining our country financially, contributing to the national deficit and providing a disincentive for African American teens to work.

The reality is quite different. The majority of welfare recipients are white. Welfare recipients are primarily women who have, on the average, two children and stay on welfare for less than two years. Only 20 percent of welfare recipients stay on the rolls for five years or more. The percentage of African American women on welfare has actually dropped in the last two decades (chideya, pps. 37–45).

Welfare does not provide more than poverty-level support. The average payment in 1993 for a family of three was $388 per month, or $4,656 per year.

If you had two children would you give up a job for this amount of money? With these meager payments, currently being cut back further, we can see why welfare accounts for less than one percent of the federal budget. Social security, in contrast, accounts for about 20 percent (chideya, pps. 37–45).

Both of the terms examined above come together in the phrase "inner city." This is supposedly where the underclass, including most welfare mothers, live. The inner city is more a site in our minds than in our cities. For most white people "inner city" means anywhere there are large concentrations of people of color, regardless of their economic status. The central sections of most large metropolitan areas in this country are highly diverse economically and racially. In many cities there are now neighborhoods of upper-income whites in gentrified houses and condos. Communities of color also have much economic diversity because of housing and lending discrimination and family ties, which keep middle income people of color close to where they grew up. Conversely, many poor people of color live in rural or suburban areas. Poor people in general, and welfare mothers in particular, can be found throughout our states, not just in urban areas. There are white communities of people who are poor, such as in Appalachia, which have longer histories, and equally severe impediments to economic recovery than "inner city" areas. All of this racial and economic complexity is concealed and distorted by the phrase "inner city."

Each of these three terms attempts to create a division between white people and African Americans giving us the illusion they are different than and lower than we are. The facts are distorted to make it seem as if white people and people of color live in different worlds with different cultures and moral values. From this framework it becomes easy to blame them for their poverty and to fail to see the interconnections between their lives and ours.

Following are four other racially coded words in common use.

Illegal aliens

>   Which immigrants are a legal or illegal has always been a function of racially determined immigration policies. Throughout most of our history Europeans have been welcomed, and immigrants from Africa, Latin America and Asia have been excluded or discouraged. Today, discussion about illegal aliens focuses on Mexicans, Central and South Americans and Asians, not on Europeans. Talk of illegal aliens justifies control of Spanish-speaking communities by extending discriminatory policies to legal residents and long-standing citizens who are Spanish-speaking, while claiming that this is a legal and non-racial issue.

Terrorist

>   This has become a code word for Arabs. When using it we

can mask anti-Arab statements and policies while ignoring the terrorist acts of white people and European and U.S. governments, such as the bombings of civilian areas in Panama and Iraq.

Politically correct

Progressives have long been challenging language that is disrespectful and abusive as well as policies and practices that are discriminatory. This phrase has become a way to divert attention from racism by counterattacking the people who are challenging it. People using this word claim to be concerned about freedom of speech while avoiding addressing issues of discrimination and harassment.

Invasion

Why don't we say that Europeans invaded North America? Or that settlers invaded the West? Most uses of the word invasion are about "us"—white Americans—being invaded by Japanese investment, illegal aliens, people of color moving to the suburbs or Haitian refugees.

We can only develop effective strategies for uprooting racism with a language that reflects reality. Racially coded words make it easier for us to focus on people of color as the problem and avoid taking responsibility for ending racism. In effect, they give us excuses for not being allies to people of color.

I Would Be a Perfect Ally If...

*W*E LEARN MANY excuses and justifications for racism in this society. We also learn many tactics for avoiding responsibility for it. We have developed a coded language to help us avoid even talking about it directly. Our training makes it easy find reasons for not being allies to people of color. In order to maintain our commitment to being allies, we must reject the constant temptation to find excuses for being inactive.

What reasons have you used for not taking a stronger stand against racism, or for backing away from supporting a person of color?

Following are some of the reasons I've recently heard white people use. I call them "if only" statements because that's the phrase they usually begin with. Our real meaning is just the reverse. We are often setting conditions on our commitment to racial justice. We are saying that "only if" people of color do this or that will we do our part. These conditions let us blame people of color for our not being reliable allies.

I would be a committed and effective ally:

> If only people of color weren't so angry, sensitive, impatient or demanding;

> If only people of color realized that I am different from other white people, I didn't own slaves, I treat everyone the same, I don't see color, I'm not a member of the KKK and I've even been to an unlearning racism workshop;

> If only people of color would give white people a chance, hear our side of things and realize that we have it hard too;

If only people of color didn't use phrases like "all white people";

If only people of color didn't expect the government to do everything for them and wouldn't ask for special treatment.

Being a white ally to people of color means to be there all the time, for the long term, committed and active. Because this is hard, challenging work, we often look for ways to justify not doing it. Rather than finding ways to avoid being allies, we need to look at what gets in our way. Where does it get hard? Where do we get stuck? Many of the reasons listed above are ways to justify withdrawal from the struggle against racism.

Another way we justify our withdrawal is to find a person of color who represents, in our minds, the reason why people of color don't really deserve our support. Often these examples have to do with people of color not spending money or time the way we think they should. "I know a person who spends all her money on..."

We often set standards for their conduct that we haven't previously applied to white people in the same position. "Look what happened when so-and-so got into office." In most instances we are criticizing a person of color for not being perfect (by our standards), and then using that person as an example of an entire group of people.

People of color are not perfect. Within each community of color people are as diverse as white people, with all the human strengths and failings. The question is one of justice. No one should have to earn justice. We don't talk about taking away rights or opportunities from white people because we don't like them, or because they don't make the decisions we think they should. Even when white people break the law, are obviously incompetent for the position they hold, are mean, cruel or inept, it is often difficult to hold them accountable for their actions. Our laws call for equal treatment of everyone. We should apply the same standards and treatments to people of color as we do to white people.

Not only are people of color not perfect, neither are they representatives of their race. Yet how many times have we said,

"But I know a person of color who..."

"A person of color told me that..."

"So and so is a credit to her race..."

(Turning to an individual) "What do people of color think about that...?"

"Let's ask so and so, he's a person of color."

We would never say that a white person was representative of that race, even if that person were Babe Ruth, Mother Teresa, Hitler, John Lennon or

Margaret Thatcher, much less the only white person in the room. When was the last time you spoke as a representative for white people?

Imagine yourself in a room of fifty people where you are the only white person. At one point in the middle of a discussion about a major issue, the facilitator turns to you and says, "Could you please tell us what white people think about this issue?" How would you feel? What would you say? Would it make any difference if the faciltator said, "I know you can't speak for other white people, but could you tell us what the white perspective is on this issue?" What support would you want from other people around you in the room?

In that situation would you want a person of color to be your ally by interrupting the racial dynamic and pointing out that there isn't just one white perspective, and you couldn't represent white people? Would you want them to challenge the other people present and stand up for you? Being a white ally to people of color calls for the same kind of intervention—stepping in to support people of color when we see any kind of racism being played out.

Being a Strong
White Ally

WHAT KIND OF active support does a strong white ally provide? People of color that I have talked with over the years have been remarkably consistent in describing the kinds of support they need from white allies. The following list is compiled from their statements at workshops I have facilitated. The focus here is on personal qualities and interpersonal relationships. More active interventions are discussed in the next part of the book.

What people of color want from white allies:

"respect"
"find out about us"
"don't take over"
"provide information"
"resources"
"money"
"take risks"
"don't take it personally"
"understanding"
"teach your children about racism"
"speak up"
"don't be scared by my anger"
"support"

"listen"
"don't make assumptions"
"stand by my side"
"don't assume you know what's
    best for me"
"your body on the line"
"make mistakes"
"honesty"
"talk to other white people"
"interrupt jokes and comments"
"don't ask me to speak
    for my people"

Basic Tactics

EVERY SITUATION IS different and calls for critical thinking about how to make a difference. Taking the statements above into account, I have compiled some general guidelines.

1. Assume racism is everywhere, everyday.

Just as economics influences everything we do, just as our gender and gender politics influence everything we do, assume that racism is affecting whatever is going on. We assume this because it's true, and because one of the privileges of being white is not having to see or deal with racism all the time. We have to learn to see the effect that racism has. Notice who speaks, what is said, how things are done and described. Notice who isn't present. Notice code words for race, and the implications of the policies, patterns and comments that are being expressed. You already notice the skin color of everyone you meet and interact with—now notice what difference it makes.

2. Notice who is the center of attention and who is the center of power.

Racism works by directing violence and blame toward people of color and consolidating power and privilege for white people.

3. Notice how racism is denied, minimized and justified.

4. Understand and learn from the history of whiteness and racism.

Notice how racism has changed over time and how it has subverted or resisted challenges. Study the tactics that have worked effectively against it.

5. Understand the connections between racism, economic issues, sexism and other forms of injustice.

6. Take a stand against injustice.

Take risks. It is scary, difficult, risky and may bring up many feelings, but ultimately it is the only healthy and moral human thing to do. Intervene in situations where racism is being passed on.

7. Be strategic.

Decide what is important to challenge and what's not. Think about strategy in particular situations. Attack the source of power.

8. Don't confuse a battle with the war.

Behind particular incidents and interactions are larger patterns. Racism is flexible and adaptable. There will be gains and losses in the struggle for justice and equality.

9. Don't call names or be personally abusive.

Since power is often defined as power over others—the ability to abuse or control people—it is easy to become abusive ourselves. However, we usually end up abusing people who have less power than we do because it is less dangerous. Attacking people doesn't address the systemic nature of racism and inequality.

10. Support the leadership of people of color.

Do this consistently, but not uncritically.

11. Don't do it alone.

You will not end racism by yourself. We can do it if we work together. Build support, establish networks, work with already established groups.

12. Talk with your children and other young people about racism.

The next sections of this book discuss how to apply these guidelines to social action in institutional settings. The final part of this section takes a last look at intervening in interpersonal situations and social settings.

It's Not Just a Joke

"*LET ME TELL* you about the Chinaman who..." What do you do when someone starts to tell a joke which you think is likely to be a racial putdown? What do you do if the racial nature of the joke is only apparent at the punchline? How do you respond to a comment which contains a racial stereotype?

Interrupting racist comments can be scary because we risk turning the attack or anger toward us. We are sometimes accused of dampening the mood, being too serious or too sensitive. We may be ridiculed for being friends of the _____. People may think we're arrogant or trying to be politically correct. They may try to get back at us for embarrassing them. If you're in an environment where any of this could happen, then you know that it is not only not safe for you, it's even more unsafe for people of color.

People tell jokes and make comments sometimes out of ignorance, but usually knowing at some level that the comment puts down someone else and creates a collusion between the speaker and the listener. The joketeller is claiming that we're normal, intelligent and sane, and others are not. The effect is to exclude someone or some group of people from the group, to make it a little (or a lot) more unsafe for them to be there. Furthermore, by objectifying someone, it makes it that much easier for the next person to tell a joke, make a comment or take stronger action against any member of the objectified group.

The reverse is also true. Interrupting such behavior makes it less safe to harass or discriminate, and more safe for the intended targets of the abuse. Doing nothing is tacit approval and collusion with the abuse. There is no neutral stance. If someone is being attacked, even by a joke or teasing, there are no innocent bystanders.

As a white person you can play a powerful role in such a situation. When a person of color protests against being put down in an atmosphere where they are already disrespected, they are often discounted as well. You, as a white person interrupting verbal abuse, may be listened to and heeded because it breaks the collusion from other white people that was expected by the abuser. If a person of color speaks up first then you can support them by stating why you think it is right to challenge the comments. In either case, your intervention as a white person challenging racist comments is important and often effective.

What can you actually say in the presence of derogatory comments? There are no right or wrong answers. The more you do it the better you get. Even if it doesn't come off as you intended, you will influence others to be more sensitive and you will model the courage and integrity to interrupt verbal abuse. Following are suggestions for where to start.

If you can tell at the beginning that a joke is likely to be offensive or involves stereotypes and putdowns, you can say something like, "I don't want to hear a joke or story that reinforces stereotypes or puts down a group of people." Or, "Please stop right there. It sounds like your story is going to make fun of a group of people and I don't want to hear about it." Or, "I don't like humor that makes it unsafe for people here." Or, "I don't want to hear a joke that asks us to laugh at someone else's expense." There are many ways to say something appropriate without attacking or being offensive yourself.

Using "I" statements should be an important part of your strategy. Rather than attacking someone, it is stronger to state how you feel, what you want. Other people may still become defensive, but there is more opportunity for them to hear what you have to say if you word it as an "I" statement.

Often you don't know the story is offensive until the punchline. Or you just are not sure what you're hearing, but it makes you uncomfortable. It is appropriate to say afterwards that the joke was inappropriate because..., or the story was offensive because..., or it made you feel uncomfortable because... Trust your feelings about it!

In any of these interactions you may need to explain further why stories based on stereotypes reinforce abuse, and why jokes and comments that put people down are offensive. Rather than calling someone racist, or writing someone off, interrupting abuse is a way to do public education. It is a way to put what you know about racial stereotypes and abuse into action to stop them.

Often a person telling a racial joke is defensive about being called on the racism and may argue or defend themselves. You don't have to prove anything, although a good discussion of the issues is a great way to do more education. It's now up to the other person to think about your comments and to decide what to do. Everyone nearby will have heard you make a clear, direct statement challenging verbal abuse. Calling people's attention to something they assumed was innocent makes them more sensitive in the future and encourages them to stop and think about what they say about others.

Some of the other kinds of reactions you can expect are:

"It's only a joke." "It may 'only' be a joke but it is at someone's expense. It creates an environment that is less safe for the person or group being joked about. Abuse is not a joke."

"I didn't mean any harm." "I'm sure you didn't. But you should understand the harm that results even if you didn't mean it, and change what you say."

"Is this some kind of thought patrol?" "No, people can think whatever they want to. But we are responsible for what we say in public. A verbal attack is like any other kind of attack, it hurts the person attacked. Unless you intentionally want to hurt someone, you should not tell jokes or stories like this."

"This joke was told to me by a member of that group." "It really makes no difference who tells it. If it is offensive then it shouldn't be told. It is sad but true that some of us put down our own racial or ethnic group. That doesn't make it okay or less hurtful."

Sometimes the speaker will try to isolate you by saying that everyone else likes the story, everyone else laughed at the joke. At that point you might want to turn to the others and ask them if they like hearing jokes that are derogatory, do they like stories that attack people?

Sometimes the joke or derogatory comment will be made by a member of the racial group the comment is about. They may believe negative stereotypes about their racial group, they may want to separate themselves from others like themselves, or they may have accepted the racial norms of white peers in order to be accepted. In this situation it is more appropriate, and probably more effective, to talk to that person separately and express your concerns about how comments reinforce stereotypes and make the environment unsafe.

Speaking out makes a difference. Even a defensive speaker will think about what you said and probably speak more carefully in the future. I have found that when I respond to jokes or comments, other people come up to me afterwards and say they are glad I said something because the comments bothered them too but they didn't know what to say. Many of us stand around, uneasy but hesitant to intervene. By speaking out we model effective intervention and encourage other people to do the same. We set a tone for being active rather than passive, challenging racism rather than colluding with it.

The response to your intervention also lets you know whether the abusive comments are intentional or unintentional, malicious or not. It will give you information about whether the speaker is willing to take responsibility for the effects words have on others. We all have a lot to learn about how racism hurts people. We need to move on from our mistakes, wiser from the process. No one should be trashed.

If the speaker persists in making racially abusive jokes or comments, then further challenge will only result in arguments and fights. People around them need to take the steps necessary to protect themselves from abuse. You may need to think of other tactics to create a safe and respectful environment, including talking with peers to develop a plan for dealing with this person, or talking with a supervisor.

If you are in a climate where people are being put down, teased or made the butt of jokes based on their race, gender, sexual orientation, age or any other factor, you should investigate whether other forms of abuse such as sexual harassment or racial discrimination are occurring as well. Jokes and verbal abuse are obviously not the most important forms that racism takes.* However, we all have the right to live, work and socialize in environments free from verbal and emotional harassment. In order to create contexts where white people and people of color can work together to challenge more fundamental forms of racism, we need to be able to talk to each other about the ways that we talk to each other.

The next section of this book looks at how whiteness has been defined against particular racial groups and how we can be more effective allies to each one.

---

* Organizational or institutional analysis and intervention against racism is the subject of Part V.

PART IV

The Effects of History

Introduction

THE FOLLOWING SECTIONS give a brief history of white people's relationships to particular "racial" groups. I include this information for several reasons. First, most of us are woefully misinformed about the actual history of interracial relationships, particularly their more devastating aspects. We have been taught lies beginning with the benign story of Columbus's "discovery" of America. Second, our history affects our current situations and experiences. The effects of slavery, the genocide of Native Americans, the conquest of Mexico, and the banning of Chinese and later all Asian immigration continue to influence our lives and the lives of people of color. Third, we cannot build trust and an honest commitment to creating equality in this country if we are denying the injustices of the past. Our good faith efforts to change the system will not be taken seriously if we continue to deny or distort the record of white racism.

Fourth, the past, even with all its horror, can give us hope for the future. White Americans did abolish slavery and end coolie labor. We expanded the vote to people of color and women and allowed them to hold elected office. We ended legally sanctioned segregation and broadened the democratic base of this country. We can easily be defeated by the challenges of the present if we don't understand the progress we have made in the past.

Finally, we have a long history of white people speaking out for economic and political justice, and we need to reclaim those heros and that commitment.

These brief histories will focus on what white people did. The history of people of color's strong, determined and diverse resistance to racism is beyond the scope of this book. There are many good sources for that history, some of which are listed in the bibliography.

Unfortunately, when focusing on white racism and its effects on people of color it can come to seem as if the lives of people of color are determined by racism, that they are nothing but victims of injustice. Nothing could be further from the truth. They are creators of their own lives and cultures. Racism is one of the social constraints that influence how people of color live, but racism does not determine how they lead their daily lives.

In this book, because the focus is on white racism, there could be the false perception that I am ignoring the cultural, political, economic and personal achievements of people of color. White people do this all the time, even those who are committed to anti-racist work. To counter this tendency it is important for you to supplement the information in this section with the writing, music, dance, speeches and actions of people of color themselves in all the diversity they represent.

The following sections are more than very brief (and inadequate) lessons about a part of our white history. They break down the monolithic racial terms we have developed for large conglomerations of different peoples. They hint at the vast richness of culture, creativity and community which lies behind the simple-minded stereotypes and misinformation we have about other groups of people.

These sections allow us some insight into how white racism has defined and controlled specific other groups. All of these sections are about white people and what we have done to people of color, even though they seem to focus on particular groups of people of color. If we keep this emphasis in mind, each section will help us think more creatively about how to be better allies to Native Americans, African Americans, Asian Americans, Latino/as, Jews, and people of mixed heritage, as well as groups not discussed here, such as Arab Americans, South Pacific Islanders, and South Asians.

People of Mixed Heritage

NOTHING CHALLENGES OUR perceptions of race more than the millions of people of mixed heritage in the United States. Still largely invisible in our culture, their presence is in sharp contradiction to our expectation that racial difference is binary, clear and simple. People of mixed heritage pose difficult challenges not only for white people, but for people of color as well. Many people of color have been pushed to claim sharply delineated identities in resistance to white racism. They have minimized the complexities of their own identities and cultures for strategic reasons. At the same time, fear and lies about people of color have pushed white people to disown and persecute white people in racially mixed relationships and people of mixed heritage—even members of their own families.

It is estimated that 30–70 percent of African Americans are multiracial. Virtually all Latino/as and Filipinos are multiracial, as are the majority of American Indians and Native Hawaiians. A significant proportion of white-identified people are of multiracial origins (Root, p.9). Racial identity is still a crucial determinant of one's opportunities in life. In the United States, a person is considered a member of the lowest status group from which they have any heritage. Therefore it is unsafe for most white people to acknowledge any part of a mixed heritage. Although the numbers are substantial, we have no way of knowing how many white people are actually of mixed heritage.

The myth of biological race and the desire to maintain the boundaries (and attendant divisions of wealth) between white people and people of color maintain white people's fear of interracial relationships and mixed heritage children. Often the justification for discrimination and persecution of interracial couples is that the difficulties of living "like that" are so bad because of the racist response of other white people. Present racial prejudice becomes the justification for continued racist practices against people of mixed heritage.

It was only in 1967 that the Supreme Court ruled remaining miscegenation laws illegal. Even today it is commonly assumed that members of interracial relationships and mixed heritage children lead harder lives, meet more prejudice, and have higher rates of divorce, suicide and other personal problems. There is no proof that this is so, and indeed there are indications that such people are more resilient and have higher self-esteem than monocultural people (Root, pp. 217 and 251).

People in interracial relationships and people of mixed heritage belie many of our common justifications for racism and racial segregation. Their health and success challenge the biological and cultural justifications commonly used for the separation and inferior treatment of people of color. They emphasize the futility of searching for genetic justification for social and political distinctions between people.

We are becoming a nation with a substantial population of people of mixed heritage. The links between physical characteristics such as skin color and either the continent of origin of one's foreparents or the cultural roots of one's ancestors will eventually become nearly indistinguishable. People of mixed heritage challenge our assumptions about racial difference and the naturalness of our "racial" categories.

The presence of large numbers of people of mixed heritage does not mean that we are moving toward the elimination of racism through the withering away of racial differences. It is perfectly possible to replace a racial hierarchy of discrete groups with a racially continuous one which still has white people on top, such as is found in Brazil. Unless we eliminate white power and privilege, people with lighter skin color, regardless of racial heritage, will be more highly valued than people with darker skin.

Racism is resilient. White people have constantly shifted the vocabulary of racism and the ways that we justify our power. There are many other ways to justify racism besides the religious and scientific ones we have used in our past. The current force of institutional racism in our society may eventually make such justifications completely unnecessary. The large numbers of visible people of mixed heritage challenge our present justification of racism, but do not necessarily challenge the ongoing force of racism itself.

In reading the sections below, keep in mind the mixed heritage of many Americans in all "racial" groups. This should be one more reminder of the arbitrariness of referring to entire groups of people as single coherent entities.

Native Americans

I GREW UP watching Roy Rogers, Gene Autry and the Lone Ranger kill Indians. I played cowboys and Indians every chance I had. We fought over who got to be the cowboys because they always won. Native Americans for me were reduced to one generic Indian male who was worth about 1/20th of a white cavalry officer. I "knew" what they looked like, what they wore, where they lived and how sneaky, brave and clever they were. I knew that part of my responsibility as a white man in the past would have been to protect white womanhood from Indian savages.

Most of all, I "knew" that they were all dead. It was precisely because they were history that we dressed up as Indians on Halloween and in Thanksgiving plays. In Cub Scouts I learned to yell and pat my mouth in the "Indian" war cry, and I was given toy tomahawks so I could pretend to scalp my opponents. I had no understanding that I was recreating a distorted and painful history and certainly no idea that Native Americans were still alive in the United States.

Today there are over five hundred federally recognized Native-American nations in the United States. At the time that Columbus arrived in the West Indies there were approximately fifteen million indigenous people in North America. Today, after reaching a low point around 1900, the population of Native Americans in the United States is around two million according to U.S. government census figures, although these figures are highly contested (Jaimes, pps. 23–53).

The population of the Taino people and other local inhabitants of the West Indies decreased from several million to 22,000 by 1514, only twenty-two years after Columbus arrived. The population of Native Americans in the continental United States decreased from twelve million to 237,000 during the first four centuries of our history. During that time white people expropriated 97.5 percent of Native-American land (Churchill, 1994, pps 28–38).

114

Please read these last two paragraphs again and stop to consider the magnitude of this genocide.

For many of us, Native Americans are largely invisible in our daily lives and are dead, romantic figures in our imaginations. They have been replaced by slogans, chants, mascots, historical replicas and new age imitations.

All the land of North America, including the land that you are on at the moment, originally belonged to Native Americans. They did not use the same legal concepts of ownership as we do, but they knew that they had rights to use it in exchange for caring for it.

There are no generalizations that we can make about Native Americans except insofar as we describe the ways that they have been exploited, and even these vary tremendously. Various Native American nations are still struggling for recognition of their sovereignty, for control over what little land they have retained, for an end to interference in their affairs, for an end to mining, logging, and toxic waste dumping that are destroying their lands, for an end to the belittlement, stereotyping and mockery of their culture, and for full respect and civil rights within American society.

The United States government systematically killed Native Americans in this country, often with the stated intention of committing genocide. This policy was consistent, from the highest levels of government down to the ordinary citizens who carried out much of the destruction.

The following is a summary of Ward Churchill's vivid description of this period in our nation's history. Cotton Mather, a noted colonial minister, referred to the burning of Indians as "a barbecue." "Referring to Indians as 'wolves'—both being beasts of prey, tho' different in shape." In 1783 George Washington ordered that those remaining within the areas of the initial thirteen states be "hunted like beasts," and that a "war of extermination" be waged against those barring U.S. access to certain desired areas, notably the Ohio River Valley. Or, as Thomas Jefferson put it in 1812, Euro-Americans should drive every Indian in their path "with the beasts of the forests into the stony mountains"; alternatively, as he'd already stated in 1807, the United States should "pursue [the Indians] into extermination, or drive them to new seats beyond our reach"; national policy should be to wage war against each native people it encountered "until that tribe is exterminated, or driven beyond the Mississippi."

Andrew Jackson characterized Indians as "wild dogs" and supervised the mutilation of about 800 Creek Indian corpses—the bodies of men, women and children that he and his men had massacred. "...Scalp bounties paid better than buffalo hides for 'enterprising citizens' in Texas and the Dakotas until the 1880s.*

---

* From Ward Churchill, *Indians Are Us?* (Monroe, Maine: Common Courage Press, 1994), pps. 309–316. Used by permission.

Racism against Native Americans, like all racism is gendered. White women were said to need protection from rape by Indian men, who were portrayed as sexual animals. Images of white women ravished by Native American men were used to incite white men to kill them. Native American women were extolled when they served white men (Pocahontas, Sacajawea) and were otherwise portrayed as exotic, shy and reserved sexual creatures. White family norms and attitudes were projected onto Native Americans whose families were then destroyed by forced adoption, residential schooling and federal policies breaking up tribal ownership of land.

As with slavery or any policy of violence and exploitation, we are not responsible for what our forefathers and foremothers did. We are responsible for acknowledging what happened, what it cost and who participated. The annihilation of Native Americans in the United States happened. It was systematic, sanctioned by all levels of society and carried out by ordinary citizens as well as by the military and state militias. Most of our predecessors participated, and every single one of them and all of us gained enormously because of this mass murder.

White people have denied the extent of the genocide by minimizing estimates of the number of Native Americans who lived here. Although now discredited by most historical research, there are still attempts to describe the country as an empty wilderness with a few bands of "Indians" here and there.

Another way to deny what happened is to make it appear to be a natural phenomenon with a momentum of its own. We talk about "manifest destiny" as if there were not real white people involved in the process of killing Native Americans and appropriating their land, as if white people were not manifesting and manufacturing that destiny.

Another justification white people have used for their violence is that Native Americans were simple, unsophisticated and, by implication, their culture was not really a loss because they were unable to compete in the modern world. In fact, there were long-term, stable, complex and sophisticated cultures in all parts of this country including the Southwest, Northwest, South, Southern Mississippi Valley, Northeast and the Great Plains. Furthermore, a people's right to exist, control their land and maintain their culture is not contingent on their sophistication.

Another way to justify the genocide was to say that Native Americans died from diseases they were biologically unable to resist. We know that diseases were introduced to Native-American populations intentionally and systematically by white people as part of a policy of extermination. For example, "In 1763 Lord Jeffrey Amherst ordered a subordinate to distribute items taken from a smallpox infirmary as 'gifts' during a peace parley with Pontiac's Confederacy.... Upwards of 100,000 Indians died of smallpox in the ensuing epidemic" (Churchill 1994, p. 343; also in Jaimes, pps 31–34).

We cannot change the past, but if we are honest with ourselves, and if we don't want to continue the injustice, we have to acknowledge what happened. It is hard to face It makes me sad and angry, depressed and frustrated. I feel guilty over what white people have done to Native Americans, yet it doesn't help them or me to remain stuck in these feelings. Many of us feel saddened by the past, while remaining ignorant of the present reality of continued exploitation and destruction of Native people, land and culture.

Throughout the United States today, in every state, Native Americans are struggling to regain control of land, to end centuries of colonization and to stop cultural exploitation. Native-American lands are being mined, logged, hunted and developed without permission, or adequate compensation. Native Americans are fighting for recognition of their sovereignty, return of appropriated cultural artifacts, recognition of their status as Native Americans, an end to police and military interference with traditional hunting and fishing rights, culturally appropriate education for their children, and for the end of stereotyping, inaccuracies and lies about American history and present realities.

At the same time that white people have vilified and annihilated Native Americans, we have constructed a mythologized image of them. We hold them up as natural, ecologically wise, at one with nature, enduring, skillful, brave, and as having rituals, stories and beliefs that we need to adopt to counter the destructiveness of our modern industrialized lives. Boy Scouts and Campfire Girls, men's lodges and men's movement retreats all mimic our generic version of Native-American culture.

Our stereotypes are so strong that very often we, or our children, don't believe that someone who is wearing contemporary clothing is a Native American because the or she "doesn't look like one." These stereotypes allow us to talk about how Native Americans *were*, without addressing who they *are*. Such symbolic annihilation is devastating to Native Americans because it renders them invisible, and their struggles for sovereignty incomprehensible.

There are many simple and immediate ways that we can counter the continued genocide of Native Americans in our society. The following questions suggest some places to start.

Questions and Actions

1. What people lived on the land you presently inhabit? How were they removed? Where do they live now? Are there any land or tribal recognition claims still pending? Where else in your state are these struggles going on?

2. Do Native Americans people have full access to jobs, social services and community resources in your community? For example, what is the unemployment rate for Native American adults and young people?

3. Are Native Americans in your area harassed for exercising, or prohibited from exercising traditional hunting and fishing rights?

4. Is there corporate mining, logging or land devastation occurring on Native lands in your region? Are toxic dumps located on Native lands?

5. Is there a climate of hatred toward Native Americans in your area? How do white people talk about them? Is there police harassment or brutality directed toward them?

6. What forms of government, foods, medical treatments, products, names and customs have white people adopted from Native Americans? How much has their contribution been recognized? How has it been exploited?

7. Are local Native-American historical sites, relics and burial grounds preserved in your community? Are museums being asked to return sacred Native American objects to the people from which they came? If so, how do they respond?

8. Are you part of a spiritual or growth community that has appropriated Native-American rituals, artifacts or customs? Have you ever borrowed Native-American spiritual practices? How might it feel to Native Americans when people from different religious backgrounds take their sacred rituals and use them as recreational activities, or mix them in with traditions from other cultures?

9. Are there schools, universities or companies in your vicinity that use Native-American names or figures as mascots, slogans or product or team names?

10. Do you hear people refer to Native Americans in derogatory ways, make jokes about Indians, or make generalized statements about all Native Americans? How can you respond when someone makes a tomahawk chop, war hoop or otherwise contributes to perpetuating a caricature of a Native American?

11. What do you remember about portrayals of Indians in film and TV when you grew up? How do you think these portrayals affected you?

12. Do your children play with toys, video games, watch TV shows or movies where Native Americans are stereotyped, portrayed as the enemy to white people, or otherwise degraded? Are there books, pictures or artifacts in your house which degrade, make fun of or stereotype Native Americans?

13. Do textbooks in your local schools accurately and truthfully describe what white settlers and government troops did to Native Americans? Do any romanticize them? Do any speak of a generic Indian? Is the full story of Columbus' and the colonialist's practices and policies told?

14. Do you and your children know about Native Americans in contemporary America?

15. When talking about Native peoples do you refer to Native Americans generically, assuming there are valid generalizations you can make about all Native Americans, or do you specify the nation or culture you are referring to and give specific examples?

16. How would Columbus Day and Thanksgiving activities have to be changed so they did not disguise the genocide of Native Americans in the West Indies and New England?

African Americans

As WITH ANY other "racial" identity, the term "African American" hides tremendous diversity. In the United States there are Africans, native-born African Americans, and immigrants from the West Indies and South America. There are African Americans with hundreds of years of history as "free blacks" and others whose grandparents were slaves. Many, if not most African Americans have Native American, white and Latino/a ancestors. Differences in class, gender, sexual orientation, physical ability and geographically specific cultures are also vitally important in the African-American community. There are no biological, economic, cultural or physiological generalizations that hold for them except for the actuality of white racism itself, which they must all deal with. Even here they are differentially vulnerable based on their gender, class, age, sexual orientation, location and other factors. Generalizations about the effects of white racism and the modes of African-American resistance to it are false and reflect the beliefs of the white people involved.

The presence and role of African Americans in the United States has been a continuous challenge to the democratic values espoused by white people since the early 17th Century. The history of white racism toward African Americans can help us understand how white people have justified racism.

The first Africans were brought to what is now the United States in 1619. In the earliest days of colonial America most Africans and 75 percent of white Europeans were indentured servants and were treated similarly if not equally (Takaki 1993, p.54). Many whites and African Americans fraternized, some intermarried, and others worked together to revolt against or escape from servitude.

By and large, Africans were seen as different than whites, but not innately inferior. Differences in economic status were explained by reasons of class and religion, by qualities which related to being poor and non-Christian.

There were already over a million slaves in the West Indies and South America, as well as a long tradition of treating darker skinned people as inferior in enlightenment Europe. Slavery expanded rapidly, and the distinction between white servants and African slaves was quickly rigidified, feeding into already existing prejudice and exploitation of people of color both in the colonies and in Europe. Over time, the white landowning class systemically codified the separation of African Americans and poor European Americans through the legalization of lifetime servitude (slavery) to control the former and to use the latter as a buffer to protect themselves from rebellion.

From 1619 until slavery ended officially in 1865, 10–15 million Africans were brought here, and another 30–35 million died in transport—a journey called the Middle Passage (Zinn, p.29). In all, 40–50 million Africans were abducted or killed by our white American and European foreparents.*

Please pause a moment and take in the magnitude of these numbers.

During slavery white people did everything possible to dehumanize, demoralize and degrade African Americans. White society systematically tried to destroy any vestige of the language, culture, spirituality, religion and family structure of the slave community. This cultural genocide was practiced throughout what was then the United States, and all white Americans, north and south, benefitted materially from the economic system of slavery.

Most of the early leaders of our country, including Washington and Jefferson, owned slaves. During the 18th and 19th Centuries the slave-based agricultural prosperity of the South fueled the industrial expansion of the North. New waves of immigrants came to a land of opportunity partly supported by the jobs this prosperity generated. White immigrants prospered not only while African Americans were enslaved, but *because* they were, benefitting from the many jobs and trades from which African Americans were excluded.

Not all white people supported slavery. There was a longstanding minority tradition of public outcry for the abolition of slavery, particularly among white women in the 19th Century.

The Civil War and the end of slavery occurred because of economic tensions between North and South, and political differences about state's rights, more than it did because of an outcry against slavery. The Civil War was a complicated political, economic and social event, and while slavery was a key issue, the abolition of slavery was not a strong concern of the American public. As Lincoln wrote in a letter to Horace Greeley,

---

* The devastating effects on African societies has been well documented in such books as Walter Rodney's How Europe Underdeveloped Africa.

> Dear Sir: I have not meant to leave any one in doubt....My paramount object in this struggle is to save the Union, and is not either to save or destroy Slavery. If I could save the Union without freeing any slave, I would do it; and if I could save it by freeing all the slaves, I would do it; and if I could do it by freeing some and leaving others alone, I would also do that. What I do about Slavery and the colored race, I do because it helps to save this Union (Zinn, p.186).

Slavery raises issues for white people that we are not yet finished dealing with. We commonly say that slavery is a thing of the past. Putting an injustice behind us is one of the tactics we looked at in Part I of this book. This tactic is not useful for several reasons.

First, we have not yet fully acknowledged as a society the extent of the devastation that white people perpetrated on West African civilization and on African Americans in this country during the period of slavery. We don't talk about the horrors of the Middle Passage, the systematic attempt to eradicate African culture, and the everyday participation of common white folks in supporting slavery. We still refer to slavery as something that most people survived. We don't talk about the millions dead, the maimed, the tortured, the broken families, the rape and daily violence. We still talk about good slaveowners and pretend that some slaves had it pretty good.

We don't talk about the benefits of slavery to white people. Most of our families did not own slaves. Most of our families did participate in and benefit from slavery, even if our foreparents arrived here after slavery ended. Immigrants benefitted from the presence of a group of people that had less respect and status than they did, from getting jobs that African Americans were barred from and from economic development based on agricultural profits from slave labor.

The second problem with "moving on" from slavery is that we rarely acknowledge the longlasting aftereffects of more than two hundred years of slavery. Although slavery was officially abolished by the Thirteenth Amendment in 1865, economic and cultural exploitation, everyday violence including lynching, rape, physical attack and other forms of mob violence, political disenfranchisement and almost total segregation in the South and the North continued into recent times. We have had over three hundred and fifty years of economic and cultural enrichment of the white community at the expense of African Americans. The effects of that exploitation are in the present.

As white people we take credit for the achievements of the past. We are proud of the democratic traditions, struggle for independence and the scientific and industrial achievements of our foreparents. We cannot be hypocritical and deny the full complexity of our heritage, including the negative aspects of it. We retain false feelings of superiority and justify further exploitation of African Americans when we deny or minimize the actions of our foreparents.

This minimization of the horrors of the past contributes to our denial of present injustices. Some of us lived through the lynchings of the 1930s and 1940s. Many of us lived through the civil rights struggles of the 1950s and 1960s. All of us are living through the criminalization of African American men, the scapegoating of African American women, and the police and state brutality of the 1970s, 1980s and 1990s. Many of us have supported and benefitted from segregation in this country during our lifetimes. Many of us and our parents fought against the dismantaling of segregation, and are still resisting the integration of schools, country clubs, recreation centers, neighborhoods and businesses. Until we have enough integrity to acknowledge our role in these injustices, we will continue to stand in the way of progress toward full equality. There is no dividing line between slavery, other forms of white exploitation of African Americans and the present. Until we deal with the past we will not lessen its overpowering influence on the future.

Although white people have systematically tried to destroy African-American culture in this country through prohibitions on learning to read and write, lack of public funding for schools, lack of public means to disseminate music, dance, games, writing and religion, lack of religious freedom and forced breakup of families, there has always been resistance to that destruction. Enslaved African Americans taught each other to read and write, passed on musical and religious traditions and resisted their dehumanization.

With the end of slavery and the beginning of migration to northern cities in significant numbers in the 1940s, the direct assault on African-American culture diminished. It was replaced by the exploitation of that culture by white society. The appropriation of music, dance, fashion, and various elements of "style" from African Americans has enriched white culture and individual white people. For example, blues, jazz, rock n'roll and rap are all African-American musical forms that white people have listened to, copied and profited from. Even elements of culture which are not exportable outside the African-American community, for example, concepts such as "Black is Beautiful" and "Black Pride," have been repackaged by white-owned corporations and marketed back to African Americans.

White racism is not just a system of economic exploitation. It is also a struggle for cultural and ideological domination. African-American cultural resistance has always been strong and persistent. It continues today, constantly taking new and diverse forms.

The impact of resistance cultures reaches far into the American mainstream, even affecting the relationships in white families, most noticeably between young people and adults and between men and women. Intergenerational conflict over clothes, music, patterns of socialization and interracial dating often trigger the perceived subversive, scary or eroticized beliefs whites hold about African-American people and culture. These fears of older whites are manipulated by the young to create more space for personal autonomy and individual creativeness. Of course, the racial icons used by white youth, such as music and clothing styles, have already been bought by white adults and repackaged for consumption by white youth. This intergenerational "discussion" tells us more about white racism and about contests of authority within white families than it does about the virtues and values of rock, jazz, or rap music.

Our national discussions about sexism and male-female relationships, especially their more difficult and troubling aspects, often use the lives and culture of African American men and women as examples. In the late 19th Century the sexual protection provided to white women was framed in the context of fear about African American male "predators." In the 1950s and 1960s the sexual freedom of young whites was often couched in terms of fears of interracial dating and marriage. (The question "Would you want your daughter to marry one?" was prevalent among whites during the civil rights period.)

More recently, national media attention has focused our discussion of contemporary male-female issues on prominent African American men such as Clarence Thomas (sexual harassment), Mike Tyson (rape), Michael Jackson (child sexual assault), and O.J. Simpson (domestic violence). Each of these issues is current, volatile and contested. Each strikes deep chords of anger, fear and pain among white people. The lives of these individuals can be held up in white Americans' conversations about these issues because African American men are presumed to represent naturally male, but less civilized or controlled sexuality, because they have less protection in a white society and because they are perceived to be clearly outside the boundaries of whiteness. These issues are less threatening to us when they are framed by white racism. If the debate gets hot and we can't reach an understanding we can write the whole issue off to the perversions of African-American sexuality.

This pattern continues a tradition of demonizing African American men, pretending they are aberrant, and condoning further violence toward them. When we use the actions of African American men as examples (regardless of what they may have actually done), we are furthering the pretense that white men are not violent. The sexual harassment, rape, child sexual assault and domestic violence committed by white men remains less visible.

The focus on fear of African American male sexuality leaves the lives and concerns of African American women unacknowledged. This is despite the fact that African American women have been in the forefront of the fight against racism and the fight for safety and equality for women. This lack of respect for African American women has meant that the concerns of African American men have been set up against the needs of white (generally middle class) women in the struggle for the right to vote, in many affirmative action programs and in concerns about women's safety from male violence.

As noted earlier, these dynamics are complex. White women have been active in fighting racism on specific issues such as abolition, education for African Americans after Reconstruction and voting rights during the civil rights movement. Male resistance to their participation in these struggles motivated them to organize around women's issues. Their work in these movements provided them with organizing skills, political models, inspiration and experience which they subsequently used in feminist struggles. But often these feminist movements ended up pursuing racist policies that subverted some of the gains they had been working for in their earlier abolition or civil rights work.

The relationship between race and gender issues as they have played out in our country's history have focused on African American men and white women. African American women have not been acknowledged for the particular needs, concerns, insights, skills and experience they have consistently provided both to the struggle to end racism and to the struggle to end sexism (see Davis 1981, Giddings).

Two other factors have been at work in white racism against African American women. White women's roles and relationships have been taken as the norm for all women (norms that were, in fact, constructed by racism), and African American women's lives are not seen or understood. White people have assumed that because many white women did not work outside the home, women of color did not either. We have assumed that because large numbers of white women were falling into poverty (the "feminization of poverty") that many women of color were also. In reality, most were already living in poverty and had nowhere to fall from. We have assumed that since white women were primarily domestic workers, taking care of children and the home, that slave women were also. In fact, most female slaves were field workers and did the same work as men. Since slavery, African American women have continued to work outside the home, often in the homes of white women.

These are examples of the assumption that African-American lives mirror white lives. The overlay of the patterns of white women's lives onto to those of African American women, in conjunction with the lack of opportunity for African American women to describe their own experience, has contributed to their invisibility and exploitation. (A parallel dynamic occurs for other women of color and poor and working class white women as well.)

These patterns have also contributed to the exploitation of white women. The wages paid to African American women as domestics have always put a ceiling on wages paid to white women domestics. The expectations and attitudes of white men toward African American women will always limit the respect and equality accorded white women. This relationship between the exploitation of African American and white women has been particularly damaging to white poor and working class women.

White exploitation of African Americans will always have a boomerang effect on white people, particularly on the poor and working class. We will not be able to recognize the source of those costs as long as our attention is focused on African Americans and not on white people.

Racial exploitation continually takes new forms as white social and economic systems change and as people of color and concerned whites resist. What remains constant is that white lives and norms remain central and opposed to those of African Americans.

When we project personal qualities onto African Americans, it reflects our images of who we think ourselves as white people to be. Statements that African Americans are lazy, promiscuous or stupid are simultaneously statements that white people are hard working, monogamous and smart. Hard working and monogamous refer to fundamental Christian values. Our statements about people of color tell us how we want to perceive ourselves as white Christians.

Our stereotyped statements about African-American relationships, families and community structure similarly tell us what we want to believe about white social organization. When we describe African-American families as matriarchal, violent, and their communities filled with drugs and violence, we are implying that white families are patriarchal and peaceful, and our communities are not filled with drugs and violence.

These characterizations set up a false norm for each community for the purpose of contrasting them. There are all kinds of family and community structures in both white and African-American communities, with much more overlap than difference. These dichotomies also establish white valuations of what should be accepted as normal. In the examples above, patriarchal is assumed to be normal and is valued over matriarchal. Matriarchal family structures are seen as abnormal, need to be analyzed and eventually become an explanation for lack of success in the African-American community. Drugs and violence are seen as natural to the African-American community—allowing us to be complacent about them—and they only become problems when we find them in the white community, or when their effects in the African American community spill over into our white neighborhoods.

The ideological systems we use to justify racism tell us a great deal about the legitimizing structures of different historical periods. The original white European settlers of this country were Protestant. Some were missionaries and others were fleeing religious persecution. People of color were demonized as pagan and "soulless." As substantial numbers of people of color were converted to Christianity, and as religion itself lost much of its power as a legitimizing agent, justifications for the brutality of slavery changed.

As the agricultural South developed into a slave-based economy, the extreme exploitation and degradation of slavery had to be justified. During this period biological, zoological and botanical theories about the natural world were extended to explain human difference and to justify slavery. The ability of these theories to justify economic arrangements enhanced the status of these sciences in particular and the public valuation of science in general. It became persuasive to call upon scientific theory to certify the naturalness of political and economic arrangements.

Within Christianity there were values of compassion, fellowship and the acceptance of other Christians which provided a base from which Christians could resist slavery and refute scientific explanations. There were also subversive scientific currents that contested the scientific "proof" of biological superiority. These countercurrents within religion and science undermined those belief systems from within even as they were pitted against each other. Together with the remarkable achievements and resistance of free blacks and slaves, these currents created space for a great national debate about the abolition of slavery.

When slavery was abolished the justification for the exploitation of African Americans continued to be scientific, i.e., biological, for several decades. As the scientific theories were discredited the explanations became more historical, often using the effects of slavery itself as the reason why African Americans were experiencing difficulties in the United States.

In more recent times biological and historical justifications for racism have been discredited, although not without many pockets of resurgence. It is now the social sciences that have become a stronger legitimizing force for the status quo in our society. Sociological and psychological explanations of the economic disparities between whites and people of color have proliferated. They deal with issues of family structure, community breakdown, individual psychology and the internalized effects of racism itself. They translate into discussions of the Black family, the role of women in the Black community, the devastation of community infrastructures, ghetto psychology, Black rage, issues of self-esteem in African American children, and "internalized oppression." Within these disciplines as well, there are currents of resistance, even as they continue to challenge biological and religious justifications of racism.

These theories and explanatory models tell us about white society. They provide keys to understanding white intellectual history and how white society thinks about itself. They describe how we have wanted to see ourselves over the centuries as first morally right, then scientifically superior, then historically justified and finally sociologically and psychologically developed. What has remained constant is the dominance of white people in power and privilege and the subordination of African Americans.

The resistance and resilience of African Americans in the face of white racism have been defining characteristics of American history and contemporary life. They force us ultimately to see that all our attempts to explain and understand racism fail to change it. These explanatory projects are, in effect, efforts to divert our attention from the practical challenge of creating a society in which African Americans have full political, economic and cultural equality. However critically they analyze the past history of white-African-American relationships, each theory reinforces and legitimizes white racism by focusing on African Americans.

White people are not directly mentioned in our discussions of African Americans and "their" problems. We are the invisible narrator as well as the only participants in the discussion. We talk to ourselves about African Americans, we describe and then "explain" their problems, and then we blame them and prescribe solutions which have to do with their changing themselves, their attitudes and their behavior.

Finally we look for people of color to testify to our conclusions. Because communities of color contain people with a full spectrum of moral and political beliefs, it is not hard for white people to find some person of color who says things that validate our theories. These people are paraded as seals of approval for white agendas.

Here again, our understanding of white racism should immediately tell us to turn our attention back to white people. What are we saying and doing? How are we implicated in this situation? What privileges, power and moral virtue are we trying to hold on to?

African Americans have been a numerically large and important part of this country's culture and economy for several hundred years, particularly in the South and East Coast. They have been the center of racial attention, and the struggles of other peoples of color have been defined against theirs. Yet we know little about them because layers of whiteness overlay our perceptions, and African Americans have had little opportunity to describe their own experience. Even today we hear the voices of few African Americans. Those we do hear are generally well educated, successful and professional. A white-controlled news and publishing network* is still the gatekeeper, deciding which African-American voices are acceptable.

Whites have created a fictitious and mythologized African-American community which we use for our convenience. African Americans are either problem or victim, aggressive or dependent, natural or barbaric. We rarely listen to what they themselves say or give them credit for the substantial contributions and leadership they have provided our society.

Beyond ending false generalizations about African Americans there is much we can do to end racism against them. Below are some questions and activities to use as a starting place.

Questions and Actions

1. List ways that at one time or another you or your family have downplayed, minimized or denied the effects of slavery and post-slavery Jim Crow segregation on the African-American community.

2. List ways your family may have colluded with or benefitted from the economic exploitation of African Americans.

3. What are ways that, actively or through inaction, you have resisted the full integration of African Americans into your workplace, school, social organizations or congregation?

4. Notice which contemporary national problems are blamed predominantly on African Americans. What national policies are being discussed to blame and punish African Americans for these problems?

5. Analyze your community. Which parts—schools, recreational facilities, job sectors, clubs—are presently de facto segregated?
   a. Which of these do you participate in?
   b. What could you do to challenge this segregation?

6. Notice what specific institutional practices contribute to de facto segregation in your community (for example red lining, real estate covenants, school district borders, suburban incorporation). List one that you are going to work with others to change.

7. Notice what kinds of individual acts of discrimination keep the segregation in place (decisions by landlords, real estate agents, employers, teachers, etc). What is one thing you can do to support public policies against discrimination, and their strong and consistent enforcement?

---

* Fifty-one percent of the newspapers in the country don't have any minority employees (Oakland Tribune, March 7, 1995, p. A–13).

8. Work to make sure the police are adequately supervised and monitored.

9. Listen to African Americans define their own lives and problems, and push for their involvement at every level in every situation you are involved in. Support their leadership.

10. Find out what you can do to work against the dismantling of affirmative action and other anti-discrimination programs and policies.

11. Find out about the agencies, local government offices and community organizations working against racism in your community.
    a. Support them financially.
    b. Support them with your time and energy.

12. Notice the sports you watch and the music you listen to. Are there any in which African Americans are major performers?
    a. Who benefits financially, and who benefits culturally from the performances of African Americans in these areas?
    b. What are the economic factors that led African Americans to be major participants in those areas?
    c. What are the stereotypes that white people use to justify these concentrations?
    d. Support the efforts of African Americans to become more powerful in these arenas through participation in management, through ownership arrangements, through less exploitive recruitment practices, etc.

13. How can you challenge other white people when stereotypes of African Americans are used to blame them for social problems? What information or other preparation do you need to be able to do this well?

14. Introduce your children to the complexities, history and accomplishments of African Americans.

15. Make sure your schools and children's programs are multicultural and that African American youth are not singled out for punishment.

Many of these suggestions apply to being allies to Latino/as, Asian Americans, Arab Americans and Native Americans as well. Others are specific to African Americans. We cannot focus on African Americans to the exclusion of other people of color, nor avoid dealing with racism against African Americans by focusing on other communities of color.

Asian Americans

W*HEN I WAS* ten, growing up in West Los Angeles in 1958, my parents were able to buy a house in the San Fernando Valley. We put our old house on the market, and the real estate agent received a bid from a Japanese family. As soon as my parents accepted their offer we began getting angry and threatening phone calls from neighbors for selling to "outsiders," "foreigners," and "Japs." This was my first experience of white hate and discrimination. My parents did not discuss the situation with my sister and me. It wasn't until years later that I realized that what we had experienced, and what the Japanese family may have experienced, was the equivalent of what was happening in the South to African Americans. At the time our attention was focused on black-white interactions in the South. Racism toward other groups, in other parts of the country, was invisible to most of us.

Asian Americans have immigrated from over twenty countries and an even greater number of distinct cultures. Like every other referent for a racial group the term "Asian American" lumps together vastly different cultural groups and subsumes the class, gender and diversity of immigrant status of millions of people.

The role of Asian Americans has always been ambiguous in a country that sees race as a polarity between black and white. The skin color of many Asians is not much different than that of many "white" people. White people have used other markers—dress, food, religious beliefs, customs and even cooking smells—to identify and justify the exclusion of Asian Americans. These differences have then been explained as biologically or genetically based and as a sign of inferiority.

We have viewed Asian Americans as inferior for much of our history. At other times we have accorded honorary white status to those who have assimilated most completely. For example, white ambiguity about the racial status of Chinese immigrants (the majority of Asians in the West and South in the late 19th Century), was reflected in constant shifts in how they were officially categorized. Louisiana's census is described by Okihiro (p. 53):

> In 1860, Chinese were classified as whites; in 1870, they were listed as Chinese; in 1880, children of Chinese men and non-Chinese women were classed as Chinese; but in 1900, all of these children were reclassified as blacks or whites and only those born in China or with two Chinese parents were listed as Chinese.

White people's relationship to Asian Americans is deeply anchored in Eurocentric beliefs that Euro-American culture and development are central in the world. We have a tradition of seeing people from Asia as irrevocably different and inferior. Although the presence of Asian Americans in the United States dates back only two hundred years, the West has had a nearly three thousand year history of relations with Asia. Early Greeks such as Hippocrates, Herodotus and Aristotle had very negative things to say about Asians, and these were commonly accepted stereotypes of their times (Okihiro, pps. 8–9).

It was Asia that Columbus was headed for. At first this fact clouded Europeans' perceptions of Native Americans more than it did their perceptions of Asians, with whom there was little contact. But when Asian Americans did arrive here they faced an already deeply entrenched system of white racism and a longstanding set of beliefs and practices toward "Asians."

White people have seldom been able to step out of a Eurocentric focus enough to understand Asian Americans as part of Asian history and culture. In the European and American invasions of Asia in the 19th and early 20th Centuries we met peoples who had three to five thousand years of highly sophisticated and continuously recorded history. Despite this history, or perhaps in response to it, we only acknowledge Asians from the time they arrive here; we only accept them once they give up, renounce or betray their broader historical culture.

Our current anti-Asian rhetoric claims that we are under attack or being besieged. We cite Japanese, Chinese or Vietnamese imperialism to feed our fears that Asian Americans have come to overrun our country and take away our jobs and industries. It is best to remind ourselves that it was we who forcefully opened up Japan and China to American trade in the 19th Century after they refused to have anything to do with us.

> Asians, it must be remembered, did not come to America; Americans went to Asia. Asians, it must be remembered, did not come to take the wealth of America; Americans went to take the wealth of Asia. Asians, it must be remembered, did not come to conquer and colonize America; Americans went to conquer and colonize Asia (Okihiro, pps.28–29).

And we might add that more recently Vietnamese, Cambodians and Laotians did not come to invade the United States, but to escape the invasion and disruption of their countries by U.S. military and economic forces.

Substantial numbers of Chinese were encouraged by American business interests to come and work in this country in the mid-19th Century to replace African Americans after slavery was abolished and African Americans began to gain power during Reconstruction. When Reconstruction ended and African Americans were forced back to the fields, Asians became less desirable as field hands. Chinese workers were used to compete with African-American labor, and this use of Asian workers against African Americans continued for decades. For instance, soon after African Americans organized the Brotherhood of Sleeping Car Porters in 1925, Filipino men were brought in and were given the jobs African Americans had formerly held. The struggles of African American and Chinese workers intertwined, and whites played one group against the other. White business leaders employed Chinese and other Asian workers when they needed them and excluded them when they didn't (Takaki 1993, pps. 202–204 and Okihiro Chapter 2).

From the beginning their presence was highly contested. Control of immigration from Asia was a touchstone for immigration battles which continue today. African Americans, Native Americans and Latino/as have always been solidly present in our society, despite practices that killed them in massive numbers and disrupted their cultures. With Asian Americans the battle has been whether to let them come to the United States, and once here whether to let them stay and become part of our society.

Beginning in 1882 with the Chinese Exclusion Act, and only ending with the 1965 Immigration Act, Asian immigration was either illegal or so sharply limited as to be virtually non-existent. During periods in which immigration was allowed, often only men were permitted to come. We did not permit Asians who were living here to become naturalized citizens for most of that period. In the late 19th and early 20th Centuries whites passed more than six hundred separate pieces of anti-Asian legislation limiting or excluding persons of Asian ancestry from citizenship (Le Espiritu, p.135). Non-citizens had no legal rights. Whites could kill Asians with impunity because Asians could not testify against them. It was only in 1952 that the last bars to Asians becoming citizens were lifted.

Although white people feared that Asians would overwhelm the white majority and contaminate white culture, such fears did not prevent government and business leaders from importing Chinese as cheap and disposable laborers whenever it was convenient to do so.

All white immigrants benefitted tremendously from the restriction of Asian immigration, even those who were only subsequently accepted as "white." In addition, they benefitted from the expanding industrial economy in the

Northeast and Midwest based on tin, rubber and other raw materials arriving from European and U.S. colonies in Asia such as Malaysia, the Philippines, China and India.

We allowed few Asian women into this country in the 19th and early 20th Centuries. Those women who did settle here have been nearly invisible to us. We tend to see Asian Americans as men, while portraying Asian women as passive, dependent, sensual, sexy and obedient—sexual objects for the use of white American men. Through our limited focus on Asian American men and Asian women, we have tried to understand Asian-American history without connecting it to the home countries from which people came. This perspective has distorted our understanding of Asian family structure, male life here, and the lives of women who remained in Asia. There are still almost no contemporary portrayals of Asian Americans in the full complexity of their gender and class relationships spanning both continents. In fact, Americans relate to Asian Americans as if their cultures and countries of origin were irrelevant except when we want to compare ourselves favorably to them.

We like to think that (white) Americans are modern and forward-looking. We often describe Asian cultures as tradition-bound. We think that innovations and "progress" come from us, and resistance to change comes from Asians. Because we have a positive regard for innovation and modernness it is difficult for us to respect alternatives to our way of doing things. When Asian Americans propose different ways of approaching problems we reject their ideas and describe their communities as more traditional than ours. Thus we reinforce our stereotypes that Asian Americans are conservative and tradition-bound, and our own self-image as modern, progressive, and forward-looking.

Indian, Thai, Malaysian, Indonesian, Japanese, Korean and Chinese cultures have survived for thousands of years and contain traditional elements which contribute stability, and innovative elements which promote change. These cultures would not have been able to adapt to changing historical circumstances if they weren't innovative and changing. Stereotypes give us static images of other people which we often generalize to say their lives are static and unchanging.

We have also done the opposite, taken these same stereotypes of other cultures and turned them into virtues. Sometimes we romanticize particular Asian traits and put down American (or African American) culture for lacking them. We may say that Asians are hardworking, patient, industrious, meditative, and steady. Recently U.S. business leaders have held up the Japanese as innovative and hard working and used them as examples to pressure U.S. workers to work harder and be more adaptable to the needs of business. These stereotypes have also been used to justify quotas on Japanese products and "Buy American" campaigns.

Our statements about Asian Americans and Asian culture reflect more on the uses we want to put them to than the qualities of the people we are describing. They also reflect our ignorance of the differences between different Asian-American peoples and cultures.

Most white Americans cannot distinguish between Chinese, Korean and Japanese peoples or languages, much less Indians from Bangladashi or Sri Lankans. We know little at all about Filipino culture, even though Filipinos are one of the oldest and largest Asian-American communities, and the United States occupied the Philippines as a colony for many years. We also lump together recent immigrants from Southeast Asia, often unable or unwilling to distinguish between Thais, Cambodians, Vietnamese and Laotians.

Most Asian Americans have been eager to assimilate into American society so they would be less subject to violence and exclusion and more able to reap the advantages that being white has always meant. White Americans' discrimination and violence have prevented them from doing so. Partly in response to our lack of differentiation and blanket discrimination, Asian Americans have joined together in political unity as "Asian Americans" for economic and political clout.

National and cultural identification is highly variable among Asian Americans. Some individuals have virtually no connections with a country of origin; others maintain substantial personal and community ties. Some practice primarily "white" American customs, and many practice mixtures of culture derived from their own, white and African American traditions. Since it often seems that participating in any culture outside the bounds of what has been pronounced acceptable by popular mainstream media is grounds for being considered un-American, it is easy for Asian Americans to feel that only if they completely "whitewash" their lives will they be accepted. So many white people believe in the primacy of white skin, blue eyes, "European" features and blond hair that Asian Americans can distrust that integration and acceptance will ever be truly forthcoming. The large number of us who bleach our own hair blond while fearing anyone who doesn't look white confirms the truth of their fears.

A good illustration of how these patterns lead to violence and discrimination against Asian Americans is the death of Vincent Chin in 1982. Chin was a Chinese American living in Detroit who was killed by two white, unemployed auto workers who believed he was Japanese. He had lived in the United States all his life. His killers had been led to believe that they couldn't get work because of the import of Japanese cars. They believed that Japanese corporations were responsible for their unemployment and that *any* Japanese American was complicit with the Japanese government. And they couldn't tell a Japanese American from a Chinese American. The sentence they each eventually received for killing Chin was three years' probation and a $3,000 fine (Le Espiritu, pps. 141–143).

Vincent Chin is dead, one of many Asian Americans blamed for economic problems and then attacked. His murderers were barely reprimanded. We must ask ourselves how many decades, generations, centuries even, people must live here before being accepted as American, if they are not white?

When it has suited our needs we have extolled the virtues of "Asian Americans" to reinforce our own virtuousness and disparage that of others. White people have used the success of some Asian Americans to demonstrate the lack of racism in this country and the opportunity that African Americans have had and not used. The phrase "model minority" codes these meanings. They are a model because they are hardworking, industrious, thrifty, future oriented, and law-abiding like all good white Christians are (or at least should be).

We must face the fact that our projections onto Asian Americans say more about our self-perception and our manipulation of racism (and of statistics) than about Asian Americans. White Americans come in all varieties: hardworking and lazy, smart and dumb, successful and unsuccessful, thrifty and spendthrift. There are no general white traits just as there are no general Asian American ones. There is also no meaningful "average" white or Asian American income level.

Statistics for a group as diverse as the Asian-American community are not useful for comparison with other groups. Average family income figures for Asian Americans hide vast disparities in the distribution of wealth. Substantial groups of Asian Americans live in poverty. Generalizations about average income lump together vastly different communities, some long established and some very recent, as well as covering over gender and class differences in income and opportunity. The unique histories and diversities of each large racial grouping (Asian American, Latino/a, African American, Jewish, Native American, white) make such comparisons invalid.

This overgeneralizing is itself a manipulation of white racism to instill fear of Asian-American success and to assign blame for African-American failure. Anti-Semites use the same tactic to set up Jewish people as economic scapegoats for poor and working class whites and people of color. Asian Americans and Jews play parallel roles in diverting the attention of poor and working class people away from white economic and political control.

That control is most evident when a "model minority" becomes too successful. At universities in California and in other parts of the country where Asian-American students have been outperforming white students, quotas have been placed on the number of admission slots available to Asian Americans. These quotas were enacted to ensure room for white students, not to preserve slots for African Americans or Latino/as. Similar quotas were also used against Jews to protect whites in earlier periods. We don't hear protests about this kind of affirmative action from white people!

The example of Asian American and Jewish "success" shows not that racism and anti-Semitism don't exist, but that both are more than systems of economic exploitation. Each of them systematically exploits people culturally and spiritually as well as materially. It keeps some people the targets of violence regardless of their financial success, and it keeps other (white) people safe and protected. Many Japanese Americans were highly successful in the Western United States but were still attacked, locked up in concentration camps and subjected to mob violence during World War II. Jews in Germany were assimilated into all areas of German society and were economically successful as a community, but they still became the victims of mass murder.

Today we have increasing middle and upper-middle class segments of the Asian, Latino/a, African American and Jewish communities. White people point to the economic success of these groups to prove that racism and anti-Semitism are no longer operating in U.S. society. Economic success does offer some protection against the worst effects of racism and anti-Semitism. However, many white Americans still consider people of color and Jews as different and inferior. White-controlled institutions continue patterns of white racism. Any person of color or Jew, even if financially or socially successful, can be attacked physically, emotionally or financially. Without the dismantling of white control and domination, no amount of economic success will protect people from continued attack and injustice. Vincent Chin could have been rich or poor, a citizen or non-citizen—what mattered to the two men who killed him was that he was Asian American.

Different groups of Asian Americans have often been held up as a demonstration of the fact that this is a country where even recent immigrants can get ahead. Koreans are only the newest group to be so used.

Most recently, in media portrayals of the 1992 uprising in Los Angeles, Koreans and African Americans were pitted against each other. This opposition distorted the reality of what took place in the uprising. It also shifted attention away from the huge role that white society has had in creating the conditions that sparked the uprising. The biggest immediate obstacles to success in both the African American and Korean communities are the exploitation and oppression experienced from white social practices such as housing and job discrimination, and the restructuring of the economy by large corporations, not the actions or personal prejudices of Blacks and Koreans toward each other's communities.

These practices set up Koreans and other Asian Americans (as well as Jews and some Arab Americans) to be buffers between white neighborhoods and African American ones. For example, structural discrimination and anti-foreign bias force well-educated Koreans to become small shop owners in

African American and Latino/a communities where they face small profits and vulnerability to violence. Then, deteriorating economic conditions coupled with media attention to their "success" directs people's anger toward them rather than toward economic policymakers. Koreans were clearly set up to be sacrificed to the rioters. Their calls to the Los Angeles Police Department and to state and local officials for protection were unanswered (Gooding-Williams, p. 201).

White people, on the other hand, could sit back and watch the show, perhaps temporarily uneasy about things getting out of hand, but nevertheless buffered from the direct effects of the violence. When rioters attacked major shopping malls in white Culver City they were quickly stopped by police (Gooding-Williams, pps. 196–211).

What does it mean for an Asian American to be successful, compared to a white American or to an African American? Why do we hold up an average income for one community and use that figure to put down or extol another one? Does economic success measure the presence or lack of racism for a particular group?

We don't need to accept the simple dichotomies of success and failure, Korean and Black, Jewish and Black. We don't need to accept simplified and misleading statistics about complex peoples. We must not accept the false conclusion that because some groups are successful economically any group can be, or that economic success itself is a sign that exploitation and injustice are no longer a problem.

In order not to accept these lies we need to be considerably better informed about the particular histories and complexity of Asian-American communities in this country. We need to break down our simplified stereotypes by going beyond an awareness of the Chinese New Year and the Japanese internment. We have to critically analyze any information we are presented and counter it with a better understanding of the actual dynamics both within and between different communities.

Within particular Asian-American communities there have been accomplishments and much resistance to racism. There has been many kinds of cross influences and effects—a constant exchange and mutual influence between many different Asian-American cultures. The cross influences between different Asian cultures and African American, Latino/a and white cultures is also dynamic, important and has a major impact on our lives.

The complexity of these dynamics defies simple generalizations about economic success or model minorities. As is always the case, such generalizations actually reflect back on what we want to think about ourselves as white people.

Questions and Actions

1. What specific Asian-American cultural communities live in your area? How can you find out more about the uniqueness of each particular community?

2. List four key Asian-American concerns in your community. If none come to mind, why might you not know? How could you find out?

3. How have parts of the Asian-American community organized to address these concerns?

4. What has been the response from the mainstream white community?

5. Are different Asian-American groups represented in your city and county governments, school boards, and other local political institutions?

6. What are some of the "positive" stereotypes that you hear about Asian Americans? What complexities and problems do these stereotypes cover up? What can you learn about white self-images from these stereotypes?

7. How have different Asian-American groups been scapegoated for economic problems in your community? How have non-American Asians been blamed?

8. What is demanded of Asian Americans for acceptance into the white community? Are there hidden reservations or conditions for that acceptance?

9. How are Asian-American and Asian culture and history represented in the schools in your community?

10. Do you and your children have accurate knowledge about the struggles for independence from colonialism of the Filipinos, Chinese, Koreans, Vietnamese, and Indians?

11. How has our relationship with particular Asian countries affected the immigration of Asians to the United States and their treatment once here?

Latino/as

LATINO/AS, OR NATIVE Spanish-speaking Americans, make up about 9 percent of the population in the United States, approximately 24 million people. In 1990 they comprised 25 percent of the populations of California and Texas, 12 percent of New York and Florida, 10 percent of New Jersey, 19 percent of Arizona, 38 percent of New Mexico and 13 percent of Colorado (Heyck, p. 450).

The variations of Spanish spoken are many, and the differences between communities of Latino/as are vast. Some groups, such as Cuban Americans or Puerto Ricans, have kept strong national identities. Others are from families which have been here for hundreds of years and have Spanish-derived cultures, but no connection with another country.

The very terminology used to describe Latino/as has been in great dispute over the years. I use Latino/a because it is broadly inclusive and tends to be preferred by Spanish-speaking people when speaking in very general terms. I use the masculine/feminine ending to remind us that we tend only to recognize the men in other cultures. The problem with "Hispanic" and "Latino/a," which derive their meaning from Spain, is that the culture no longer has much connection to Europe. These words conceal the connections to North and South American land struggles and the intermingling of Spanish-derived culture with Native-American cultures.

I also use the term "Spanish-speaking" because most Latino/as in this country are connected to longstanding and complex Spanish language cultures that span the hemisphere. This term also emphasizes that many of the issues we are addressing are cultural as well as economic or political.

There is no national identity or set of interests uniting Latino/as except their concern for the end of white racism toward Spanish-speaking people. Many Latino/as prefer to be called Cubanos, Mexicanos or Puertoriqueños.

These are the three largest groups of Spanish-speaking people in the United States; many Latino/a identities are formed primarily within these communities.

The first permanent European settlement within the current United States borders was established at St. Augustine in 1565. From settlements in Florida, Mexico and the West Indies, approximately one-third of the present territory of the continental United States was invaded by Spanish soldiers and missionaries and conquered in the most brutal way. A combination of Spanish (male) administrators, conquistadors, ranchers and missionaries killed, tortured and enslaved most of the Native American men and killed, raped and intermarried with the Native American women in what is now California, Utah, Nevada, Arizona, New Mexico, Texas and parts of Colorado and Wyoming.

Part of our white "creation" story (which we tell on Thanksgiving) relates how our roots are deep in this country and how we were the original European settlers. Contrary to our story, descendants of Spanish colonists have lived in the Southeast, Southwest and West for considerably longer than have most English-speaking people. Spanish-speaking Americans and many Africans arrived in this country from the very earliest period of colonization. Some were here before any northern Europeans.

When our ancestors arrived in this country—whether four hundred years ago or last week—should not be important. But we can probably agree that misrepresenting the facts of our history is morally wrong and reflects on our integrity as a people. It also fuels anti-immigrant violence because we conveniently forget that many of us were immigrants ourselves not so long ago, and many of the people we target as unwelcome have roots far back into our history.

White people whose foreparents have arrived within the last hundred years lay claim to the false history that white people were the original colonists in this country. We then look at recent immigrants from Asia, and Central and South America and forget that we haven't been here that long ourselves.

Most white people don't distinguish between recent immigrants and people whose foreparents preceded ours, lumping all Spanish-speaking people together. Our attacks on recent immigrants or immigrants without papers become a way of abusing all Latino/as. Cracking down on immigrants without papers promotes police harassment, job and housing discrimination and denial of health and educational services to anyone who a white person "mistakes" for an undocumented immigrant.

A substantial number of Spanish-speaking Americans in the United States are here because they were conquered and colonized by U.S. forces seeking new territories to provide markets for U.S. goods. Most white Americans also felt they had a mandate from God to spread Christianity and white hegemony over the rest of the continent and overseas. President McKinley's words about his decision to take the Philippines illustrate the mixture of economic, nationalist, racist and moralistic reasoning involved in justifying U.S. expansion throughout the Spanish-speaking world.

> Before you go I would like to say just a word about the Philippine business....The truth is I didn't want the Philippines, and when they came to us as a gift from the gods, I did not know what to do with them....I went down on my knees and prayed Almighty God for light and guidance....I don't know how it was, but it came: 1) That we could not give them back to Spain—that would be cowardly and dishonorable. 2) That we could not turn them over to France or Germany, our commercial rivals in the Orient—that would be bad business and discreditable. 3) That we could not leave them to themselves—they were unfit for self-government—and they would soon have anarchy and misrule over there worse than Spain's was: and 4) That there was nothing left for us to do but to take them all and to educate the Filipinos, and uplift and civilize and Christianize them, and by God's grace do the very best we could by them, as our fellow men for whom Christ also died (Zinn, pps. 305–6).

In 1830 the Mexican government outlawed slavery and prohibited further American immigration into Texas. Americans were outraged, and thousands continued to move into Texas as *illegal aliens*. They rose against Mexican rule in 1836 and, although initially defeated, were eventually victorious, claiming independence as the Lone Star State. Texas was annexed by the United States in 1845. Further border skirmishes led to an U.S. invasion of Mexico resulting in the Treaty of Guadalupe Hidalgo in 1848 in which Mexico ceded all of California, New Mexico, Nevada and parts of Colorado, Arizona and Utah. As one congressman wrote at the time about our "manifest destiny" to rule the hemisphere, "This continent was intended by Providence as a vast theatre on which to work out the grand experiment of Republican government, under the auspices of the Anglo-Saxon race (Takaki 1993, p. 176).

In 1898 we declared war on Spain and took over a war of independence that Cubans had started in 1895. Within three months we defeated the Spanish forces and required them to turn over control of Cuba to us, completely ignoring the Cubans who had been fighting for their freedom. We also took over Puerto Rico, annexed Hawaii, occupied Wake Island and Guam in the Pacific, and claimed the Philippines. Filipinos had been engaged in a long-term war of independence with Spain, and in 1899 they rose up against U.S. rule. President McKinley sent in 70,000 troops. Three years later one sixth of the Philippine population was dead and the war was over (Zinn, pps. 306–310).

More recently, substantial numbers of Spanish-speaking people have arrived from Cuba, Haiti, and many Central and South American countries. These immigrations have been connected with U.S. foreign policy and economic expansion. The blockade of Cuba, intervention in Haiti, support for dictatorships in Central and South America, economic dislocation in Mexico from U.S. corporate development, and the need for agricultural laborers in the fields of California and the Southwest have all contributed to large numbers of people being uprooted, exiled or forced to migrate. Groups of refugees came to the United States seeking asylum and economic opportunity. U.S. government and corporate policy also directly encouraged migration through the Bracero program which brought more than 5 million Mexican workers to the United States between 1942 and 1964 as cheap agricultural labor (Heyck, p.6).

It is not accurate to say that people of color within the United States make up internal colonies. While there are some similarities to the colonial process, by and large this model doesn't help us to understand how racism works in this country, nor to develop strategies to end it. We do have to understand and take responsibility for the history and dynamics of colonialism because the presence of people of color, and particularly of Spanish-speaking people, in the United States is intertwined with the colonial expansion of the United States during the 19th Century and the continuation of those patterns in the 20th.

The Monroe Doctrine, written in 1823, was the first attempt to articulate the American perception that all of the Western Hemisphere was our "backyard" and we could control what happened there. We have initiated hundreds of invasions and interventions in Central and South American countries in the last two centuries, leading to the deaths of tens of thousands of people and wreaking havoc with the lives and economies of local populations. At the same time we have invited millions of workers to come here and work for low wages on our corporate farms and in our manufacturing centers. We are clearly hypocritical when we blame recent Spanish-speaking immigrants for our economic problems, and when we try to enforce a rigid border separation between Mexico (or Cuba, or Haiti) and the United States. Corporate interests want to have free movement of capital and resources throughout the Americas and have pushed through the North American Free Trade Association (NAFTA), the General Agreement on Trade and Tariffs (GATT) and other policies conducive to their ends. But they want the rest of us to blame low wage Mexican and Central American workers for the lack of jobs and economic dislocation which result from those policies.

White Americans have long been concerned with both expanding and maintaining our national borders. The expansion has always been seen in terms of economic opportunity. The maintenance has consisted of keeping Spanish-speaking people on the fringes of our society and not allowing them into centers of power and control—maintaining white privilege. The struggles of many Spanish-speaking people in this country have therefore been focused on the borderlands, both physically and figuratively, between Anglo and Spanish land and culture.

Spanish-speaking Americans have occupied various positions in the overall racial hierarchy of the United States depending upon economic and cultural factors. After the annexation of the Southwest in 1848 Spanish-speaking people had enough economic clout and "civilized" habits that they were accepted as white and given the rights of citizenship in California (Almaguer, pps. 54–56). This was in contrast to the few Blacks there, who were ranked far below Mexicans; to the Chinese, who were ranked slightly above Indians and had no rights; and to the Indians, who were considered barely human and were killed indiscriminately (Almaguer, pps. 7–9). This racial hierarchy still has white people on top, but today Spanish-speaking people are considered, along with African Americans, to be at the bottom of the racial hierarchy, and Asian Americans are held up as closer to white and treated far better.

Latino/as are underrepresented, undercounted and underestimated. Their lives, culture, and the deprivations they have suffered are invisible to us. For example in the Los Angeles uprising in 1992, the greatest number of people killed from any ethnic group were Latino/as. The greatest damage done was to property owned by Latino/as. Immediately following the uprising there was a massive immigration crackdown and hundreds of Spanish-speaking Los Angeles residents were deported, most without trials or legal recourse. Very few non-Latino/a Americans know these facts because the media was focused on African Americans as the villains and on Black-white and Black-Korean interactions.

Latino/a communities are exploited and oppressed by white-controlled political, economic and cultural practices. I will focus on some of the cultural dimensions of racism in this section because our relationship to Latino/a communities illustrates some salient features.

Spanish-speaking people can participate in literary, musical, dramatic, political and popular developments throughout the Spanish-speaking world. They have access to a major international culture that is largely invisible to monolingual white people. These dynamic, cosmopolitan and creative currents could be brought into mainstream U.S. culture by the Spanish-speaking people of this country. Some of them obviously are, yet most of the time they are resisted. White people have fought against the use of Spanish in schools and workplaces, and have ignored, denigrated and attacked Spanish language culture as being inferior, uncivilized, rural, traditional, monolithic, subversive and dangerous. What are white people trying to maintain, and what do we fear when we attack a vital, international culture of which we are ignorant?

We are saying that English is *the* language of culture and achievement, and European-based civilization is the source of all beneficial contributions to the world. We are also saying that the lives, thoughts, feelings and cultures of Spanish-speaking people are insignificant and do not count. We are, in addition, demonstrating that white racism is not only about economic and political domination, it is also about cultural hegemony. It is about white people and white institutions being able to define what culture is, who gets to participate in it, and what language, literature, art and music are included in it. White racism is about control of the cultural content of people's lives.

It is crucial for us to understand the importance of white racism as a system of cultural domination. White people have long denied or minimized the importance of culture to people's everyday lives. We have appealed to universal, international and human standards and values in our politics, science and philosophy. This makes it very difficult for us to recognize the value of culture in our own lives, much less in other people's. We don't want to understand the crucial and devastating role culture plays in white racial domination. We fail to see the inspirational role that culture plays in resistance to that domination by people of color. Even the cultural aspects of our everyday "white" lives are impossible for us to see or understand.

When we aren't remotely familiar with the music, literature and dance of people we live with, we cannot expect to understand what they experience or what moves and guides them. We cannot honor and respect their concerns and life choices. In addition, using music as an example, when we are unfamiliar with the contributions of Reuben Blades, Celia Cruz, Tito Puente, Carlos Santana, Flaco Jimenez, Los Lobos, Selena and Villa-Lobos, we deny ourselves access to the richness, creativity and inspiration that their culture could provide us. Instead of maintaining cultural borders, we need to become much better at crossing them.

Today's international cultures are complex, without clear boundaries, in constant flux. Boundaries and borders are permeable. Nothing we do—the food we eat, the words we use, our gestures, rituals, music or celebrations—is purely white, Latino/a, African American, Asian American or Native American. There are no traditions unchanged by contact with others.

We cannot eliminate racism without understanding its cultural dimensions. White racism is supported by economic, political and cultural practices which operate partly by marketing to us other people's cultures and packaging them as exotic, original, natural and authentic. Their cultures are distorted by this marketing and packaging and by the separation of their cultures from themselves as people living those cultures. At the same time, white cultural practices are rendered invisible by our focus on other people's. In this sense the border keeping Spanish-speaking people out of the mainstream of our society is maintained by economic and cultural domination, language barriers and geographic segregation.

Use the following questions and the suggestions in the sections on Native Americans, African Americans and Asian Americans to guide your work as an ally to Latino/as.

Questions and Actions

1. Which Spanish-speaking people live in your town, city or rural area?

2. Which Spanish-speaking people provide labor or services on which you personally or the economy is dependent (farm workers, low-wage manufacturing workers or workers in factories near the Mexican border)?

3. What do you gain and what do you lose when these workers are poorly paid, work in unsanitary conditions, are exposed to dangerous chemicals and have unsafe working conditions?

4. In what ways are Spanish-speaking groups under attack at this time? Which social problems are they being blamed for?

5. How well are Spanish-speaking communities represented in your local governments?

6. Are there adequate support services for Spanish-speaking families and Spanish-speaking youth in your area? How could you find out?

7. How have the histories of U.S. involvement with Mexico, Cuba, Puerto Rico and El Salvador influenced the status and position of the immigrant communities which arrived here from those countries?

8. How have stereotypes of Latino/as helped prepare for or justify invasions and control of South and Central American countries?

9. Have you been involved with solidarity work with Spanish-speaking countries? How might that work have been connected to the exploitation of Latino/a communities closer to home?

10. Did your foreparents speak a native language which has been lost in your family or community? What other losses accompanied the pressure to be a monolingual community?

11. How has the emergence of English as the language used in international communication been an advantage and a disadvantage to us?

12. How has this role of English in world discourse affected people whose primary language is not English?

13. Do you speak Spanish? If not, what might be reasons for learning to do so? Why haven't you in the past?

Jewish People

W*HEN I'M IN* a workshop on racism and the facilitators tell everyone to break up into a white group and a people of color group, I immediately want to say, "Wait a minute, I'm not white."

To some extent this gut-level response is similar to the "I'm not white" response of other white people as described in the first part of this book. When the subject is racism nobody wants to be white, because being white is "bad" and brings up feelings of guilt, shame, embarrassment and hopelessness.

There are other reasons why I want to say "I'm not white" which have to do with the particularities of being Jewish. I want to explore these other reasons because to understand them is to understand some of the complexities of being Jewish and of the ways racism and anti-Semitism operate as systems of power and domination.

When I say that I'm not white there are many white people in the United States and throughout Europe that would immediately agree. "Of course you're not white. Jewish people are part of the contamination of the white, Christian race, along with people of color, Romany, the mentally challenged and lesbian, gay and bisexual people." These attitudes and policies are based on the conjunction of whiteness with Christianity.

Jews were considered inferior and a threat to Christians, because they rejected Jesus as the son of God from the beginnings of Christian church history. In addition, they were falsely accused of killing Jesus in the New Testament. Various anti-Semitic stereotypes were disseminated by early Church leaders such as St. John Chrysostom who wrote,

> The Jews are full of hatred for the rest of mankind and are the enemies of all gentiles: they are parasites on the gentile societies that harbor them; they are addicted to money, and through the power of money, they aspire to be rulers of the world (Rose, p. 3).

Early Christian church leaders continually attacked Jews on theological grounds and condoned the actions of Christians who attacked synagogues and killed Jews. When the church became the official religion of the Roman Empire in the early 4th Century, Jews became even more vulnerable to violence from Christians. They were banned from public office, from many occupations and some were forced to become tax collectors. They were subject to special taxes, prohibited from practicing their religion and building or repairing synagogues, not allowed to intermarry with Christians and prohibited from holding any civil or economic position higher than any Christian. They were subject to forced conversions and commonly referred to as a source of religious pollution, contagion and disease, setting the stage for later racially based anti-Semitism (Ruether, pps. 184–204).

Large-scale attacks on Jews by Christians occurred during the Crusades when Jews were seen as the European agents of the Moslem/Arab "infidels" who controlled the Holy Lands. Although the goal of the church was to attack Arabs and reclaim Jerusalem, most crusaders never left Europe. As they pillaged their way toward Jerusalem, they rounded up and killed thousands of Jews and destroyed their communities.

In the following centuries Jews were subject to forced conversions or banished from such regions as England (1290), France (1306, 1322, 1394), Hungary (1367), Strasburg (1381), Austria (1421) and Cologne (1426). Jews fought to protect themselves, fled, converted or looked for protection from secular rulers, but were generally not powerful enough to protect themselves from Christian violence.

On July 1, 1492 the Spanish monarchs, pressed by the Inquisition, gave all Jews thirty days to pack up whatever they could and leave the country they had lived in for centuries. A month later Columbus had to depart from a different port than originally planned because of the congestion caused by the Jews' departure. Some of their confiscated possessions were used to finance his voyages.

Even after the Spanish expulsion, the Inquisition continued to persecute those suspected of idolatry. Under the laws of purity of blood, any person with even one drop of Jewish blood was condemned. To prove their innocence, suspects had to display genealogical charts proving they had no Jewish ancestry. They Inquisition, drawing on anti-Semitic stereotypes from early church teachings, combined religious and biological justifications fro persecution, setting the stage for the later development of biologically-based theories of racism.

Many Jews fled from Spain to Portugal, but within a few years were forced to flee again after being given the choice of forced baptism or death. Subsequently they faced persecution and expulsion from the Italian peninsula and from many German cities and principalities in the 16th Century as well as pogroms in the Ukraine in the mid-17th Century (Friesel, Gilbert).

Anti-Semitism became rooted in Protestantism during the "Enlightenment" through the writings of such key figures as Martin Luther. In 1543, in "Against the Jews and Their Lies," he accused the Jews of being not only the bloodthirsty murderers of Christianity, but specifically of the German people. He wrote,

> We are at fault in not avenging all this innocent blood of our Lord and Churches and the blood of the children which they have shed since then, and which still shines forth from their Jewish eyes and skin. We are at fault in not slaying them (Rose, p. 7).

He goes on to suggest that Germans burn the houses and synagogues of the Jews, ban their rabbis under pain of death, withdraw Jewish safe-conduct on the highways, prohibit usury, institute manual labor for young Jews, and finally, confiscate their wealth and expel them from Germany (ibid.).

Protestantism imbued whiteness with a set of normative Christian values which included belief in Jesus, original sin, individual salvation through one's work, the equation of sex with procreation, a belief in heaven and hell and the condemnation of those who are not Christian.

Jews were held to be a nation of outcasts who had killed Christ, rejected Christianity, used the blood of Christian children in Passover rituals and prevented the Second Coming by their failure to convert. Even before biological theories of race, they were believed to automatically pass on these traits to each succeeding generation regardless of where they lived, what they practiced, and even, in many cases, whether or not they converted to Christianity.

These were official policies of the Catholic Church and many Protestant denominations and the common beliefs of many Christians. It was only in 1965, for instance, that the bishops of Vatican Council II voted to absolve contemporary Jews of any guilt for the crucifixion of Jesus and to repudiate the belief that God rejected the Jews because they refused to accept Jesus as the savior (Singer in Gerber, p. 386).

Because of the conjoining of whiteness, Christianity and various forms of nationalism, Jews were prohibited from becoming part of the general community in many European countries and were often forced to relocate elsewhere on short notice. No matter how long Jews lived within a country or principality, or how successful they were economically, they were not immune to persecution and violence. For example, Jewish people lived in Germany for over a thousand years, were financially and socially successful, but were still subject to mass murder during the Holocaust.

Jewish people were originally Arabs. Whatever their original distinguishable Arab or "Semitic" characteristics, through rape, intermarriage, forced exile, conversion and assimilation, Jews today are part of many cultural groups on several continents. Jewish people are not only not a race—we have seen how this is not a meaningful concept—but come in many shades and colors from nearly black Ethiopian Jews, to dark brown Jews from the Cochin coast of India, to light brown Jews from Argentina and Morocco, to blond and light-skinned Jews in Denmark and England. While this diversity is a refutation of racial stereotypes, it can make Jews more vulnerable when another group of people is claiming some kind of national identity, religious unity or genetic purity.

Dark-skinned by northern European standards, light-skinned by standards in the United States, in either case Jews of European origin are not Christian. Even if they have the right color skin, many Christians still believe they can contaminate the "purity" of white Christian culture. The membership application of the Invisible Empire of the Knights of the Ku Klux Klan requires one to "swear that I am a White Person of Non-Jewish ancestry" (Bulkin, p. 104).

When Jews walk down the street their skin color is immediately visible, while their cultural practices and religious beliefs are not. If they pass for white and don't voluntarily give away the fact that they're Jewish, they enjoy the same respect and privilege that other white people are given in our society. Their presence is accepted, their words are listened to, they have more police and judicial protection. If their name is recognizably Jewish, if they are wearing traditional clothes or religious objects, or if their appearance or mannerisms fit certain stereotypes of what it means to be or look or act Jewish, then passing is not an option. If they can't or don't want to pass they are vulnerable to the same jokes, harassment, discrimination and violence that other non-white, non-Christian people are vulnerable to. That in itself is a strong incentive to try to pass.

In order to pass they have to give up, minimize or downplay any aspects of their life and appearance which are visibly Jewish. They can't say or do anything which will give away to people that they are really Jewish. Since being Jewish is inherently a range of ways of being, talking and doing things that are not Christian, the more they pass the less they are who they are. They have to give up parts of themselves and become more Christianized and "white" in order to pass. At any time they might be found out and lose everything they thought they had gained in compensation for giving up their core identity.

It also becomes dangerous for them to be associated in any way with other Jewish people who are visibly Jewish. Either they fear they might be condemned along with them, or they fear they might pick up "Jewish" speech or mannerisms which would make it harder for them to pass. If they are in any way visibly Jewish then they know that many of the white Christians they encounter will treat them as non-white and they will face mistrust, ignorance, discrimination or outright abuse.

When I say in that workshop that I'm not white because I'm Jewish there are lots of people who would agree with me. Then there are others who would not. People of color often say, "What do you mean you aren't white? You look white, you act white and you enjoy all the privileges of being white including the direct benefits of exploiting people of color such as better jobs, better schooling and better housing." They are right too. As a Jew descended from Eastern European Jews, I am white.

I am white in the sense that my particular Jewish ancestors lived in Europe for nearly a thousand years before coming to the United States. During that time we assimilated a tremendous amount of European culture in order to survive. We have learned how to adapt, camouflage, assimilate, sabotage, resist and undermine some of that culture. During that entire time we have never been safe from spontaneous and systematic violence and exploitation. Sometimes we have even had to exploit other people in order to stay alive, or to be allowed to stay in a place we had lived for hundreds of years. And sometimes we have come to believe the lies of racism, the justifications for economic and cultural exploitation that European culture is built on.

In the United States, besides the threat of violence and the constant pressure to assimilate, one of the prices people pay to be accepted as white is to collude in perpetuating racism. This is a price that many Southern and Eastern Europeans as well as assimilated Jews have paid. They come to believe that economic improvement for themselves is different than economic justice for everyone. Some Jewish people, probably no fewer or no more than other groups, have paid that price. Today in this society there is some privilege attached to being white, or, we might say, conditionally white. We will accept you as white *on the condition* that you support the racial hierarchy which keeps people of color on the bottom. Jewish people who are "white," like Irish, Polish, Finnish or Spanish people, are safer, have greater educational and economic opportunity, and are generally more accepted than African Americans, Latino/as, Asian Americans, Arab Americans and Native Americans. That is what being white is all about.

Many Jewish people have accepted this racial hierarchy in exchange for feelings of safety and acceptance. Consequently, they have established, in this country and in Israel, parallel race-based systems within the Jewish community. Jewish people of color are the majority of Jews in the world and in Israel. Despite this fact, European-descended Jews dominate culture and politics in the Jewish communities of both Israel and the United States. This has rendered invisible non-white Jewish people and made it seem that racism is an issue that Jewish people are separate from, something out there in

American society. Yet we carry the pain, violence and confusion of racism within our own bodies, and in the distribution of economic and cultural power within our Jewish communities.

Many Jewish people have also accepted the American bipolar focus on black-white relationships. In this book we have seen how the bipolar perspective is a distorted one. Yet most within the Jewish community do not understand or pay attention to the Latino/a, Asian American or Native American communities, maintaining a focus only on Black-Jewish relationships.

That binary focus is itself distorted because there is no monolithic Black or Jewish community. What does it mean for a people of millions—including conservatives, liberals, radicals and fundamentalists, old and young, women and men, rich and poor—to have a relationship with another people of millions with similar diversity? We need to ensure that we don't let journalistic representation simplify and distort the complexities of the interactions of two vastly diverse peoples because it can only lead to more stereotypes, misunderstanding, racism and anti-Semitism. This dynamic focuses attention on Blacks and Jews and encourages us to attack each other rather than challenge white, Christian racism.

It is important to challenge anti-Semitism wherever it occurs. However there is a clear difference in who has the power to carry out anti-Semitic violence in our society. One way white people retain power is by attacking strong and powerful individuals of color who are mobilizing people. Whether it's Louis Farrakhan, Sister Souljah, Jesse Jackson or Malcolm X, we can expect that white people will try to set up Jewish people to attack African American leaders and vice versa. Then they don't have to take the heat directly. If we are challenging Louis Farrakhan's anti-Semitic statements but not Pat Buchanan's or Rush Limbaugh's, then we are contributing to racism and being strategically ineffective. White Christian leaders like nothing better than to see groups taking potshots at each other.

Some people argue that racism and anti-Semitism are different because one is based on skin color and the other on religious and cultural differences. It is true that historically the two have taken on different characteristics. Ruling classes have always used cultural differences to exploit people and to determine the roles that outside groups would play in the economic system. Racism and anti-Semitism are strategies ruling classes use: 1) to divide people, exploiting some groups more heavily than others; 2) to strengthen white cultural solidarity and chauvinism; 3) to make white workers feel lucky they have some privilege or status no matter how heavily exploited they are; and 4) to divert working and middle class attention from the wealthy by focusing on scapegoats "above" them (Jews) and "below" them (people of color).

Colluding with anti-Semitism, even through silence, contributes to inequality and *racial* injustice. European and American political and economic elites have set up Jewish people as scapegoats for their economic and political decisions. Fighting against anti-Semitism is fighting for economic justice. Whenever the stereotypes of Jewish money or power go unchallenged, the injustice of our economic system is strengthened and racism is continued. Blaming Jewish bankers or African American women on welfare are parallel strategies to divert our attention from the corporate elite which makes the economic decisions that affect our lives. These strategies give the majority of white people the mistaken impression that they are controlled by Jews and competed against by people of color—squeezed on both sides.

There are other complex strands in anti-Semitism. People of color who are Christian have adopted and passed on anti-Semitic lies about the role of the Jewish people in Western history. Many Christians of color are capable of condoning violence against Jews even while they are themselves the targets of racism. This leads many people who are fighting racism, whether they are people of color or white people, to downplay the importance of anti-Semitism and not respond vigorously when Jews are attacked.

Moslems also have a long history of anti-Jewish practices and justifications. At the same time, in Europe and America, Jews and Arabs have been categorized together as infidels and as threats to Christianity and to Western civilization. The word anti-Semitic itself points to the intertwined history of anti-Jewish and anti-Arab violence in Western countries. Jews and Moslems were both exiled from Spain in 1492. Although it is not discussed in this book, we have much to learn about how racism operates by analyzing the ways anti-Arab racism is part of anti-Semitism, how Arab societies have contributed to anti-Jewish violence, how European-based parts of Jewish American and Israeli society have contributed to anti-Arab racism, and how white Christian-dominated Western societies have set up Jews and Arabs to fight each other in the eastern Mediterranean region.

Looking in detail at how anti-Semitism operates gives us further insight into the dynamics of racism. It helps us see that racism is not simply a religious, biological or cultural persecution. It rests, instead, on a hierarchy and on institutionalization of power and violence. Those who benefit most from that power use economic, religious, cultural, biological, historical or sociological justifications *as needed* to maintain their control. They can offer safe haven, economic success, voting rights, tolerance and even status as honorary whites to various groups when their support is needed. Just as quickly they can withdraw those favors and set the wrath of the rest of the populace against selected scapegoats when a diversion is called for. The only long-term corrective to anti-Semitism and racism is the democratic dispersion of political, economic and social power to all people within a society and the creation of a democratic, anti-racist, anti-sexist and secular multicultural state.

Sometimes in a workshop it is useful to divide into a white caucus and a people of color caucus. If we don't acknowledge the differences between those who have access to material benefits from being "white" and those who don't, we are not adequately addressing racism. But if we don't acknowledge the issues of Jewish people's lives we aren't adequately addressing racism either. We need to do both.

I need non-Jewish people to recognize that my participation in the struggle against racism is part of my identity as a Jewish person fighting for justice, equality, the end of exploitation and for my personal and group safety. To ask me to fight racism as a white person without recognizing my Jewish identity renders me invisible, at risk for further violence from white Christians and from non-Jewish people of color, and ultimately renders me ineffective.

I am not a white Christian, I am a white Jew. I can fight racism best by understanding that it is a strategy, like anti-Semitism, used to justify economic and cultural exploitation *and* to keep power and control in the hands of white people, particularly the white Christian upper class. Racism exists within that part of the Jewish community that accepts economic and cultural exploitation. We need to challenge racism within the Jewish community, racism directed toward both Jewish *and* non-Jewish people of color. Since Jewish people know directly the results of racist ideology, institutionalized violence and economic injustice, we can do that best by drawing on our own history and experience.

European-descended Jews can be powerful allies to people of color because we are often in positions to intervene or interrupt racism among white people. We don't need to overlook anti-Semitism in order to do this. We can't. We are often the targets of anti-Semitism as soon as we raise concerns about racism! Our fears of arousing anti-Semitism when challenging racism give us a deep understanding of how both oppressions work. We need to confront anti-Semitism wherever it occurs, including from people of color, because racism cannot be eliminated unless anti-Semitism is as well.

Bringing up anti-Semitism does not distract from the struggle to end racism, it enhances it. Dealing with anti-Semitism makes it clearer how racism works and how Christian values are a cornerstone of racism. My greatest effectiveness as an ally to people of color comes from my history and experience as a Jew.

I will return to the subjects of Christianity, religion and racism in the next part of the book. For now, consider the following questions as they apply to you.

Questions and Actions

If you are Christian or of Christian background:

1. What did you learn in religious school or church or from the Bible about Jewish people? What did you learn about people of color?

2. What non-explicit messages did you receive about both groups from your Christian heritage?

3. In what ways is it true and in what ways is it not true to say "America is a Christian country?" How would you respond if someone said this in your presence?

4. What are ways that Jews are blamed for social problems?

5. Beginning with the fact that Jesus and Mary were Arab Jews with skin coloring, hair and facial features that were clearly not European, in what ways has Christianity "whitewashed" its origins?

6. How can you challenge anti-Semitism expressed by other Christians and within your church?

If you are Jewish:

1. Are you generally treated as white or as non-white in Jewish society? In gentile society?

2. What forms does racism take within the American-Jewish community?

3. What kind of support do you need from Christian allies when anti-Semitic statements or actions are being committed?

4. How can you draw on your Jewish identity, history and experience to be an ally to (other) people of color?

5. When you or other Jewish people raise issues of racism do you find yourselves targets of anti-Semitism? What support do you need from Christians when this happens? What support do you need from other Jewish people?

6. How could you challenge racism within the Jewish community?

Conclusion

THESE PROCEDING SECTIONS have been brief and cursory. Some parts of certain sections apply to other groups of people of color because our response as white people to people of color is complex and overlapping.

Again I remind you that this entire section was about white people and our treatment of people of color. People of color are not just the result of what white people have done to them or even just of how they have resisted racism. The lives and cultures of people of color can only be conveyed through their own voices, and I encourage you to listen to those voices. Your life will be changed as a result.

To broaden our narrow thinking which constrains our worldview and understanding, we need to promote the thinking, creative expression and leadership of people of color. We should do this not because the result will be better than white thinking, but because we have systematically controlled, exploited and stymied such expression for hundreds of years. We have an historic responsibility to work for the end of white cultural, political and economic exploitation. We shall certainly gain from the process.

Some of the benefits we can expect include the fact that the burden of guilt, blame, shame and sadness will be lifted from our shoulders. We will no longer be standing on the backs of other people with all the precariousness that position entails. We will have an active role to play in the end of injustice. We will gain immeasurably from the contributions that people of color make to the world without exploiting them for it. And we will have a more accurate assessment of the contributions of white people. We will better see that leadership, wisdom and creative expression have nothing to do with racial groupings, but are the result of the rich interplay between individual creativity, culture, circumstances, politics and history, and that they defy categorization of any kind.

The final part of this book looks at the structures and values we need to facilitate a democratic, anti-racist, multicultural society. But first, in Part V, we look at institutional racism and how we can take more effective social action to end it.

PART V

Fighting Institutional Racism

Institutional Racism

*R*ACISM IS NOT just the sum total of all the individual acts in which white people discriminate, harass, stereotype or otherwise mistreat people of color. The accumulated effects of centuries of white racism have given it an institutional nature which is more entrenched than racial prejudice. In fact, it is barely touched by changes in individual white consciousness. We often find it difficult to see or to know how to challenge institutional racism because we are so used to focusing on individual actions and attitudes.

One example of institutional racism is that professors of color (and white women) make considerably less money than their white (and male) counterparts. Prejudice and acts of discrimination by individual white faculty and administrators contribute to this disparity. But even if all white people were completely racially neutral, the disparities would persist.

Some of the reasons for these systemic disparities are that past discrimination excluded students of color from academic programs. Segregated and inferior schools have forced students of color to play catch up in college taking longer to complete their studies. Established networks of white academics have made it easier for white students, particularly males, to get into the best universities, thereby getting better training, credentials and research opportunities. These networks help them to find out about scholarship opportunities and to find postdoctoral positions, thus advancing their careers faster.

People of color have only recently been allowed into many academic professions. The factors mentioned above result in white professors being hired at higher starting salary levels than corresponding professors of color. Lack of peers of color for support, racism from white colleagues and pressure on the limited number of professors of color to advise students of color contribute to higher workloads and less support than for their white peers. In addition, recent cutbacks, salary and hiring freezes in many universities have prevented faculty of color from catching up with white faculty who have already reached the highest salary levels.

The result of these patterns is that faculty of color earn approximately 75 percent of what white faculty with comparable qualifications earn. A faculty member of color, working in the same department, who was equally qualified, the same age and with the same years of experience as her white colleague could be making $10,000–$15,000 less a year and have considerably less job security and other benefits. This could be true without a single overt act of discrimination in the department or the university.

Nor is this pattern of institutional racism eliminated in one generation as some of us might hope. There are few professors of color in most disciplines and therefore few role models, mentors and advisors for current students of color, discouraging some and making it harder for others. This situation reproduces many of the above effects into the next generation.

Disparity in public school funding is another example of institutional racism. Although in most states there is a standard reimbursement per student to school districts, the actual amount spent on students' education depends on many factors including local property taxes, contributions from parents, volunteer hours from community members and business and foundation contributions. The average spent per pupil in the same metropolitan area varies enormously from $3,500 to $15,000 (Kozol, pps. 236–237).

Most students in the United States go to schools that are highly segregated by race because of discriminatory housing and lending practices, and estate tax laws which promote the transfer of wealth through generations. Predominately white schools spend much more per student than schools in which the majority of students are of color. The average difference in spending is probably about 2:1, although in many areas the greatest differences can run 8:1 or 10:1. An additional $1,500 per year per student gives a class of thirty $45,000 more a year. Without a single overt act of discrimination the educational opportunities of most children of color in our country are vastly deficient when compared to those of white children. Today we have an educational system that is nearly as racially segregated and unequal as before the Supreme Court's Brown vs. Board of Education ruling outlawed intentional school segregation. This is institutional racism.

We could take examples from any area of contemporary American society. White Americans no longer need to overtly discriminate against people of color to maintain a racial hierarchy. Because of the vast disparities of wealth, power and privilege, and the historical injustices upon which that wealth and power is built, we cannot rely on neutral legal remedies, on bans against overt acts of discrimination, or on individual white people unlearning prejudice as sufficient means to overcome racism—although these are all important.

Racism is self-sustaining. It can allow white people to be friendly to people of color, support the policies listed above, and still collude with institutional policies that continue racial injustice. The patterns are so well set in place that we can even allow some people of color to become successful, and little will change.

We can only stop racism by taking present and past institutional racism into account (as well as sexism, classism and other historically significant injustices). *We must judge our efforts at justice by the justice they produce.* Public policy should be directed at producing equality of opportunity and justice for all Americans, regardless of race. The rest of this book considers how we can be more effective in combatting racism in institutional settings and in public policy arenas.

Public Policy

*P*UBLIC POLICY REFERS to government planning, decision making and allocation of public resources. Government officials and the public are constantly confronted by an array of issues affecting our lives and communities. Which issues are addressed, how they are addressed, who gets to participate in the discussion, and what solutions are considered viable answers to all of these questions are influenced by racism. As informed and active citizens we can influence the nature of public policy discussion and decisions.

Americans can influence public policy at several levels. The most powerful is when we organize around particular issues or programs and create pressure that public officials must respond to. The civil rights movement, women's movement, disability rights movement, lesbian and gay movement, American Indian movement, Chicano movement, and anti-Vietnam War movement are examples of large scale organizing that led to new laws, executive orders, funding appropriations, federal guidelines and other specific results.

Another way to influence public policy is by electing officials who represent our interests. This is always complex because candidates run on a platform of interests some of which may be progressive and others of which may not be. They also make promises during elections on which they do not or cannot follow through. Unless there is public pressure while they are in office, they don't have the leverage to fight entrenched interests.

We are also able to respond to proposed legislation, state initiatives, nominations of public officials and public planning documents. Here again, concerted mobilization of people dramatically increases our effectiveness in responding to issues.

We are asked to respond to a constant barrage of proposals, budgets, elections, special-interest agendas and planning documents. Unless we analyze the issues carefully and critically, keeping a focus on how they affect racism and race relations, we will not be able to marshall our forces effectively. In the following section, I look at some current public policy issues in a way that can be used as a guideline for critically analyzing others not covered here.

We will not get very far in the struggle for racial justice unless we have significant national public support and leadership for addressing racial injustice directly and forcefully. This calls for no less than massive reinvestment in communities of color to begin to redress the long term effects of racism on those communities. Some people might call this reparation, such as the Germans paid the Jewish community after World War II, and the American government paid the Japanese who were interned and had their property confiscated during World War II.* Some might call it reinvestment for what was taken out of communities of color by white people. Others might call it retributive justice. Whatever we call it, it means taking responsibility for the killing of millions of people, the stealing of the land and the exploitation of the labor and culture of Native Americans, African Americans, Latino/as and Asian Americans during the last five hundred years of European settlement in North America. We can't make up for the lives, communities, land and culture lost. But we can acknowledge our responsibility and make a commitment to ending racism and other forms of injustice.

Public reinvestment needs to be focused and accountable. It needs to be controlled by the people whose lives it will affect and be directed toward building infrastructures which will promote personal and community development.

People of color do not want handouts. They say they want an end to racial exploitation; they want the same opportunities white people have. These opportunities include meaningful and effective education for themselves and their children, decent jobs, adequate health care, safe streets, quality childcare, adequate social services and the chance to be represented by people who truly share their interests. These are opportunities that all people deserve and that, according to our founding documents, we are honor bound to provide equally for all Americans. We can certainly afford to do so, and we cannot afford not to.

How do we pay for reinvestment? It is no secret, but still little discussed among us, that wealth is concentrated among a relatively few in the United States. In 1987 the top 0.5 percent of the population, or about 1.25 million people controlled three times as much wealth as the entire 90 percent or 210 million on the bottom (*Monthly Review*, September 1987, pps. 4–6). The top

---

* The first reparations bill was introduced in the Massachusetts state senate by Senator Bill Owens. More recently a bill was introduced in congress by John Conyers which would set up a reparations fund to compensate the African-American community for slavery.

10 percent controls about three-fourths of the nation's wealth. The top 1 percent of the population of the United States averages $2.3 million per household (*New York Times*, April 17, 1995). The astoundingly high concentration of wealth in this country is the direct result of hundreds of years of exploitation of poor, working and middle class people by the rich, and of people of color by white people. We need to put the redistribution of that wealth at the very top of our agenda.

In the last two decades that disparity has become worse. By 1994, the 1986 tax "reform" alone had transferred over $200 billion to about 150,000 individuals and families with annual incomes over a half-million dollars (Barlett and Steele, p. 17). We have corporate welfare policies, such as unlimited deduction for interest on corporate debt, intangible asset write-offs, foreign tax credits and write-offs for banks for foreign debt losses, costing us over $160 billion a year. In addition, it is estimated that corporate fraud costs us $200 billion a year. In contrast the FBI puts the loss from burglary and street robbery at a comparatively small $4.64 billion in 1992 ("Third Force," March/April 1995, p. 7).

One example of corporate fraud is the Savings and Loans debacle in which hundreds of millions of dollars were transferred to the rich at a cost to the country of over $500 billion which we will be paying off well into the next century. This will cost each of us over $2,000. (That adds up to $10,000 for my family of five.) A bill was passed in Congress and signed into law which made it impossible to prosecute individual corporate officers or others who had been instrumental in the failure of Savings and Loans and who had benefitted from those failures. This law was passed *at the same time* as the Omnibus Crime Bill which ostensibly cracks down on crime. Clearly white collar crimes by the rich are being treated much differently than crimes committed by the poor and people of color.

Such government policy favors the rich over the rest of us, and white people over people of color. To end racial injustice we need to take money from where it has accumulated and move it to where we need to invest for our future.

This is an economic and a racial issue. Racial justice cannot be achieved when there are such huge disparities in wealth, much of which has been created through racial exploitation. Economic democracy and redistribution of wealth will not necessarily end racial injustice unless white people end the practices which exploit and oppress people of color.

We need to tax the income and accumulated wealth of the small percentage of individuals, families and corporations that control our economy and our communities. Then we need to reinvest that money in community-controlled and racially just development. Poor, working and middle class people of all races, women and men, young and old, people with disabilities, rural, urban and suburban dwellers would benefit if we did so.

The tax structure of the United States is complex, at least partly to protect the tremendous accumulation and concentration of wealth. A detailed analysis of it is beyond the scope of this book. We could make the entire system simpler and substantially more with just a few major changes. Following are some suggestions that are adapted from Barlett and Steele's *America: Who Really Pays the Taxes* (pps. 338–341):

1. Eliminate all tax credits and exemptions except the personal exemption.

2. Eliminate all itemized deductions.

3. Lower the lowest rates and raise the highest rates in a simple scale.

4. Eliminate special treatment for capital gains.

5. Impose the income tax on the increase in value of all holdings at death.

6. Withhold on all income.

7. Have a means test for all individual government benefits such as social security.

8. Impose a 1 percent excise tax on all securities and options trading.

9. Eliminate corporate tax preferences and increase corporate taxes to generate about 31 percent of total income tax collections.

10. Tax income earned in the United States regardless of country of filer's residence.

11. Eliminate write-offs for taxes paid to foreign governments.

12. Raise taxes on overseas investors.

13. Raise taxes on foreign companies earning money in the United States.

There are many areas of public policy that we need to address to end racial injustice, but redistribution of the wealth of this country should be the first and primary one.

We must stop exploiting and start rebuilding what we have devastated. We need to publicly invest in the creation of meaningful, safe and well-paid jobs for everyone, universal and comprehensive health care, safe, challenging and democratic schools for all young people, the end of discrimination based on gender, race, sexual orientation, age, physical or mental ability, religion or other "differences," the participation of every person in the decisions which affect their lives, and reconstruction of our devastated urban and rural environments.

Public policy issues change over time, but every public policy issue in the United States is at least partly an issue of race. We must always pay attention to the racial consequences of any issue that is being considered. We must also be sensitive to the racial implications of any "progressive" policy we are advocating so it doesn't have racist effects.

At the same time we need to be aware that almost every public policy is already intentionally coupled with a racial perspective to gain support for the policy and to elicit the collusion of white people. We have already seen how public policy responses to issues of inner city decay, poverty, welfare reform and teenage pregnancy are coded for race. Both Republicans and Democrats routinely use these codings to build support based on our shared interests and fears as white people.

We must do three things to take strategic action on public policy issues. We must assume that there are substantial racial implications for every issue before us. We must understand the ways that issues are framed in racial terms, in code or openly, to build support for an upper class agenda. And we must keep revisiting issues that we thought were once settled because our gains are subject to erosion and counterattack.

Issues which were important to pursue a few years ago may not be today. Stands that were originally progressive may be co-opted very quickly. Battles won can subsequently be lost when opponents regroup and counterattack. That is why we must strategically evaluate current realities—political, cultural and economic—and keep in mind that our goal is effective action for racial justice.

It is easy to become mesmerized by public policy debates because the personalities and issues are fascinating. We can forget that the point of understanding the issues is to be able to influence the decisions that get made. Some of us are tremendously well informed on current affairs, passionately hold progressive opinions and take a principled stand on issues—but we don't translate that stand into public action.

We want to respond effectively to public policy initiatives through public action. More importantly, we want to shape public policy through educational and organizing efforts. Public action is what influences and shapes public policy debates in the first place. During the first two-thirds of the 19th Century African Americans and white people worked to make abolition an issue that could not be avoided. Civil and voting rights for African Americans became public policy issues as a result of grassroots organizing that occurred during the civil rights movement. Japanese Americans struggled for many years to make reparations for the internment of Japanese American citizens during World War II an issue the government had to address. These are the kinds of campaigns we can support. This is the kind of public action we need to take.

Here are some questions to ask yourself when responding to public policy issues.

Questions

1. How is the problem being defined? Who is defining the problem? Who is not part of the discussion?

2. Who is being blamed for the problem? What racial or other fears are being appealed to?

3. What is the core issue?

4. What is the historical context for this issue?

5. What is being proposed as a solution? What would be the actual results of such a proposal?

6. How would this proposal affect people of color? How would it affect white people?

7. How would this proposal affect the rich?

8. How would it affect women? Young people? Poor and working people?

9. What are other options?

10. How are people organizing to address this problem in a more progressive way? How are people organizing to resist any racial backlash this issue might represent?

11. What is one thing you could do to address this problem?

Any public policy issue can be analyzed through these and other questions. They stimulate our critical thinking so we are not misled into colluding with an agenda that benefits a few and distracts us from the source of our problems.

Throughout this book we have seen how people of color are routinely scapegoated for social problems that they have little influence over. One of the most vulnerable groups of people of color are recent immigrants. Although some immigrants come to this country highly skilled, highly trained or with family and economic resources, most are poor, isolated by language and culture and disoriented by a new society. Many are fleeing war, poverty or political repression. Many of our own foreparents faced similar conditions when they arrived one, five or ten generations ago. Recent immigrants, especially those without legal papers, are currently being attacked as a cause of economic deficits, the lack of jobs, and the deterioration of American values and cultural unity.

Who has legal papers and who doesn't, who is welcome here and who isn't, are not questions of impartial legal standards. Immigration policy has always been an arm of foreign policy as well as an instrument of white racism. Cubans fleeing Castro have been preferred over Haitians fleeing Duvalier; Vietnamese fleeing communism have been preferred over Salvadorano/as fleeing U.S.-supported dictators; and Europeans have been preferred over people of color. These are examples of how political factors influence immigration policy which in turn determines who is here legally or illegally. The current debate over services to residents without papers, reflected in the 1994 California ballot initiative 187, is an example of an issue that can be looked at through the questions posed above. In brief, here is how it might be analyzed.

Critical Analysis

The problem is being defined as "illegal" immigration producing a disproportionate burden on the states to pay for services provided to these immigrants. This is said to produce state budget deficits when the federal government mandates services but doesn't pay for them. White political leaders, the media and states rights advocates are primarily defining the problem while poor and working people, people of color and immigrants are excluded from the discussion.

Recent immigrants without papers are being blamed for these problems. This becomes a way to blame the entire Latino/a and Asian-American immigrant communities, allowing the government to keep them under tight control and surveillance and to further cut back social services to the poor. Defining immigrants without papers and the Latino/a and Asian-American immigrant communities as the problem appeals to white people's fear of people of color and immigrants, our fear of losing jobs and our fear of budget deficits and further cutbacks.

The stated issues are funding sources for federally mandated services, reduction of federal and state budget deficits and the loss of jobs in the United States. The primary issue, however, is a white backlash against the increasing size, influence and eventual majority status of communities of color. This backlash uses "illegal alien" as a racially coded word for immigrant of color, playing into the economic and racial fears of working and middle class whites.

Historically white people have used issues of states' rights to fight against reliquishing white power. The Civil War was fought over whether the states or the federal government had the right to set policy on slavery, not on whether slavery per se was right or wrong. Much of the resistance to the civil rights movement was based on similar arguments about states' rights and the role of the federal government in enforcing desegregation, voting rights and access to education. Once again white people are trying to roll back gains in government policy which benefit the poorest and most vulnerable members of our society by claiming that the federal government has no right to tell the states what services they must provide. This is a familiar pattern in which communities of color are attacked indirectly through a challenge to the government's role in enforcing their rights. The specific proposals being advanced would cut off all services to immigrants lacking legal papers. The intended result is a net savings from not providing services to them.

Not surprisingly, the cost of services to immigrants with or without papers is often inflated, and the contributions they make are ignored or minimized. Most studies indicate that they actually contribute more to the community in taxes, job creation and the revitalization of neighborhoods than they require from it in economic support. Over time their contribution increases and costs decrease further. They do take jobs—usually those that whites don't want or won't do—but their needs for services creates jobs as well.

In the long term this proposed "solution" would affect people of color in several ways. It would further impoverish the Latino/a and Asian-American immigrant communities while holding them responsible for declining employment, wages and benefits in the U.S. economy. It would cut them off from schooling, health care and other essential public services while targeting them for further police and INS harassment and intimidation as well as violence from individuals.*

Anti-immigrant bills would further segregate white people from people of color, reinforce our racial stereotypes and contribute to further racial injustice. These proposed solutions would focus our attention on the immigrant community rather than on the true source of the loss of jobs, decreased earning power and economic dislocation we are currently experiencing. The increasing disparity of wealth, and the source of the economic decisions that have impoverished many of our lives would continue to be covered up. Businesses would have an increased ability to exploit immigrants because of their fear of being deported or of being mistakenly identified as illegal.

Under these proposals certain groups would be hit particularly hard. Bearing primary responsibility for the health and welfare of the family, immigrant women would have less access to work, education, safety and health care, and fewer resources for raising children. These proposals make all Asian American and Latina women more vulnerable to sexual and racial harassment at work, and to physical and sexual violence within the family.

---

* "According to the Los Angles County Commission on Human Relations, hate crimes against Latinos increased sharply last year. The Commission attributed the 23.4 percent increase in hate crimes against Latinos in Los Angles county to the passage of Proposition 187." Newsletter of the Coalition for Immigrant and Refugee Rights and Services, Spring 1995.

They would cut off children of immigrants without papers from schooling and health care, and increase the two-tier system in which some children have future opportunities and other children are without future prospects of work.

There are many other options for balancing state budgets and paying for social services, if that is the concern, than blaming and punishing immigrants of color. We could increase taxation of the rich and of corporate wealth. We could use some of that money to create jobs, job training, school programs and social services to integrate immigrants more quickly into the economy.

A great deal of organizing against anti-immigrant proposals and policies has already occurred. Some programs provide services and legal assistance to immigrants without papers. Some are organizing immigrant workers so they will have a stronger voice in the political system. There are organizations addressing economic dislocation and redevelopment, while others are organizing and doing educational work against ballot initiatives and legislative proposals that attack immigrants. There are also campaigns of non-compliance with initiatives already passed coordinated by teachers and health care workers.

There are many ways to become involved. You can join an organization supporting immigrant rights, and you can make a financial contribution to an organization working with immigrants and refugees. You can write letters, phone, or send faxes and E-mail to policymakers, and you can work with others to protest the enforcement of policies that discriminate against immigrants. You can challenge other people when you hear racially prejudiced or misinformed statements about this issue. You can help others think critically about how racism operates in an issue like this.

This is an example of the critical analysis of social issues that can lead us to effective political action.

Using the questions listed a few pages ago, do your own assessment of the three-strikes, Omnibus Crime Bill, or of welfare "reform."

Affirmative Action

*A*FFIRMATIVE ACTION HAS been one of the primary public policy controversies of the last thirty years. Even now debates about its effectiveness continue. Following is an overview of some affirmative action issues as another example of how to think critically about public policy issues.

Affirmative action is more than a legal issue. Every section of this book describes steps you can take to eliminate racism. Everything you do in this area is an affirmative action. Affirmative action to end racism should be the challenge and responsibility of every single person in our society, as well as of the institutions and organizations which have such a large impact on our lives. Yet today we have a vocal minority who are saying we should stop affirmative action not only as a legal remedy, but also as a social commitment. They are saying we have gone too far in correcting racial injustice. Of course, they are not challenging traditional forms of preference and discrimination that favor the rich, the educated, white people and men.

Affirmative action is practiced in many areas of our society. We have hiring and recruiting preferences for veterans, women and the children of alumni of many universities, special economic incentives for purchase of U.S.-made products, import quotas against foreign goods and agricultural and textile subsidies. These practices have led to a huge overrepresentation of white people, men and people of middle, upper middle and upper class backgrounds in our universities, in well-paid jobs and in the professions. One indication that attacks on affirmative action are part of a white backlash against equality is that affirmative action in the form of preferences that primarily benefit white people is not being questioned.

Many forms of discrimination in our society are illegal. The federal government mandated affirmative action programs to redress racial inequality and injustice in a series of steps beginning with an executive order issued by

President Kennedy in 1961. The Civil Rights Act of 1964 made discrimination illegal and established equal employment opportunity for all Americans regardless of race, cultural background, color or religion. Subsequent executive orders, in particular Executive Order 11246 issued by President Johnson in September 1965, mandated affirmative action goals for all federally funded programs and moved monitoring and enforcement of affirmative action programs out of the White House and into the Labor Department. These policies and the government action which followed was a response to the tremendous mobilization of African Americans and white supporters during the late 1950s and early 1960s pushing for integration and racial justice.

There are many ways to attack racism. In this section I would like to address the particular legal remedy called affirmative action. It is a policy aimed primarily at correcting institutional discrimination where decisions, policies and procedures that are not necessarily explicitly discriminatory have had a negative impact on people of color. Affirmative action policies address and redress systematic economic and political discrimination against any group of people that are underrepresented or have a history of being discriminated against in particular institutions. Beneficiaries of these programs have included white men and women, people with disabilities and poor and working class people, but their primary emphasis has been on addressing racial discrimination.

There is pervasive racism in all areas of U.S. society. For example, in 1991 Diane Sawyer with ABC-TV filmed two men, one African American and one white, who were matched for age, appearance, education, and other qualities. They were followed for a day by a camera crew. The white man received service in stores while the African American was ignored, or in some cases, watched closely. The white man was offered a lower price and better financing at a car dealership, jobs where the African American was turned down, and apartments for rent after the African American man was told they were no longer available. A police car passed the white man while he was walking down the street but it slowed down and took note of the African American (Horne, pps. 40–41). Many other studies like this one demonstrate discrimination against people of color in different areas of everyday life.

Racism, rather than being self-correcting, is self-perpetuating. The disadvantages to people of color and the benefits to white people are passed on to each succeeding generation unless remedial action is taken. The disadvantages to people of color coalesce into institutional practices such as those noted in the beginning of this section which, although they may be race neutral in intent, adversely affect people of color. We have to take positive steps to eliminate and compensate for these institutional effects of racism, even when there is no discernible discriminatory intent.

For example, most job opportunities are heard about through informal networks of friends, family and neighbors. Since the results of racism are segregated communities, schools and workplaces, this pattern leaves people of color out of the loop for many jobs, advancement opportunities, scholarships and training programs. Federal law requires widespread and public advertisement of such opportunities so that not only people of color, but white women and men who are outside the circles of information, have an equal opportunity to apply for these positions.

Another area affirmative action addresses is preferential hiring programs. Many times people of color have been excluded from hiring pools, overtly discriminated against, unfairly eliminated because of inappropriate qualification standards, or have been rendered unqualified because of discrimination in education and housing. Court decisions on affirmative action have rendered illegal those qualifications that are not relevant to one's ability to do the job. They have also mandated hiring goals so that those employed begin to reflect the racial mix of the general population from which workers are drawn. There is no legal requirement to ever hire an unqualified person. There is a mandate that in choosing between qualified candidates, the hiring preference should be for a person of color when past discrimination has resulted in white people receiving preferential treatment.

Sometimes people argue that affirmative action means the best qualified person will not be hired. However, it has been demonstrated many times in hiring and academic recruitment that test and educational qualifications are not necessarily the best predictors of future success. This does not mean unqualified people should be hired. It means basically qualified people who may not have the highest test scores or grades, but who are eminently ready to do the job may be hired. Employers have traditionally hired people not only on test scores, but on personal appearance, family and personal connections, school ties and on race and gender preferences demonstrating that talent or desirability can be defined in many ways. These practices have all contributed to a segregated work force where whites hold the best jobs, and people of color work in the least desirable and most poorly paid positions. Affirmative action policies serve as a corrective to such patterns of discrimination. They keep score on progress toward proportional representation and place the burden of proof on organizations to show why it is not possible to achieve it.

Affirmative action programs have been remarkably effective in dampening discrimination and opening up work and educational opportunities for groups of people previously excluded. When these policies receive executive branch and judicial support, vast numbers of people of color, white women and men have gained access they would not otherwise have had.

It has been argued that affirmative action benefits people of color who are already well off or have middle class advantages, not the poor and working class people of color who most need it. Affirmative action programs have benefitted substantial numbers of poor and working class people of color. Access to job training programs, vocational schools, and semi-skilled and skilled blue-collar, craft, pink-collar, police and firefighter jobs has increased substantially through affirmative action programs. Even in the professions, many people of color who have benefitted from affirmative action have been from families of low income and job status (Ezorsky, p. 64).

Middle class people of color have also benefitted from afirmative action. All people of color have experienced the effects of racial discrimination. Having more money may buffer the most extreme effects, but it doesn't protect people from everyday racial discrimination. The middle class in various communities of color is small and often fragile. It's members own less wealth and have less financial security than their white counterparts because of the past effects of racial discrimination. They also experience the full range of cultural racism and white prejudice that all people of color have to deal with.

Another argument raised against affirmative action is that individual white people, often white males, have to pay for past discrimination and may not get the jobs they deserve. It is true that specific white people may not get specific job opportunities because of affirmative action policies and may suffer as a result. This lack of opportunity is unfortunate and we need to address the causes of the lack of enough jobs. We tend to forget that millions of specific people of color have also lost specific job opportunities as a result of racial discrimination. To be concerned only with the white applicants who don't get the job, and not with the people of color who don't, is showing racial preference.

But how true is it that white male candidates are being discriminated against or are losing out because of affirmative action programs? If we look at the composition of various professions such as law, medicine, architecture, academics and journalism, or at corporate management, or at higher-level government positions—or if we look overall at the average income levels of white men—we see that people of color are significantly underrepresented and underpaid in every category. People of color don't even make up the proportions of these jobs equal to their percentage of the population. They don't earn wages comparable to white men. White men are tremendously overrepresented in almost any category of work that is highly rewarded except for professional athletics. According to a 1995 government report, white males make up only 29 percent of the workforce, but they hold 95 percent of senior management positions (Sklar, p. 115). Until there is both equal opportunity and fair distribution of education, training and advancement to all Americans, we need affirmative action for people of color to counter the hundreds of years of affirmative action that has been directed at white males. We cannot reasonably argue that white males are discriminated against as a group if they are overrepresented in most high status categories.

We should note two other aspects of this dynamic. We have seen how all white people benefit from racism. White men receive more of the economic and other benefits of racism than white women of the same socio-economic status. White men have always been favored in families and schools and preferred for jobs, training, educational programs, athletic programs, military careers and job advancement and promotion. Men still make more than women for comparable work, are given better educational opportunities, have more leisure time and are accorded higher status than women.

The second and equally important part of this dynamic is that not all white men are equal. If you are a white male you may or may not have gained a lot from racism. If you are not well-off, well educated or well rewarded in your life, you should look at white men who are and analyze how they accumulated such rewards. Why do many corporate executives make more in a week than their workers make in a year? Why does the average CEO "earn" as much as 157 factory workers (Sklar, op. cit. p. 9)?

Business leaders are able to exploit male workers by appealing to common bonds and common fears among white men. They have played on white male fears of losing their jobs (and their manliness) to keep them working hard, claiming that only white men had the strength, skill, intelligence, independence, strength of character and virility to do the job. White workers have often bought these arguments feeling pride and increased self-esteem in their working abilities, and feeling personally threatened by the presence of people of color and white women in the workplace. Their ability to fight against low wages, unsafe working conditions, the restructuring of their jobs and plant closures has been diminished even while they thought they were protecting their jobs through race riots, anti-immigration laws, attacks on affirmative action and workplace discrimination, harassment and exclusion.

Collusion with well-off white men against affirmative action is not in the best interests of poor, working and middle class men. Yet many have bought the lie that who they are is based on the manliness of the work they do* and their ability to keep their workplaces as white male preserves.

Affirmative action programs have been effective in many areas of public life because they open up opportunities for people who would not otherwise have them, including white women and men. Attacks on affirmative action are part of a systematic attempt to roll back progress in ending discrimination and to curtail a broad social commitment to justice and equality. Attacking affirmative action is self-destructive for all of us except the rich.

---

* Manliness is defined differently, but no less exclusively in the computer industry than in trucking or construction.

Affirmative action helps mitigate the effects of institutional racism. It also counters the effects of current discrimination, intentional or not. We know that not all white people are well intentioned. Others of us believe that everyone should have an equal chance but still hold deep seated prejudices against people of color. For a substantial number of us those prejudices lead us to practice discrimination. Without specific, numerical goals, it has been found that many people and organizations continue to practice discrimination while professing agreement with affirmative action.

There are so many subtle and not-so-subtle ways to eliminate people of color from the job application process it is not surprising that employers have found ways around affirmative action unless it is tied to visible hiring and promotion targets. In a society with such overwhelming evidence of racism, we must assume that individuals and organizations will resist efforts to end it. For instance, in 1993 the Equal Employment Opportunity Commission had a backlog of 70,000 discrimination cases (chideya, p. 110). We have to set goals and enforce and monitor standards because it is the only way we can measure compliance. These are the mechanisms we need to ensure that affirmative action is more than a facade.

Quotas have been used in the past to exclude particular groups of people from jobs or educational opportunities. They have been used to limit the number of Asian Americans or Jews in universities so white people would continue to have unequal access. Setting minimum goals for inclusion is the opposite of setting maximums. We need numerical goals to guarantee compliance with affirmative action policies. Numerical goals promote democratic access to education, jobs and job training.

Some people have claimed that affirmative action programs lower self-esteem in those who are favored by them, perhaps even in those who do not directly benefit from them. There is no systematic evidence for this effect. It seems to be something that white people worry about more than people of color.

Persistent denial of equal opportunity—and therefore inadequate access to good jobs, good education and housing—leads to poor self-esteem. If we are truly worried about low self-esteem among people of color, then we need more effective affirmative action programs to counter discrimination. It is discrimination that seems to be the more important harm we should be trying to eliminate.

Affirmative action is not a cure-all. It will not eliminate racial discrimination, nor will it eliminate competition for scarce resources. Affirmative action programs can only ensure that everyone has a fair chance at what is available. They cannot direct us to the social policies we need to pursue so we do not have to compete for scarce resources in the first place. In the larger picture we must ask ourselves why aren't there enough decent paying, challenging and safe jobs for everyone? Why aren't there enough seats in the universities for everyone who wants an education? Expanding opportunity for people of color means expanding not only their access to existing jobs, education and housing (affirmative action), but removing the obstacles that cause these resources to be limited (social justice).

Affirmative action has been a symbol of white people's acknowledgement of and serious commitment to eradicating racial discrimination. It has been interpreted as such by most people of color. It is crucial that at this stage of backlash against the gains of the last three decades, we don't abandon one tool that we know works.

When whites attack affirmative action—if they are truly committed to American ideals of justice and equality—they should be proposing other remedies for racial inequality in our society. The hypocrisy is clear when white people who say they support equal opportunity attack affirmative action, yet want to leave intact the basic economic and racial injustices it is designed to correct. Ask people who oppose affirmative action how they propose to eliminate racial discrimination. You can learn a lot about their true beliefs from their answers.

Questions and Actions

1. List some of the obvious and subtle ways that people of color may be discriminated against in the hiring, promotion and benefits processes at your workplace or other workplaces you encounter in your daily life.

2. Which of these areas do you have some control over or participation in?

3. What leverage do you have as a manager to make changes? What leverage as a worker? As a client or consumer?

4. What is the role of any labor organizations related to your workplace regarding affirmative action? Does the membership reflect the diversity of the community?

5. How are people recruited to the organizations you are involved in?

6. How might these recruitment practices discriminate against people of color?

7. Have there been charges, lawsuits or public action against discrimination in any institution you use such as a bank, school, city government, retail store or manufacturer? How was it resolved? Did you ignore or feel angry about the disruption? Did you support the action against discrimination by:
   a. joining the action?
   b. boycotting the store or product?
   c. writing letters of support?
   d. encouraging your friends, family, or co-workers to be supportive?

8. What would the composition of your workplace look like at all levels if it truly reflected the racial diversity of the community?

9. What effect do you think it would have on your metropolitan area if all people had access to good education and decent jobs? What would have to happen for this to become a reality?

10. Affirmative action is a tool for full inclusion and equal opportunity for all people, not only people of color. Go back through these questions and substitute women for people of color. Substitute lesbians and gay men for people of color. Substitute people with disabilities. Substitute seniors and young people.

11. What fears, doubts, questions or concerns do you have about affirmative action? Where do your fears come from? What could you do to answer your questions? Who could you talk with about your concerns?

12. Have you ever been chosen for a job, training program, college level program or housing opportunity in which you were less qualified than others? Have you ever been given preference because of family connections, economic background, age, race or gender?

13. Think again about #12 and try to understand ways that family connections, economic background, race, age or gender may have given you the benefit of the doubt compared to other applicants.

14. Do you think that veterans, sons of alumni, farmers or other people who receive preferential treatment experience self-doubt, lowered self-esteem or feelings of guilt because of it?

15. Besides numerical goals, what measures would you suggest be used to monitor racial and other forms of discrimination?

16. How are you going to respond to people who say that affirmative action unfairly discriminates against white males?

17. List three things you can do to defend or strengthen affirmative action programs in your workplace, community or state.

18. Choose one that you will start doing.

Although institutional change seems difficult to tackle, we are already involved in several institutions in our daily lives. Our workplace, the schools we or our children attend, the stores we patronize, the places we socialize, the community with which we congregate for religious worship—we have some leverage at each of these institutions. We need to analyze the institutions we are a part of, evaluate the influence we and others with us have, and devise effective strategies for challenging racism. The next sections look at some of the ways you might focus on institutions you are already involved with including your workplace, your school system, the police, the criminal justice system and your religious organization.

At Work

W*HITENESS HAS LONG* been related to racism in the workplace and economy. As David Roediger explains in his book *The Wages of Whiteness*, part of the campaign to entice white male workers into industrial jobs during the 19th Century was the rationalization that at least they were not slaves. They could keep their white masculinity intact even while giving up their economic independence because they were told that being a worker in a factory was not the same as being a slave working for a master.

Male industrial workers eventually borrowed the language of slavery to describe their "waged slavery." They played on similarities between their work situation and that of slaves, at the same time trying to keep the differences clear so they could preserve industrial jobs for whites. The relationship of racism to work issues is complex. In general, early white industrial workers were manipulated by racism, and in turn, used racism to gain economic benefits. Employers manipulated racism to create a false sense of pride and opportunity among white workers, which workers then used to separate themselves from male workers of color.

Work in the United States is still highly segregated by class, race and gender. The overall economy, as well as most large organizations, is vertically segregated. Upper middle and upper class white men have access to the jobs with the most money, power and status. Women, working class whites and people of color are strung out on the economic hierarchy, but are found disproportionately at the bottom in the least secure, most unsafe, poorest paid jobs.

We saw in the section on benefits that there are many, specific economic advantages to being white. One early purpose of racism in the United States was to justify economic exploitation. Racism has always been intimately tied to the economic hierarchy. While this section focuses on the realities of fighting racism in the workplace, winning the broader struggle for economic democracy is crucial for truly ending racism.

Women comprise 50 percent of the world's population, perform two thirds of the work, earn one tenth of the world's income, and own 1 percent of the property (United Nations Report, 1980).

The United States, containing 5 percent of the world's population, consumes 30 percent of the world's total use of resources (Durning 1992).

As the above figures indicate, inequality and injustice exist at every level of our economic system. Racism contributes to an international system of economic exploitation. A key to achieving economic justice is solidarity between white workers and workers of color, between U.S. workers and workers from other countries. Racism undermines both levels of solidarity.

In addition to challenging racism where you work (see the workplace assessment below), following are some labor and race issues that deserve attention outside the workplace.

The recent collapse of the Mexican monetary system makes the interdependences of the world economy evident. What may not be so clear to us in the United States is the devastation of non-Western countries which results from the economic policies imposed by the International Monetary Fund, the World Bank and other U.S.-dominated institutions. The colonial practices of European countries, beginning in the late 15th Century and later taken up by the United States, have concentrated international power and wealth in the hands of white people and have given us the ability to dictate the economic fortunes of the rest of the world.

One way to challenge these patterns is to organize against new attempts by U.S. financial interests to further consolidate their dominance through such trade agreements as NAFTA and GATT. These agreements enhance the ability of multinational corporations to move jobs and factories from country to country, to pollute and destroy environments and, in general, to wreak havoc on the lives of hundreds of millions of people, including ourselves. These treaties encourage us to believe that our own (white) U.S. jobs will be protected at the expense of those of people of color in other countries. In reality, we get played off against foreign workers and are able to exert even less control over corporate policy.

The result of these policies is that jobs are moved overseas to countries where multinational companies and local elites buy up land that is then diverted from growing food for local consumption to growing cash crops for U.S. consumption. Foreign workers cannot grow their own food and are forced to move to the cities. If they are lucky they can find work on plantations or in multinational factories to earn enough cash to buy food that they could formerly grow. Treaties like NAFTA and GATT make it easy for companies to move to where wages are lowest and where there is the least labor and environmental regulation.

We have created an international racial hierarchy of wealth, power and control which mirrors our internal one. This international hierarchy subjects us to economic and cultural exploitation camouflaged by racist justifications that blame workers of color and foreign capitalists of color for our declining standard of living and social problems instead of blaming the decision makers in our corporate boardrooms.

We are not powerless against multinational corporations if we overcome our training in racism to work together with people from other countries. We can challenge the dumping of toxic waste and unsafe products in other countries, the exploitation of foreign workers by U.S. companies, the sexual exploitation of women of color overseas by U.S. tourists and corporate and military personnel, the economic policies of the IMF and the World Bank, the displacement of local agricultural production to grow export crops for the United States, the manipulation of unequal trade and other agreements, the scapegoating of foreign workers for U.S. generated problems, and the scapegoating of foreign capitalists of color such as the Japanese and Arabs when (white) British and Canadian capitalists go unmentioned.*

Many of us work for these same corporations and can challenge their policies from within. We all have specific opportunities to confront racism where we work.

To identify where you have the most leverage related to your work, it is important to make an assessment of your workplace. Use the following questions. Talk with others, particularly people of color, to help you do the assessment.

Assessment

1. What is the gender, race and class composition in your workplace? Which groups holds which positions?

2. Who, by race, gender and class, has the power to make decisions about hiring, firing, wages and working conditions in your workplace? Who gets promoted and who doesn't? Are there upper levels (glass ceilings) beyond which some groups of people (i.e., people of color, white women) cannot go?

---

* The British own as much U.S. property as the Japanese and are increasing their stake at a faster rate.

3. Is hiring non-discriminatory? Are jobs openings posted and distributed? Do they attract a wide variety of applicants? Are certain groups excluded? Does the diversity of your workplace reflect the diversity of the wider community?

4. Do layoffs, reassignments, workplace closures or other cutbacks disproportionately affect people of color?

5. What are the salary differentials between those least well paid and those most well paid? Are salaries for comparable work equal?

6. Are there "invisible" workers, people who cook, clean or do maintenance, for example, who are not generally noticed or paid well?

7. Do the board of directors and top level management of your employer include significant numbers of people of color?

8. What is the racial composition of the people who actually own your workplace? Who makes money from the profits of your work?

9. Are there jokes, teasing, put downs or harassment of people based on race, gender, sexual orientation, age, religion or other differences?

10. Has there been or is there any racial or sexual harassment or discrimination, or charges of such, or investigations by any outside agency about such things? Do people of color describe discrimination or harassment at your workplace?

11. Does your organization provide products or services to people of color? If it does, is the clientele treated with respect and dignity? Do staff make racial comments about clients? Is there any discrimination in how people are served or treated?

12. Do the advertising and publicity images that your employer produces convey a multiracial image, or do they reinforce racial or sexual stereotypes?

13. Are there any workplace groups such as unions or affirmative action committees that monitor or respond to racial discrimination? Are they effective? Are they supported or hindered by management? Do they challenge or do they support racism?

14. Is your employer part of a larger organization with manufacturing or other facilities at other sites? Are those sites in communities of color? If they are, are workers paid the same and treated equally to workers at your site?

15. Has your employer closed down or moved facilities to areas of the United States or to other countries in order to pay workers less or to avoid unionization, workplace safety regulations or other oversight?

16. Does your company produce any kinds of toxic waste? If so, in which communities is the waste dumped?

As you can see from these questions, racism affects every level of our workplaces. Starting with an assessment you can pinpoint just how racism operates. Then you can figure out where you and other workers can start to use your own knowledge to make changes. It is difficult to do alone, although individuals can make a big difference. Even more powerful is working with others who are similarly committed to eliminating racism.

Look to the leadership of the people of color you work with, if there are any. They know where the racism lies in your organization. They may be quite clear about what kind of solidarity they need from white co-workers. Ask them how they see things, what are their priorities.

You will also need to work with other white workers, building a core group dedicated to eliminating racism. Many of your white co-workers may not have questioned the racism in your workplace. They need information and support for making changes in workplace practices and environment. You may meet with solid resistance from others who feel they have something to lose from eliminating racism. Challenging them will require more strategic thinking.

Many workers have such pressing financial and emotional needs they may not understand at first why racial equality and economic justice need to be a priority. The information provided in this book can lead you to effective strategies to help them see the costs of racism in their lives.

A good way to begin, once you have the information you need, is to ask questions. "Why is this person of color paid less than that white person who was hired more recently?" "Why aren't there any people of color at management level?" "Why don't people of color stay with this organization very long?" "What effect does that kind of comment (e.g., to a racial put down) have on other people around here?"

Asking questions raises issues for people to think about. Sometimes that alone will make other people want to make some changes. Often you'll get excuses, justifications or cynicism in response. Those responses will help you and others see how white people are thinking about racism and what level of awareness they have. It will also help you map out where you'll meet resistance to further actions.

It is generally not useful to label people as racist. This strategy produces defensiveness. You will do better to document racism within the organization, build allies and propose concrete changes. If you attack people personally, they will probably counterattack. Everyone within the organization will feel unsafe. Instead, you want to focus on policies, practices and procedures.

This is not to say you won't meet resistance, innuendo, slander, isolation and threats. But where injustice and inequality are the focus, it is harder for people to present a reasonable defense of previous patterns than if they are personally attacked.

Eliminating racism is not a question of economic cost but of injustice. But in organizing against specific forms of racism, it can be a useful short-term strategy to point out the economic benefits of the changes desired or the economic costs of the old patterns. What does it cost an organization when there are high turnover rates for personnel who are people of color, when clients of color are not well served or when the leadership talent of people of color is not utilized? What does it cost when there are discrimination lawsuits, strikes, boycotts or government investigations because of racism within the organization? Organizations are differentially vulnerable to such costs. What does it cost you and those you work with when injustice is allowed to continue without protest?

An effective cost analysis may be difficult to make when corporate investment in personnel and infrastructure is scandalously low and when many company policies are based on such short-term considerations that financial payoffs must be almost immediate.

Specific struggles against racist practices can also be used to raise consciousness about management policies and economics. Each particular fight against racism is part of the long-term struggle, and even when it is unsuccessful, it can educate and organize other workers. Our long-term goal is to create a broad movement of people committed to eliminating racism in all aspects of our lives.

I am not going to romanticize the power of workers; in most circumstances multinational companies can play off workers from many sites against each other. However keeping the issue of race and gender based exploitation on the table in every workplace struggle will further the move toward economic justice. Doing so keeps people of color and white women in leadership positions, demonstrates the interconnected ways that people are exploited and produces the informed solidarity that is essential to the success of any struggle for economic justice.

Education and Schools

MOST OF US spent a considerable amount of our childhood in school. Our children still do. Social activism is needed to create equal opportunity in the educational system which is a major gatekeeper for the distribution of the social and economic benefits of this society. What's going on in this system in the 1990s?

Most students in the United States are still attending segregated schools. Within schools, students are segregated by race and tracked by class or by smaller divisions of economic difference. Segregation and tracking destine most students from a very early age for a particular socio-economic role in their adult life.

There is a vast disparity in what is spent per student. White suburban schools have approximately twice the funds per student as compared with urban schools where students of color are congregated (Kozol, pps. 236–237). When this is multiplied by the number of students in a classroom or school, the disparity is enormous. That money buys fewer students per teacher, classroom necessities like books, pencils and paper, not to mention computers, art and music classes, recreational equipment, teacher's aides, special events and field trips, and in the long run, the best teachers. Students are given a direct measure of their social worth and future chances by the amount of money they see being spent on their education.

When we look at the disparities in educational expenditures we have to acknowledge that most white students have tremendous educational advantages over students of color. I am not saying that enough money is spent on their education, or that it is spent effectively or that all white youth have the same opportunities. We need to school all our children better than we have. But money makes a difference. As parents we know this is true. That is

186

why, when we can afford it, and sometimes even when we can't, we move to school districts with better schools or send our children to private ones.

Given the economic and educational realities of this society it makes sense for us to give our children the best education possible. We shouldn't feel guilty for doing so. But insofar as many children of color are abandoned to the disaster of inadequately funded public schooling, our individual actions do contribute to the overall gap between white children and children of color. Furthermore, it is hypocritical for us to contend that everyone has an equal chance to succeed when white children systematically have better educational opportunities than children of color.

It is a continuation of racism to spend different amounts of money on students according to race, class or any other factor. Yes, there is waste in the school system. Yes, there is bad management, poor teachers and poorer administrators. We need to attend to those problems. And we need to increase and equalize our spending so that every student has a chance.

Find out per student expenditures in your district and others. What disparities do you find? Where does the money come from? How can you work with others to develop new school funding strategies? We urgently need to develop different, more equitable ways to finance our educational system.

Education is more than money. It includes teachers, curricula, school buildings, safety to learn and many other factors. Racism affects the quality and quantity of each of these resources. Teachers in the United States are disproportionately white, far beyond their representation in the general population, and this disparity is increasing. Few students of color have role models of their own ethnicity, and few white students have contact with people of color in positions of authority. In additon, challenges to white culture-based curricula are harder to organize because there aren't sufficient numbers of teachers of color to counter traditional curricula.

White teachers, like all white people, have racial assumptions and prejudices which they carry into the classroom. These assumptions affect what is taught, how it is taught and how teachers interact with students. Teachers are part of the middle class which has traditionally had the function of supervising, training and disciplining the poor and working people of this country and of acting as a buffer between them and the wealthy. Their livelihoods depend on their ability to instill particular values and attitudes in their students so that the economic system runs smoothly. When middle class white teachers are preparing poor and working class students of color for a future of mostly unskilled jobs, economic and racial prejudices work to the double disadvantage of the students.

Who is teaching in our schools? How are they trained? What do they do in the classroom? How does racism in schools affect teachers of color? The answers to these questions can guide us to action. For instance, knowing about changing teacher demographics leads us to work against changes in educational policy, such as the National Teacher's Exam and longer teacher education courses, that present unnecessary obstacles to teachers of color and contribute to their increasing exclusion from our classrooms.

We also need to eliminate racism in the curriculum. School curricula in the United States have a European/American historical focus that emphasizes the development of ideas and political processes from Greece through Rome and Europe to the United States.

"Western" knowledge is actually a conglomeration of ideas and developments from every part of the world. Much of what we call the Greek or classical roots of our civilization was borrowed from Egypt and the Near East. The Greeks themselves acknowledged the source of their learning and made many references to their Egyptian mentors (Bernal).

In our classrooms we still deny or diminish the importance of other world civilizations. Textbooks often present them as if they were only significant when they were impacted by Europeans or Americans. The dynamic interchange between the West and other cultures is glossed over. Cultures from other geographic regions are presented superficially, particularly in the lower grades, through their food, holidays, traditional clothes and little else.

Our curricula also omit the history of white colonialism as colonialism, and they don't address racism and other forms of exploitation. People of color are marginally represented as token individuals who achieved great things rather than as members of communities of resistance who contributed to the welfare of all of us. The enormous contributions that people of color have made to our society are simply not mentioned. (See Weatherford, Bernal and Van Sertima.)

For example, textbooks describe the influence of British and French philosophers on our founding fathers and completely ignore the equally important influence of Iroquois theory and political practice on the roots of our democratic traditions. This is despite the fact that key participants, including Franklin and Jefferson, explicitly describe the Iroquois models as influential in their thinking (Mohawk).

Arab contributions to mathematics, astronomy, geology, minerology, botany and natural history are similarly unmentioned. The Arabic numbering system, which replaced the cumbersome and limited Roman numeral system, and trigonometry and algebra, which serve as cornerstones of modern mathematics, were all contributions from Muslim society (Nasr, pps. 75–88).

As a result children of color do not see themselves at the center of history and culture. They do not see themselves as active participants in creating this society. The roles played by their foreparents have simply been written out of history giving white children and children of color distorted understandings of their own histories.

We need to challenge all aspects of racism in educational curricula, including but not limited to the teaching of Europe-focused history, the use of literature texts in which only white authors are presented, the trivializing of other cultures by focusing on their food and holidays or by caricaturing their people, the exclusion of poor and working people from written histories of the struggles which shaped our country, the glossing over of European and U.S. colonialism, the exclusive use of white cultural examples for math problems, the teaching of science as a purely Western tradition, and the ommission of racism as a pervasive and central component of lessons in history, social studies and other subjects.

There are further questions we need to ask. How are students treated? Are students of color systematically harassed, disciplined or tracked by teachers or administrators? Does the school have anti-racist policies in place, and are these known and enforced?

How are students prepared to deal with racism? Social scientists once thought that if white students and students of color would just have contact with each other then prejudice would diminish. It has since been found that contact by itself doesn't necessarily eliminate prejudice. White people often claim that the people of color they know are different. In any case, most white students don't go to school with students of color. Because of tracking even those who do may not share the same classes.

Some schools took the next step and developed policies against racial teasing and targeting to help eliminate racism between students. These policies help but don't go far enough.

Students need support for taking an explicitly anti-racist stand. They need to be taught critical thinking skills so they can see where racism is operating and know how to intervene. Schools must be challenged to provide these skills.

Many people are already involved in the struggle to make our schools more democratic, safer and less racist. These efforts include two kinds of interventions.

The first approach is to help individual students of color succeed in spite of the limited opportunity provided by their family or community. Tutoring programs, scholarship funds, special training programs—these are effective in helping specific individuals acquire higher education or better jobs. Such programs do not address the systematic inequality between the educational opportunities of white students and students of color. On the contrary, as the results of these programs, a few highly successful people of color, are often used by whites to put down the rest of the community and blame those who fail to succeed.

The second approach is to attack the structural roots of inequality. People are organizing around the issues of school funding, curriculum development, resource allocation, teacher training and the control and administration of educational programs. Such activity is probably already occurring in your community, and you can join. If it isn't, get together with concerned parents, teachers and educational activists to get something going. The questions to keep asking ourselves in analyzing the status quo or evaluating changes we want to make are: "What are the effects of these policies on students of color?" "Who is going to benefit from the changes?" How can we achieve greater equality of opportunity?"

The Police

JUST AS TEACHERS have the middle class function of training young people for their future roles in the economic hierarchy, police officers have the working class function of disciplining those who don't follow the rules. Teachers are primarily women because women are trained to be caretakers of young people. Police officers are primarily men because men are trained to enforce class, gender and racial roles. Both occupations are primarily white because their function is also to train people of color to accept their place in U.S. society and to punish them when they don't. They act as a buffer between people of color and the rest of the white community. They maintain and enforce the economic and racial hierarchies we have developed in the United States.

For these reasons we have a very different relationship to the police than do people of color. Our economic status also influences our experience with and trust of the police. We are more respectful and trusting if we are middle class because they are protecting our property and upholding our values. If we are poor or working class we have more likely experienced harassment from the police and have less at stake in their role of maintaining the status quo.

As a middle class white child I was raised to trust the police and to look upon them as a source of help. The ensuing decades have worn off much of that trust, but in general, I do not fear being stopped and searched arbitrarily by the police. People of color, particularly young African American and Latino men, are very likely to be stopped and searched by the police for no apparent cause. This happens not just to young men hanging out on the street. Groups of young people of color, men and women, are stopped, searched or otherwise harassed in many situations where we would not even imagine fearing police interference. If the police think you look suspicious, and to some police any man of color looks suspicious, you may be stopped, even if you are with your family, even if there is no apparent cause for suspicion, even if you are just driving by somewhere.*

Every year there are hundreds of reports of police brutality. In Los Angeles alone a recent Amnesty International study found abuses too numerous to count. The Los Angeles Police and Sheriff's Departments have paid out tens of millions of dollars to victims of brutality and surviving families (chideya, p. 204). Frequently the results of police brutality investigations are never released to the public. A May 1993 conference of gang leaders in Kansas City had as one of its demands that these cases be opened to the public and that the national travesty of police brutality be stopped.

The riots in Harlem in 1935 were in response to police brutality, as were many of the riots in the 1960s, the riots in Miami in the 1980s and the uprising in Los Angeles in 1992. Nothing makes more of a mockery of our legal system than police abuse of African Americans, Latino/as and Native Americans. We have allowed them to criminalize an entire segment of our population under the pretense of protecting us.

At this time in our history, the police are seen as the representatives of white power in communities of color. When they trample people's rights they are acting in our name. When they are protecting the lives and property of white people at the expense of those of people of color, they are a visible tool used by white people to enforce the racial and economic hierarchy in our country.

The racism behind much police brutality makes people of color unsafe in two ways. First, they are vulnerable to attack from the police. Most people of color know of someone who was stopped arbitrarily by the police; many know someone who was shot without justification. Everyone saw the footage of the Rodney King beating. To most people of color, particularly Native Americans, Latino/as and African Americans, such occurrences are common knowledge.

This knowledge of police brutality prevents many people of color, particularly women, from seeking protection from non-racial crimes such as domestic violence. Many women of color are understandably hesitant about handing their men over to a racist and violent police force and a discriminatory criminal justice system, even though their refusal to do so might increase their own vulnerability to violence.

These dynamics also make it unsafe for white people. Police resources are directed at communities of color and not at the interpersonal and economic crimes that we are most likely to be victims of.

Many of us are afraid of being robbed, beaten, raped or burglarized. Some of us have been already. Most of the crime we experience is committed by

---

* See "Anatomy of a Party Gone Wrong: When Police Brutality Hits Home" a chilling account of police attack on a private party, by Mandisa-Maia Jones and Valerie Willson Wesley in "Essence," December 1991.

other white people, many of them people we know. When there are racist patterns to police practices we are even more at risk because the police are looking in the wrong direction.

This is not to say that white people are never robbed by people of color. You may even know someone who was. You have certainly read about someone who was, because the racial bias of the news media presents us with a disproportionate number of these cases, giving them wide publicity, which in turn exacerbates our fears. We then allow the police to continue their practices justifying their "excesses" by attributing them to rogue officers who, it is claimed, are the exception.

Police racism and brutality fuel the anger of communities of color which, in turn, gets directed at us. But we are differentially vulnerable to that anger. Poor and working class white people live closer to and are less protected from retaliatory racial violence than are the wealthy. Working class white men are hired for the dangerous work of police and security guards to protect white neighborhoods and businesses. The wealthy live in secluded, secure areas.

When we don't respond strongly and actively to police brutality in our communities we increase polarization and justify the anger of people of color who say that the police represent the interests of white people. If we want to deal with racism we have to rein in, retrain and redirect the police so they don't initiate acts of violence in our name while defending the lives and property of the wealthy.

I am discussing the police in general, as they actually manage relations between the white community and communities of color. Individual officers may be better or worse in how they carry out this role. The answer is not simply more multicultural awareness for police, or more "community" policing.* We need to make the police accountable to the entire community, and, at the same time, challenge the racism of our society which continues to use the police to enforce inequality and injustice.

How should we redirect the police? There are obvious areas upon which they could focus. Most acts of physical and sexual violence are between people who know each other. Police response to incidents of domestic violence, child sexual assault and rape are crucial indicators of the safety of our communities. White collar crime and high level drug importation and distribution are more devastating to our lives and pocketbooks than petty thievery and small scale drug dealing.

Where do the police devote their time and attention? How do they allocate resources? How well are they trained, including training in racism, domestic

---

* Community policing refers to the practice of having police assigned to specific neighborhoods and getting to know the area and the people.

violence, community relations and community building? These are the kinds of questions we need to ask. Here are some places to start.

Assessment

1. Is there an *independent* police review board or commission in your city or county? How effective is it?

2. Are there allegations of police brutality or civil suits against the police or sheriff's department? What is their status, and how have law enforcement officials responded? What is the history of allegations, lawsuits and police response in your local police and sheriff's departments?

3. Are the police and sheriff's departments fully integrated? Are they trained to deal with a multicultural population? How do they respond to different kinds of calls? Do they work well with community agencies and organizations?

4. Is the response to family violence racially biased? Is there a policy of mandatory arrest for incidents of domestic violence? Are reports of child sexual assault and rape investigated and prosecuted vigorously and nondiscriminately?

5. Is community policing used by the police department? How is the community involved? Are people of color from within the communities represented and empowered?

6. White adults and adults of color can collude to blame and criminalize young people for high crime and drug abuse rates. This conveniently ignores the responsibility adults have for youth safety, education, family support and recreational opportunities. Do the police in your area respond without prejudice and undue force to the needs of young people in your community? (Ask young people.) How can young people be more involved in police-community relations?

When you see the police stop people of color slow down, drive around the block, let them know you're paying attention. Don't assume that because the detained are people of color they must have done something wrong. Don't assume that because you respect the police that they respect everyone in the community.

Get together with other concerned citizens to monitor police activities. The single biggest deterrent to police abuse is an alert community. Good, community based policing can help make all our lives safer. And we can each help ensure that police action does not further racial violence.

The Criminal
Justice System

*M*OST OF US don't have an active, everyday role in the criminal justice system, but we do have some influence in what happens within it. Our advocacy of crime legislation the death penalty, police practices and our funding of prisons, jails and wars on crime and drugs all play a part in how different people are treated on a daily basis by the legal system.

The legal system has been controlled by wealthy white people since its inception in feudal England. Our country's founding legal documents were written by white men who owned property—about 10 percent of the population at that time, and they limited most rights to white men who owned property (Feagin and Vera, p. 189).

The history of racism within the British and U.S. legal systems is well documented. Even today there is ample evidence of substantial racial bias in police arrest policies, charging practices, trial and sentencing procedures, judicial attitudes and the use of the death penalty, not to mention manifest bias in the laws themselves.

I will briefly describe two examples of institutional racism in the criminal justice system. Powder cocaine is purer than crack and worth more. Yet it takes possession of 500 grams of powder (worth $40,000 in 1994) to equal the five-year sentence that someone possessing five grams of crack (worth only $250) would receive. Whites are the main users of powder cocaine, and African Americans primarily use crack (chideya, p. 195). This discrepancy has resulted in fewer arrests and lighter sentences for whites than for African Americans.

Whites do use and sell crack, and even here there are disparities in arrests, prosecution and sentencing. The *Los Angeles Times* reports that law enforcement in southern California waged its war against crack almost exclusively in minority neighborhoods. When they are arrested, whites are prosecuted in state court, where sentences are lighter. Not a single white was convicted of a crack cocaine offense in federal courts serving Los Angeles and the surrounding areas between 1988 and 1994. This pattern creates a two-tier system when African American and Latino crack dealers get ten-year mandatory sentences in federal courts and whites get a maximum of five years, often receiving no more than a year in jail from state courts ("Crack penalties appear to hit minorities harder" *Oakland Tribune*, May 21, 1995, p. A–5).

Unequal enforcement of the law undermines respect for and compliance with it. White criminals, especially those that are well off, have less fear of being caught or prosecuted. People of color have less respect for the legal system because of the arbitrary and racist patterns of abuse within it.

As noted earlier, Americans are afraid. We have turned our fear into the unconstitutional criminalization, incarceration and surveillance of communities of color. These practices are particularly aimed at Latino, Native American and African American male youth. Such policies are shortsighted and ineffective. Our fears are used to promote the building of more prisons, the mandatory sentencing of juveniles and the continuing surveillance and control of communities of color by the police. Funding appropriations support a vast prison construction industry and an army of professionals, guards and other staff, but do little to reduce crime. When we are spending more to lock up youth of color than to educate them we know something is wrong.

Would you want white youth to be treated just as harshly as youth of color are now? What about your own children, grandchildren, nieces, nephews or the children of friends? Should thirteen and fifteen year-olds be treated as adults and imprisoned for life? What responsibility does our society have for their behavior?

We need to look within the criminal justice system to understand and eliminate the ways that racism blames and then punishes youth of color. Young people of color don't grow, make, import or transport drugs, (primarily white) adults do. Young people of color don't manufacture and sell guns, white adults do. Young people of color don't move jobs and stores out of neighborhoods, white adults do. Young people of color don't keep information about birth control, sexually transmitted diseases, drugs and violence away from young people, white adults do. Young people of color don't decrease funds for education while increasing spending on defense and prisons, white adults do.

Young people of color are the focus of our attention and our wrath when it comes to behavior we don't approve of. As white adults, we need to take responsibility for the policies and decisions that set them up to fail and then punish them for their lack of success.

We also need to look at the broader social context to understand the root causes of violence and criminal behavior. We know what the answers are for crime prevention—well-paid and safe jobs, challenging and supportive educational opportunities, recreational activities, adequate health care and adequate economic and psychological family support services. We must measure every dollar we spend on prisons and jails, which can never be a long-term solution, against the other ways we know we can make a dent in the violence we all fear.

Religion

S*PIRITUALITY REFERS TO* our experience of being connected to a reality greater than ourselves. Religions are the organized social structures in which some of us put our spirituality into practice. We are all spiritual beings. Many of us are also connected to a particular religious institution through our upbringing or through current affiliation.

Most white people who are part of an organized religion in the United States are Christian, so I am going to focus this discussion on Christianity. There are also white people who are Moslems, Jews, Buddhists or pagans, or who belong to a new age spiritual community. Much of this section will be relevant to these people as well with some adaptations.

The major denominations of the Christian church have contributed to racism and anti-Semitism in both Europe and the United States for many centuries. At the same time, many individual Christians and church leaders have been inspired by Christian teachings to work for social justice and for an end to racism and anti-Semitism. In other words, the Christian church and its teachings have been used by Christians both to support and resist racism.

In U.S. society many white people have assumed a correlation between whiteness and Christianity. As I discussed in Part I, some of the attributes of whiteness have been based on Christian values. Defending whiteness has sometimes been seen as defending Christianity against unbelievers, sinners, witches, pagans and infidels. Various sectors of the Christian church have contributed to this confusion as a result of specific teachings about Jesus, evangelism, salvation and sin.

This is not the place for a detailed discussion of Christian history or theology. Nor can the important role that faith plays in white Christian resistance to racism be addressed. It is important that we build on the inspiration our religious faith gives us to work for social justice, while resisting racism in our religious institutions. Use the following questions to guide you in these tasks.

Assessment

1. What is your religious upbringing?

2. What did you learn about people of color in Sunday school or sermons? About Jewish people?

3. Was your religious community all white? Was the leadership of your religious organization all white?

4. What attitudes were expressed about people of color through discussion of missionary work, charity or social problems?

5. What connections, if any, were made in your church between sin, evil and the lives or situations of people of color or Jewish people? What Christian virtues were used for making negative judgements about people of color. (e.g., hardworking, industrious, thrifty or patient)?

6. What religious or historical role do the Jewish people have in your denomination's teachings? How may that role have contributed to anti-Semitism?

7. What do you know about the history of resistance to racism in your religion or denomination (e.g., abolitionist or civil rights struggles or the resistance to Nazism during World War II)?

8. What Christian values did you learn that have directed or might direct you to work against social injustice? What values specifically inspire or support anti-racism work?

9. How does racism manifest in your current religious organization, if you participate in one?
  a. In the leadership?
  b. In the theology?
  c. In the membership?
  d. In the educational curriculum?
  e. In the practice of the church as a community institution that owns land, employs people, develops projects and allocates resources?

10. Is your religious group actively addressing racism?

a. Is addressing racism seen as a priority by the membership and by the leadership of the church?

b. Is racism defined as a problem in the community and/or within the church?

c. Does your church have an active committee or program to address racism?

d. Is it equipped and authorized to make real changes?

e. What has it accomplished?

f. Where has there been resistance?

g. How can you be more involved?

You probably participate in other institutions besides work, school and church, such as social service agencies, recreational clubs, youth service organizations or volunteer agencies. Think about each in turn and ask yourself some of the questions from the previous sections. What do you notice? Where are you going to become involved?

The final section of this book looks at how we might create democratic, anti-racist, multicultural organizations and institutions. Many of those ideas can be applied to the previous sections on work, school, the police, the criminal justice system and religion.

PART VI
Democratic, Anti-Racist Multiculturalism

Introduction

*A*NY FOURTH GRADE history textbook will tell you that living in the United States commits one to a common set of legal rights and responsibilities which are supposed to apply equally to all people. All people means all people regardless of gender, race, class, physical condition, sexual orientation, religion, place of residence, length of time here, level of education and English-speaking ability.

Beyond that, our differences are vast. In fact, our diversity is what makes us a strong, dynamic, energetic and creative nation.

We are not all the same. Other Americans do not look like you, think like you, cook like you, eat like you or act like you. For many of us this is hard to accept. We are used to having things done in ways that are familiar and comfortable. Most of us have experienced tremendous upheaval and change in our lifetimes. We may not be anxious to invite more by embracing diversity.

Being a multicultural nation does not mean that we all fit together easily, or that our differences complement each other. We should expect conflict and get good at it! As a nation and individually, we need to develop tools for dealing with conflict without resorting to violence. The word "multicultural" describes a process in which we all participate in making the decisions that affect our lives. It is a strategy toward full inclusion, participation and justice for all Americans.

When any principle is turned into practice, it can fuel greater inequality or it can fuel further progress toward ending racism. Multiculturalism can be used as a way to deflect attention away from racism or to dilute attempts at racial inclusion. It can be used to address broader issues of inclusion and social equity, issues of gender, sexual orientation, class, religion and disability. We have to examine how multiculturalism is conceived and put into practice. We need to look at who has power, who retains power, who benefits and who doesn't. Let's look at this matter more closely.

Democratic, Anti-Racist Multiculturalism

W *E LIVE IN* a multicultural society. This is not something we're striving for, it already is our reality. However our multicultural society is neither democratic nor anti-racist. We have much to do to achieve those goals. In our daily lives, most of the organizations we are involved with are not even multicultural, they are segregated. One way to achieve racial justice is to build democratic, anti-racist multicultural organizations.

What does it mean for an organization to be democratic, anti-racist and multicultural? At a minimum the membership, staff, administration and board of directors would all have to reflect the ethnic, gender, economic, religious and other diversity of the larger community. The organization would have to be serving the needs of a broad-based section of the community. What the organization does, how decisions are made and who is served would have to reflect an inclusive process.

That is not enough. We need to look more closely at the internal process, structure and context of the organization to see if it meets our criteria. Before we do that we have to develop a basic framework for understanding what multicultural, democratic and anti-racist mean.

As we have seen, our dominant Western tradition is based on an either/or logic. Even complex racial matters get reduced to black-white contrasts, win-lose situations. We have also seen how this simplified perspective distorts our perception of reality and can make our actions ineffective.

When people come together to make decisions affecting their lives, their differing perspectives, needs and desires will probably not reduce to an either/or choice. If we expect differences to lead to conflict then we come in defensively, ready to protect our own interests. We won't be striving for common solutions that take into account everyone's needs.

How would it make a difference in your interactions with other people if you always assumed there was a cooperative solution possible that would benefit all parties?

The assumption of competition built into Western modes of thinking strongly influences our interactions with each other. Boys are particularly well trained through academic competition, sports and the military against finding cooperative solutions to problems. One reason they get into fights with other guys so often is the expectation that there can be only one winner. One reason they hit young women is they feel they cannot afford to lose to anyone, much less a "girl." This binary opposition with one person on top is expressed in many ways. We talk of winners and losers, champs and chumps, bullies and wimps. We don't teach people to negotiate, compromise, or work out creative solutions. Instead, particularly for men, aggression becomes the best defense. Action precedes discussion.*

We need innovative ways of thinking about reality that embrace diversity and cooperation. Otherwise we are stuck in a competitive framework with every party feeling that if they don't win, they will lose—that they can only win *if* others lose. We need a different framework for thinking about reality and for making decisions.

Some people have suggested that we adopt a "both/and" way of thinking. In this framework we assume that the needs and perspectives of different parties are not necessarily conflicting. Using this approach allows us to embrace both sides' perspectives and draw up a solution that includes elements of each. This kind of thinking shifts the emphasis from fighting to negotiating.

People who employ both/and thinking understand that truth is not absolute. Truth comes from the understanding, traditions and experience of the people whose lives are involved. Different people have different experiences, and what is true for one person or culture may not be true for another. Although there may be simple truths in science (and even those are hotly debated), our social reality is much more complex. One mark of a mature person is the ability to accept differing opinions and ideas respectfully and without attack.

---

* For a discussion of male training, see Kivel, *Men's Work: How to Stop the Violence that Tears Our Lives Apart.*

Both/and thinking is an improvement over either/or thinking because it helps people reduce conflict and develop cooperative solutions. Yet even both/and thinking assumes there are two sides, and they are mutually exclusive. There may be as many "truths" as there are people or groups involved in the process. How do we deal with three, four or eight different sides?

None of our truths are mutually exclusive. We share a lot as human beings, even though we come from different cultures, families and personal experiences. There is usually common ground on which we can build our decisions. Finding that common ground needs to be a process in which everyone is included.

Beyond either/or and both/and thinking is inclusiveness. In a democratic multicultural process everyone is included. Each person's opinions are respected, and each person's needs are taken into account. Even more importantly, each person participates in making the decisions that affect her or his life.

Democratic, anti-racist multiculturalism requires time, inclusion and more complex decision making processes than most of us are used to participating in. Such processes necessarily take time because each person has the opportunity to be heard. We need more versatile decision-making tools than simple majority rule or majority take all. We need to refine consensus models, systems of proportional representation and other group processes that are more inclusive than what we have relied on so far.

Full inclusion can only occur if we don't throw anyone away. Our society discards people whenever there is trouble. One common way we deal with conflict is to label some people as the problem and then try to make them disappear by locking them up, isolating them or segregating their communities. Often those thrown away are people of color, lesbians, gays, bisexuals, women, people from different religions and cultures than ours, people with disabilities and young people. We cannot throw some of the participants away and then claim that we are being inclusive just because we have included everyone who is left.

For example, labeling students troublemakers and kicking them out of our schools, which consigns them to a future with little prospect for success, is a way of throwing them out rather than working to include them. Locking up teenagers for long prison terms is a way of throwing them out.

A cardinal rule of conflict resolution is to attack the problem, not the person. More often we attack the people and leave the problem unattended. We talk about the poor rather than about poverty, the unemployed rather than the lack of jobs, the homeless rather than homelessness, women who are abused rather than male violence, and violent youth rather than violence against young people. The people who are suffering the effects of discrimination or violence become the objects of our discussion but are not themselves participants in that discussion. Most of the solutions we come up with are based on blaming and then punishing the victims.

We cannot possibly solve problems if we have excluded the people who are experiencing those problems from the discussion of solutions. Their active participation in problem solving is essential to its success. If we exclude them we guarantee that they will remain part of the problem. Multiculturalism has to be based on inclusion.

Multicultural Competence

IN ORDER TO make sure that everyone is not only present, but can participate fully, we need to be what many people call "culturally competent." Cultural competency is the ability to understand another culture well enough to be able to communicate and work with people from that culture.

We are all culturally competent in our own culture. We know the language, the nuances and the assumptions about how the world is defined and organized. We know where there are disagreements and differences and generally what the rules are for solving problems. Most of us know how to get around in our cultural neighborhood. Multicultural competence is being fluent in more than one culture, in whichever cultures are part of your surroundings.

"Culture" is a vague, shorthand word to name the complex ways that people who form a "community" (another vague, shorthand word) interact with each other. There are usually cultural norms within a community, but cultural practices can change, can be contradictory and usually overlap with practices of other cultures. Cultures form around specific identities, geographies, beliefs and daily practices. Besides our ethnicity and race, our gender, class, religion, sexual orientation, physical ability, work and family history influence the cultures we are a part of and our roles and experiences within them. Multiculturalism means more than racial balance and inclusion. All members of the community must be competent to communicate with each other for an effective multicultural process.

Learning to be sensitive to the cultural expressions of another group is not difficult but does require time and energy. We must learn to observe, empathize, and appreciate other people's ways of doing things to become culturally competent. Even beginning levels of such competency open doors to understanding different perspectives. People who are culturally competent in even one culture besides their own have a broader, richer and more accurate view of the world. They are able to work with others as full and equal partners.

It is difficult for white people to become multiculturally competent because we are the mainstream culture. Wherever we look we see ourselves, our language, our values, our images and our history. We are given little sense of the importance of cultural competency and an over-inflated sense of the importance and centrality of our culture. We have learned how great European-based American culture is. Most of the heros we studied were white men like Shakespeare, Washington, Jefferson and Lincoln. We were taught that our values, form of government, literature, science and athletic accomplishments are not only the best of all, but an entire level above any others. We have been trained to think that other cultures are less literate, less civilized, less efficient, less practical, less worldly and not sanctioned by God. It is impossible to make a good faith effort to respect and learn about other cultures when we hold a core assumption that they are inferior to ours. Operating from that assumption, we naturally believe, even if at a very subtle level, that we, white people, are the ones who should be in control, who should make the important decisions.

The difficulty of valuing multicultural competency is increased for white people who are Christian. Christianity places such importance on the individual's relationship with Jesus that culture has often been seen as a distraction to faith. (This is less true for Christians of color.) Since people who don't believe in Jesus are consigned to damnation, many denominations focus exclusively on saving the souls of non-Christians. The primary value in understanding another group's language is to translate the New Testament and win them over to God. This perspective makes it difficult for Christians to respect and value the beliefs and cultural expressions of non-Christians. Sometimes non-Christian come to think they are only of interest to Christians as potential converts. Multicultural understanding can only be achieved when there is no ulterior agenda, when other people's cultures are treated as already complete, not needing improvement by whites or Christians.

Many women, people with disabilities, people who are poor or working class, Jews, lesbians, gays and bisexuals are already competent in two or more cultures. They understand mainstream American culture and are fluent in their own. Sometimes this understanding gives them the impetus to challenge the cultural assumptions of whiteness. It can give them insight into how the dominance of one culture oppresses and exploits people outside the mainstream.

White cultural dominance puts pressure even on alternative cultures to be white. Women's cultures, lesbian, gay, bisexual, disability, Jewish and working class cultures often accept white norms and fail to be inclusive.

Furthermore, the more economically privileged we are, the more racially isolated we tend to be. We have less opportunity to learn from different cultures. The people of color we do come into contact with are in less powerful roles or are in jobs that provide services for white people. We are trained to value them less highly and to devalue the contributions of their cultures. Without a good understanding of how white racism has set up this hierarchy of status, we don't have much incentive to value or understand other cultures.

Our culture has drawn from many different cultural traditions. We have valued them enough to appropriate their strengths and achievements. It is time to explicitly, sincerely and publicly acknowledge these contributions. It is not a question of valuing diversity, but of acknowledging rather than exploiting the contributions of all people to the American enterprise.

Cultural competence is not something we have or don't have. It is a process of learning about and becoming allies for people from other cultures, thereby broadening our own understanding and ability to participate in a multicultural process. The key element to becoming more culturally competent is respect for the ways that others live in and organize the world and an openness to learning from them.

One way we retain our assumptions of white superiority while increasing our cultural competency is to split off the culture from the people who live it. White people have appropriated music, art, spiritual practices, stories and beliefs from other cultures while killing or excluding the people who created them.

For example, it is not difficult for a white person to become a connoisseur of jazz—learning to appreciate, collect and even perform the music—while remaining opposed to the full participation of African American people in American society. It is possible for a white person to become an expert on the Hopi while supporting the federal government in exploiting their culture and land. One of the ways that white people have traditionally become experts in other people's cultures is by participating in these kinds of exploitation.

There is also the danger that we will use our knowledge of another culture to feel superior to the people whose culture it is. Even if we know a lot about the holidays, practices, cooking, music or beliefs of another culture we still have a lot to learn from the people who live it.

We need to use what we learn to be stronger allies for people of color. An ally is an advocate, a person who supports other people's right to speak for themselves, who resists the temptation to speak as an expert on their behalf. Other white people will ask us to speak for, translate for, or have an expert opinion about people of color we know, have studied or lived with. We will be pressured to use our knowledge and professional expertise against those whose lives it is based on. If we do not defer to the leadership of people of color and defend their ability to speak for themselves, we will end up using our expertise to promote ourselves. Only if we are clear that we do not want to reinforce white dominance can we resist the temptation to profit from the accomplishments of people of color.

Making multicultural processes work is essential to our success as a 21st Century society. Our nation faces complex social, political, economic and interpersonal challenges. Diverse experience, complex approaches and critical thinking are tremendous assets to us. We must learn how to value the experience and thinking that people of color possess. Diversity is absolutely essential to the vitality, strength and maintenance of our society. Valuing diversity is not just a personal preference. Nor is it something we can choose not to do. We have no choice but to draw on the rich and multifaceted experience of all peoples in this country if we are to survive and thrive.

People of color have to be minimally competent in at least two cultures to survive: their own and white mainstream culture. They have to learn to operate in white work, school and public institutions and to understand mainstream white values and norms. There are many white subcultures and many different communities of color. Insofar as most people of color are highly segregated, both from white society and from other communities of color, they also need to become more culturally competent.

The goals of multicultural competency are increased understanding, respectful communication and full inclusion of all people, not cultural competence by itself. We are striving for a democratic, anti-racist multiculturalism in which all people are part of the decision-making process. At least a minimum level of understanding, cultural competency and openness to learning from other people's cultures is a prerequisite for participating effectively.

Anti-Racism

WHY DOES ANTI-RACISM, including anti-Semitism, have to be one of the components in a multicultural process?* Isn't it enough that we are inclusive and democratic, that we are culturally competent and value diversity?

If we were starting out today, without five hundred years of history, we might be able to ignore racism and anti-Semitism. When we come together in a multicultural environment, we come in a context of white, Christian-based racism. Even if we are all included, even if we listen, value and respect each other and even if we focus on the challenges we face, we still need to address this ongoing legacy.

Anti-racism is the process of actively and consistently confronting racism and anti-Semitism wherever they occur. The only way to build a democratic multicultural society from a society dominated by white, Christian-based racism is through a commitment to use anti-racist analysis and action.

We have seen how white people hold power in ordinary interactions and in institutional settings and receive unequal and unjust benefits from the social system. We bring this history of inequality and injustice and our training in racist assumptions of power and privilege with us wherever we go. All too often people who are proponents of multiculturalism refuse to acknowledge or address the devastating effects of racism on our ability to create an inclusive process.

Other dynamics of racism make it difficult to achieve our goals unless we focus on eliminating them. For instance, people of color and Jews carry with them varying levels of distrust, unease and internalized racism and

---

* It is important to include anti-Semitism with racism because we have seen how intertwined whiteness is with Christian values. In this section, I will use the term anti-racism to include the struggle to eliminate anti-Semitism

anti-Semitism from their experience in this and other Western societies. In addition there are the many levels of institutional racism which influence particular situations. Unless we pay explicit attention to the specific, ongoing dynamics of racism, it will inevitably sabotage our efforts to build an inclusive, diverse and respectful society.

The first efforts at creating a multicultural event, program or staff may be greeted with great anticipation and fear by all parties. Whether it's a new employee of color, a new policy, inclusion of new material in a program or even one new song or book in a curriculum, pent-up feelings hoping for and fearful of change can interfere with the normal process of interaction and evaluation. That person, policy, program or item becomes the test of whether multiculturalism will work. The high stakes may well jeopardize the long-range prospects for successful change, as white people quickly judge something or someone as less than perfect, and therefore as a failure. If we pay attention to the way that racism undermines the considered responses of both white people and people of color, we are better able to counteract its effects.

A clear anti-racist agenda can also help prevent multiculturalism from being watered down. It is possible to use our emphasis on inclusiveness to divert attention from racial issues. Concerns of gender equality, sexual orientation or physical access can become dominant issues while the struggle against racism is ignored. Even concerns about anti-Semitism can play out this way if they are not understood in their relationship to racism. This occurs in part because we tend to treat any other inclusion issue as a white issue. This is another manifestation of racism.

It is often more comfortable, even if we disagree or are violently opposed to each other, to talk about lesbian and gay rights, for example, if we have created a white context. We define issues of disability, gender, class and sexual orientation as white issues, not having to do with race. (Most of us would actually say these issues are racially neutral, but in a racist society "neutral" means not taking into account the reality of racism, and therefore is a code for "white.") In trying to be so broadly inclusive we end up excluding people of color with disabilities, women of color and lesbians, gay men and bisexuals of color. Without a strong and continuous focus on racism we can end up with a group of heterosexual white men and women, white lesbians, white gay men, white people with disabilities, white Jews and some people of color who "represent" their racial groupings. This setup perpetuates racism under the guise of multiculturalism. We do need to focus on complete inclusion, but we cannot let that become a substitute for dealing with racism.

The effects of racism will linger with us for a long time, even if we immediately institute massive changes to create a democratic multicultural nation. Unchallenged racism makes a mockery of our democratic multicultural values. It turns multiculturalism into the same kind of false promise that integration has been, camouflaging the continued dominance of white people in our society. A commitment to anti-racism encourages us to pay attention to the effects that racism and anti-Semitism continue to have so that we can take action against them.

Unequal distribution of wealth is a keystone of racism. We haven't achieved much if we produce a multicultural ruling class. Our government, large corporations and other institutions are capable of becoming multicultural while continuing to exploit the majority of us.

The word "democracy" implies more than a cultural democracy where every culture is represented. We also need to make sure that the word "democratic" includes the concept of economic democracy, that this multicultural agenda includes the goal of ending economic injustice. We have already noticed sections of the African American, Latino/a, Asian American and Jewish communities who have been given economic opportunities in exchange for supporting the status quo. Without an economic analysis we can continue to support injustice while appearing multicultural.

There are many ways that inattention to the distribution of wealth can subvert our efforts at democracy. We might bring only middle or upper class people of color into the organizations we are involved with, and this will do little to redress the unequal participation of broad groups of poor and working class people of color. We can become professionals specializing in multicultural or diversity trainings, and not change the segregation in our schools, neighborhoods and work places. Diversity training now supports an industry generating millions of dollars a year for professional trainers. Multiculturalism without attention to issues of wealth and power can become a collusion among professionals, both white and of color, to maintain control of the movement to end racism and to benefit themselves.

Multiculturalism supports the articulation by each person or group of their economic, political and cultural needs and concerns. It also demands that people work toward solutions that are inclusive and for the good of everyone. We each must learn to address the entire agenda, not just our own particular concerns. There are multiple, complex issues before us, and only full inclusion and cooperation will lead to lasting democratic solutions.

This collaboration is inherently difficult because our society is large and complex, and no one can represent the interests of very many others. People of color have come together around racial identities in response to political and economic exclusion. People can act as if these racial boundaries are well drawn and clear, even though we know that they are not. We may find ourselves negotiating for the participation of people from particular racial groups in an organization, even though we know such homogeneous groups with clearly defined agendas do not exist. We must begin by focusing on the racial configurations that have developed under racism while understanding their provisional and historically contingent status.

This means that people cannot represent "their" group. A Korean American cannot speak for all Korean Americans, much less for Asian Americans or people of color. People speak as individuals, perhaps sharing interests with others. When we bring a group of diverse individuals together, they must be allowed to speak from their own understanding, experience and integrity, not as representatives of some group or constituency. We don't want multiculturalism to degenerate into a collection of individuals jockeying for power by claiming to represent different constituencies. We don't want to become complacent and believe that we understand the needs of a community of people through hearing from a few "representatives." We must eschew the tendency to think of multiculturalism as a device for representing the interests of different constituencies, while holding onto the necessity for our organizations to be diverse enough to reflect the diversity of the larger society.

We also need to be looking out for the interests of whoever is not included in the process. We can't represent them. But we can push to have the broadest possible inclusion. We should be thinking seriously about how the needs and interests of anyone not already involved can be taken into account, how their voices can be heard. In this sense multiculturalism is a strategy toward full inclusion, i.e., democracy. If any policy, practice or program labeled multicultural increases exclusion, tokenism, false representation or the unequal distribution of resources, then it is not an effective strategy for ending racial injustice.

You can become an advocate for democratic, anti-racist multiculturalism in every setting you participate in. Many of the exercises in this book have probably started you thinking about how you can be effective at work, at home, in school and in community settings. Pick a group that you are a part of, formal or informal, and use the following questions to sharpen your strategic thinking.

Questions and Actions

1. Describe the group you are thinking about in terms of composition, purpose and decision making process.

    a. Is it multicultural? Who is involved and who is excluded?

    b. Is it democratic? Who holds power and how are decisions made?

    c. Is it anti-racist? Is racism talked about and dealt with effectively within the group?

2. What needs to change?

 a. Who needs to be brought into the group?

 b. How would the group need to change to truly be open to their participation?

 c. How could the group be more democratic?

 d. How would this change affect how the group operates?

 e. What forms of racism need to be dealt with?

 f. Who can you talk with about these challenges?

 g. Who might be allies in changing the dynamics of the group?

 h. What is one thing you will do to begin this process?

 i. What fears or concerns do you have about raising these issues?

 j. What will you and the group lose if you don't raise them?

Integration and Tokenism

MANY PEOPLE OF color have expressed concern that multiculturalism will become (or already is) a new form of integration and tokenism. Unless we are vigilant it certainly can become so.

Integration is based on the belief that people of color have been segregated from the mainstream of U.S. society and need to be incorporated into it for full participation. Since the Brown vs. Board of Education decision in 1954 (and even much earlier), the discussion about racial equality in the United States has revolved around integration. I want to look at these issues more closely because they influence our efforts to build a democratic, anti-racist multiculturalism.

Our belief in the importance of integration is based on the assumption that there is one mainstream, normal set of (white) values, practices and procedures that other people can learn and adapt to. We assume that people of color want to be included in the mainstream but have previously been excluded because of prejudice and discrimination—racism.

There is real cause for concern about the exclusion of people of color from mainstream institutions in the United States. To a great extent people of color and white people live separately, pray separately, go to different schools, do different jobs and socialize separately. Insofar as people of color are not only separate but unequal, this is a tragedy of injustice, as the Supreme Court ruled in 1954.

Integration is not necessarily the solution to racism. Integration assumes that people of color will adapt to a white, mainstream way of doing things, and that the institutions they integrate into will accept them as equal

216

participants. There is certainly some question whether present U.S. institutions will ever welcome people of color as full and equal participants because of the deep levels of white culture and racism embedded in them. Many people of color also feel that having to give up cultural, traditional and ethnic ways of thinking, acting and relating to others in order to "integrate" simply maintains white power. Integration fails to address the problem of white racism. It's a form of tokenism—small or insignificant change in lieu of fundamental transformation.

The question is: "Integration into what, on whose terms?" When we assume that the terms and the institutions are fixed, we are advocating continued control by those who have traditionally held it. Under pressure from African Americans, many traditionally white colleges and universities integrated their classrooms in the 1950s and 1960s. When students of color started to demand participation in decisions about the curriculum and policies, these same institutions reacted by calling the students ungrateful and irresponsible. When students demanded that the faculty and administration include people of color, with the power to make decisions, school officials dismissed such demands as impossible.

Today, over thirty years after integration of those schools, most public and private school administrators, deans and professors are white. Obviously most college and university student bodies are integrated to varying degrees. Just as obviously white people remain at the center of power and decision making. This "you can join us, but we're going to keep control" form of integration does not deal with the fundamental inequalities of racism.

Not everyone wants to be integrated. Some people of color are cynical about the ability of white people to fully accept them as equals. Others are skeptical about most white people's willingness to seriously question their own privilege. Many people of color have rich cultures, practices and identities they don't want to give up. There are some Native Americans and Black Nationalists who want cultural and political sovereignty. Still others are only willing to integrate into democratic, multicultural and explicitly anti-racist institutions because only these will protect them from further white racism.

We need to develop a much more sophisticated view of racial progress in which we don't make assumptions about what people of color want or don't want. In some cases, for some people, integration is an appropriate strategy. In other cases it may be a step backwards. In still others, it may be a way to sidestep demands for justice. Integration can only be a strategy for justice and equality, not a goal. As a goal, it too often leads to various forms of tokenism and isolation.

Tokenism plays out in our society in many stages. When people of color demand greater power and participation they meet with white resistance at each stage. White people seldom voluntarily give up control or willingly look at our role in resisting change. If people of color push hard enough, we slowly and reluctantly accept their participation. We meet each stage with cries of, "We've already done so much, what more do they want?" or "They're so unappreciative of what we've done, they'll never be satisfied until they control everything," or "We're moving as fast as we can." All the tactics of denial, minimization, blame and counterattack discussed in Part I are marshalled to justify the slow pace toward equal participation.

The first and simplest stage of tokenism occurs when a small and insignificant number of people of color are allowed to integrate a school or workplace. Or we add a few names and pictures of people of color to a textbook or a wall. We treat people of color and their contributions as the exception. People of color are extremely isolated in these situations and acutely vulnerable to personal abuse. They do not have much support and usually succeed only if they thoroughly internalize the values of the institution.

Another early stage of token integration occurs when white people include only those people of color who fit a certain mold or support the traditional values of the institution. Any who might challenge traditional patterns are screened out, isolated, fired or otherwise neutralized. People of color are accepted for their decorative role and to deflect concerns about discrimination or diversity, not to be full participants.

This is also the stage where we quote particular people of color, such as well-off men in academia or politics like Shelby Steele, Clarence Thomas or Thomas Sowell, to give a seal of approval to our policies and statements.

These tactics may not work to derail integration. There may be significant numbers of people of color who are demanding equality. We will then seek input from people of color. We allow them to speak out or testify, we study the situation, we do research and we remain in control. This process creates the illusion of participation, but there is still no sharing of power.

This stage might be coupled with another form of tokenism which involves paying attention to racism only when people of color are in the room, outside the door or in the streets. When they are not visibly present, it is business as usual. Racism is viewed as a problem for people of color and only of incidental concern to the main business of the organization.

If these tactics don't succeed in quelling protest, white people will give up some control, but only in special areas that are deemed culturally appropriate to people of color. We may allow them to teach in ethnic studies departments but not in the sciences, or to write about news in their community but not about mainstream events.

These are some of the ways that white people control the participation of people of color and prevent a democratic multiculturalism from developing. Each involves a token form of integration in which white people retain ultimate power and control.

Many organizations can look multicultural from the outside—they are often intended to. Multiculturalism can become token integration hiding our failure to redistribute power and resources. To break these patterns of white control we must see through these tactics and understand why the democratic and anti-racist components of multiculturalism are crucial. Most importantly, we must be willing to share power.

We should be actively organizing to create a democratic, anti-racist, multicultural process in our workplaces, schools, police and fire departments, religious organizations, athletic clubs, unions and city, state and national governments. The assessments we did in the last section can be guidelines for proceeding. The four key questions are:

1. Is this organization multicultural?

2. Is it democratic?

3. Is it anti-racist (and anti-sexist, etc.)?

4. What are you going to do about it?

Up to this point we have been talking about institutions that may have more effect on us than we have on them. There is much that we can do to change them, particularly if we work in concert with others. But they can present formidable challenges to our ability to organize and sustain social action.

There is one institution over which we have a lot of control. It is a place where we can work to make changes with the people who are closest to us. This is a place where we can practice the skills we want to develop and model the kind of society we want to build. This is a place which can nurture and sustain our struggles against social injustice "out there." This place is at home with our family.

Home and Family

VERY OFTEN WE think of racism as an issue out there, in the community. We don't think of social action as including how we live with other family members. The walls separating us from the community are permeable, and racism doesn't stop at the door. This section will give you ideas for eliminating racism in the ways you live with others and raise your children.

Although your family members may all be white and your neighbors appear so, there may well be people of other cultures, people in interracial families, people of mixed heritage or people who are passing as white among your friends. People of color may also be providing services for you, your children, your apartment, house or yard. Our environment is seldom as white as we assume it to be because we generally don't notice people of color when their presence doesn't challenge our sense of their proper role.

Our homes are less separable from the greater community than they have ever been. They are connected to the outside world through TV, including cable channels, computer games, the internet, toys, music from CD's, cassettes and radio, books, magazines, the daily newspaper and direct market catalogs. Each of these provide vehicles for racism to enter your home and opportunities to respond to it.

Is racism talked about where you live? When you and other family members watch a movie, discuss the news or talk about daily events is racism noticed and talked about?

Talking about racism is not easy for most of us to do. Few of us grew up in homes where racism or other difficult and emotional issues were talked about at all. We come from backgrounds of silence, ignorance or a false belief that to talk about racism is to further it. When talk about race did occur, some of us experienced conflict with family members because we disagreed over racial issues. We can acknowledge and overcome these past experiences and create an atmosphere in our own homes where issues of race, gender or class can be openly and respectfully talked about.

We have an impact on family, friends and neighbors by the physical environment we create in our home. Do the calendars, pictures and posters on your walls reflect the diverse society we live in? Are there books by women and men, lesbian, straight and gay people from many different cultures? Are there magazines from communities of color? We don't get extra points if there are. Nor are we trying to create an ethnic museum. But paying attention to our environment broadens our perspective and counters the stream of negative racial stereotypes which otherwise enter our home through the media.

It is even more important to discuss racism and to pay attention to our home if we have children. As responsible parents we need to think about the toys, games, computer games, dolls, books and pictures that our young ones are exposed to. It is not just children of color who need Latino/a, Asian American, Native American, and African American dolls. It is not just children of color who are hurt by computer games that portray people of color as evil, dangerous and expendable.

I am not recommending that you purge your house of favorite games and toys or become fanatical about the racism you find in your child's life. Children don't need to be protected from racism. They see it all the time. They need to be given critical thinking tools for recognizing, analyzing and responding to the different forms that racism takes. Discussing the racism (or sexism) in a children's book or movie, helping them think about the injustices of racism, and providing alternative, anti-racist materials—all these contribute to your children's awareness and their ability to respond to injustice.

You might want to initiate family discussions about racism by talking about this book and how you don't want your home to support racism. You can describe what racism is and how it affects white people and people of color in terms appropriate for the ages of your children. You can solicit their help in doing an assessment of your home and thinking about how different games, books, videos or posters might be racist.

Let your children help decide what to do to make your home different. It is one thing to create an anti-racist, multicultural environment by yourself. It is an entirely different level of education, empowerment and activism to include your children as valued participants in the process. The goal is not to create an ethnic museum but to acknowledge and celebrate the diversity of people and cultures represented in our society.

Obviously, this kind of assessment and interactive process should address issues of gender, class, disability, sexual orientation and religious and cultural difference as well as race. We don't want to foster stereotypes that people of color are not also women, poor or working class, people with disabilities, lesbian, gay or bisexual and/or Moslem, Buddhist or Jewish. These issues are inseparable. When dealt with in a context of social justice, young people are quick to develop principles of fair treatment and equality, eager to become co-participants in creating a healthier environment and challenging injustice. They may well end up inspiring and leading us with their readiness to challenge authority, take risks and stand up for fairness.

Questions and Actions

1. Were people of color and racism talked about in your childhood home? Think about particular incidents when it was. Was there tension around it? What was the general tone? Who initiated discussions and who resisted them?

2. Were Jews, the Holocaust, or anti-Semitism talked about? Think about particular incidents. What was the general tone? Who initiated discussions, and how was tension handled if there was any?

3. Was there silence in your home on issues of racism or anti-Semitism? What did you learn from the silence?

4. Was there conflict within your family because of racism or anti-Semitism (over integration, interracial or interfaith dating, music, busing)? Think of particular incidents. How was the conflict dealt with?

5. Were there people of color who cared for you, your parents, building, house or yard? If so, how were they treated? How did their presence and your family's attitudes toward them influence you?

6. As a child, what stories, TV shows or books influenced you the most in your attitudes about people of color? About Jews? What do you carry with you from that exposure?

7. Talk with your partner, housemates and friends about these issues. Notice the whiteness of your surroundings out loud to family and friends. This needn't be done aggressively or with great anger. You don't need to attack other people. Ask questions, notice things out loud, express your concerns and give other people room to think about and respond to what you say.

8. If you did a room-by-room assessment of your home today would you find a diversity of images and items?

9. If the answer to #8 is no, what do you and other family members lose because of that lack? How does it contribute to racial prejudice and discrimination?

10. Bring up feelings or thoughts about reading this book at dinner or other family time. What is difficult or awkward about doing this? What is the response?

11. Do an assessment of your home including the following items:
   a. books
   b. posters

      c. cookbooks

      d. calendars

      e. paintings

      d. magazines

      f. newspapers

      g. videos

      h. games

      i. computer games

      j. toys

      k. art materials

      l. religious articles

      m. sports paraphernalia

      n. music

12. What would you like to remove?

13. What would you like to add to what you have? (Try to go beyond the tokenism of putting up pictures of Martin Luther King, Jr. or Michael Jorden or adding a book or two to your children's collection). Explore the roles and contributions of people of color in areas where you and other family members share an interest, such as sports, science, music, reading or movies.

14. Are women well represented in the items in your home? Are poor and working class people? Are people with disabilities? Are Moslems, Jews and Buddhists? Are lesbians and gay men? Are children? Are the creations of children themselves included?

15. Do you employ people of color? How well are they paid? How well are they treated? How do your children respond and relate to them? How will you talk with your children about these relationships? How will you balance these relationships with friends and neighbors from different cultures who are not employees? Are your children exposed to professionals such as teachers, doctors and dentists who are people of color? How could you increase such exposure?

    These are small, personal steps, but they have two important consequences. The more contact we have with people of color and with images and information about them, the more we are motivated and equipped to challenge racism. We are able to see more clearly the tremendous gap between average white perceptions about people of color and the lives and communities of people of color themselves. This awareness can guide our action and enrich our lives.

    Second, we prepare our children to notice how racism operates and to become champions for racial justice. There are resources in the bibliography for enhancing your parenting skills and continuing this process.

For the Long Haul

RACISM IS NOT going to end tomorrow or next year. Every delay and setback saps our strength and strains our hope. It is easy to despair, easy to give up. How do we nurture and sustain ourselves for what may well be a lifetime struggle? How do we keep alive the vision of racial justice and multicultural democracy that guides our action?

This section describes ways to approach social justice work that sustain our efforts. The first step is to stop and think about how we are taking care of ourselves for the long term. Our guilt, desperation, anger, fear, the immediate pressure of events or even our enthusiasm, may make it difficult for us to think about how to keep going after this next action, campaign or crisis.

If we are not thinking about how to nurture ourselves in the coming years, we are probably also not thinking strategically about the future. We may have become bogged down reacting to everyday events. We may have lost sight of our goals, not noticed how the world is changing and forgotten that we are going to have to renew ourselves to remain effective.

We need to create time in our over-worked, over-committed lives to reflect on the future. Some of us do this best alone, others with friends and family. In either case we must start with time for reflection.

Take a moment to think about how you center your energy or calm yourself amidst the pressures and stress of your daily routines? How could you strengthen this part of your life.

Reflection is a spiritual practice for some of us. Any spiritual practice that connects us to a reality greater than our individual lives—that connects us to other people, to animal and plant life and/or to a larger energy in the world—can increase our respect for life and our valuing of difference. It can renew and guide our pursuit for a better world. We each have, or can find, our own unique way to reflect and connect. What activities help you connect to a greater reality? How could these activities support your work for social justice? How might you create more time for reflection in your life?

We also need to take care of ourselves physically and emotionally. We need to live as if we wanted to be alive when our visions are realized. It goes without saying that we need to eat, exercise, relax, have fun, play, enjoy and smile. Yet how many of us don't take these parts of our lives seriously until we can't continue our work because of exhaustion or poor health? How do we expect to continue in the struggle? What are we modeling for the young people around us?

For those who are from white Christian backgrounds there may be a big dichotomy between work and leisure. Taking care of oneself, goofing off, having fun may seem self-indulgent, even sinful. Some people can even turn exercise and other forms of recreation into work, cancelling out some of their value to us. These attitudes can also make it difficult to exult in the singing, dance, drama and other celebratory rituals that can be so renewing to our lives.

Reclaiming or developing cultural rituals can heal and reinvigorate us. Rituals build community, connect people, and inspire new visions and strategies. Singing or going to hear music, writing, reading or listening to a poem, participating in a holiday ritual, sharing a meal with friends—we need to allow ourselves the cultural activities that nurture our souls.

Mainstream male, white and Christian traditions also push people to be rugged individuals. The message is, "Go it alone." There is an individual path to salvation, and people shouldn't make mistakes or ask for help. We become isolated, scared, confused and lost. We don't know where to turn for support. Many of us find it easier to support others than to ask for help. We have to overcome our pride and fear to admit that we can't do it all by ourselves.

We can't fight racism alone. We can't create social justice by ourselves. Cultural activities and broad-based community support and action networks are essential to sustain us in this work. Friends, family members and community networks keep us connected, supported and inspired. They help us maintain perspective on who we are and what we can do. Working with others aids us in evaluating what we can or cannot take on, what our share is.

Who are family and friends you could talk with about doing racial justice work? Who will you talk with first?

Who are co-workers who might help you form a racial justice action/support network? Who will you talk with first?

Who are people of color that you know or know of that you want to talk with about fighting racism? List the one you will talk with first. Ask if he or she has time and is willing to do this with you.

Name one network, action committee or support group that you are going to join.

Taking care of ourselves through healthy lifestyles, rituals, cultural activities and support networks builds and sustains a community of people dedicated to the struggle for social justice.

What kind of cultural events, rituals or celebrations have inspired you to fight racism? What kind of cultural activity brings you together with others? Which ones renew your spirit?

Finally, we need to celebrate our successes, no matter how small; our victories, no matter how tenuous. We need to see how far we've come as well as how far there is to go. Although racism is still a central constituent of American life, we have made progress, things have changed. They have changed because multitudes of courageous people of color and white people have fought, resisted and refused to be overwhelmed by racism. They have changed because the human spirit is indomitable and we each share that spirit. We can only sustain our efforts by building on and celebrating the achievements of the vast numbers of people who have contributed to getting us as far as we are today. How could you make your work to end racism an honoring and a celebration of the efforts of those who have preceded you?

Conclusion

A *FEW YEARS* ago my colleagues at the Oakland Men's Project and I did a five-day workshop in Ohio in which we focused extensively on racism. Six months later we were back for a two-day follow-up with the same participants. To start the workshop we asked them to talk about how the previous workshop had affected them.

I sat listening to several people describe how the workshop had changed their understanding of racism, how it had affected their relationships with co-workers and how it had sensitized them to racial injustice in their community. I was pleased that our work had a positive impact, but was a little uneasy without knowing why. Finally a white man, Mark, began to speak.

> That workshop has influenced me in more ways than I can say. But I think it made the biggest difference at work. This fall we needed to hire five new staff (he works at a large county social service agency) and I made sure that three of those five people were people of color because our staff has been mostly white until now.

"That's it," I said to myself, realizing what had been missing from the others' accounts.

It is important for us to unlearn prejudice, broaden our understanding of racism and learn to recognize racist acts when we see them. But unless we are actively involved in the fight against racism we haven't taken it far enough. Mark understood that he needed to take his awareness and turn it into concrete action. He changed his workplace. He didn't just try to get one person of color into the organization because he knew that one person would probably not have lasted long. He wanted to make a significant impact so he focused on the difficult but reachable goal of making three of the five new hires people of color.

Mark was not a high level manager or director. When I talked with him later he described in more detail what he had done. It had taken him many discussions both one-on-one and with the full staff to convince his peers and supervisors of the importance of hiring qualified people of color. He had prepared a staff presentation about racism, looking at the agency, its staff, policies and clientele. He had lobbied long and hard, at some personal risk, to convince people that they needed to address racism concretely in their hiring practices. He had helped with the job search and interviewing so that qualified candidates would be found. Now he was supporting the new staff as they came on line.

We don't always have the visible impact Mark had in fighting racism. Even if he had not been able to diversify the staff, he would have made a difference. By raising the issue of racism within the organization he was questioning established patterns and expectations. He challenged everyone to rethink how hiring was done and what the implications were for the organization and for the community.

Sometimes change comes not in the first round, but at the second, third or fourth. Change starts with one person questioning, challenging, speaking up and doing something to make a difference. We can each make a difference.

We can make a difference because each of us is already part of the community where racism exists and thrives. We are connected to neighborhoods, workplaces, schools and religious organizations. Our connections, our relationships, our positions in these organizations give us some leverage to make a difference.

This book is intended to be provocative rather than definitive. I have tried to draw a balance between the need to understand the issues and the need to take effective action to confront racism. Both understanding and action are needed, one to guide and nourish the other.

It is difficult to know what to do in these tumultuous times. Some white people are trying to extend the roots of racial injustice more deeply into the foundations of our society. There is no broad progressive movement of people to challenge injustice on any front, much less on racism. It looks like we have made progress in some areas and lost ground in others. People of color have many different strategies for challenging racism, some of which seem confusing or contradictory to us. There is no one to turn to for a simple answer to the question "What should we do to end racism?"

I have tried to show that there is much to be done without our having all the answers, if we pay attention. What should we pay attention to?

The actual difference that race makes today in our society.

The configuration of economic, political and social power and privilege on which racial injustice is based.

What people of color and white people have done in the past to make a difference.

The effects of our actions so we can refine our strategies and become more effective in the future.

How people of color are building communities and resisting racism.

What people of color say about what they need from white people.

What tactics white people are using to resist progress toward equality.

How we can build democratic, anti-racist multicultural organizations as we begin building alternatives to inequality and injustice.

And finally, we should notice and celebrate all the ways that white people and people of color are taking steps to end racism.

We can intervene at work, at home, in our schools, in the criminal justice system and in areas of public policy as well as in our interpersonal relationships. We can focus on different "racial" groupings of people and challenge the particular ways each group experiences racism. We can assess our strengths and sources of power and resources to see where we can leverage the most support as a personal ally for people of color. In all of this we must understand the complexities of how racism works without becoming paralyzed by our understanding. We can acknowledge the depth of our emotional response to racism without becoming paralyzed by our feelings. We can join and strengthen the efforts of vast numbers of white people who have always fought against racial injustice.

In the beginning of this book I said that we all need to get on the lines to fight the fires of racial injustice. I did not mean that we should rush about simply reacting to racist acts and policies. For us to be able to sleep in peace in our homes without the threat of fire, everyone else must be able to sleep in peace with a roof over their heads and the conditions of conflagration eliminated. Building a democratic, anti-racist, multicultural society is the only way to provide us with that deep level of security. Nothing less will do because only justice will put out the fire.

Bibliography

Abrams, Grace Contrino. *Creative Conflict Solving for Kids*. Miami Beach, Fla.: Peace Education Foundation Inc., 1986.

Acuna, Rodolfo. *Occupied America: A History of Chicanos* (2nd ed.). New York: Harper and Row, 1981.

Adair, Margo and Sharon Howell. *The Subjective Side of Politics, Breaking Old Patterns, Weaving New Ties: Alliance Building*, and *Democracy at Work*. San Francisco: Tools for Change, 1988, 1990, 1995. (Tools for Change, P.O. Box 14141, San Francisco, Calif., 94114.)

Adleman, Jeanne and Gloria Enguidanos, eds. *Racism in the Lives of Women: Testimony, Theory and Guides to Antiracism Practice*. New York: Harrington Park Press, 1995.

Aguilar-San Juan, Karin, ed. *The State of Asian America: Activism and Resistance in the 1990s*. Boston: South End Press, 1994.

Albrecht, Lisa and Rose M. Brewer, eds. *Bridges of Power: Women's Multicultural Alliances*. Philadelphia and Gabriola Island, B.C.: New Society Publishers, 1990.

Allen, Paula Gunn. *The Sacred Hoop: Recovering the Feminine in American Indian Traditions*. Boston: Beacon Press, 1986.

Allen, Robert. *Black Awakening in Capitalist America: An Analytic History*. Cambridge, Mass.: MIT Press, 1970.

Allen, Theodore W. *The Invention of the White Race*. London: Verso, 1994.

Allport, Gordon. *The Nature of Prejudice*. New York: Doubleday, 1954.

Almaguer, Tomas. *Racial Fault Lines: The Historical Origins of White Supremacy in California*. Berkeley, Calif.: Univ. of California Press, 1994.

Amott, Teresa and Julie Matthaei. *Race, Gender, and Work: A Multicultural Economic History of Women in the United States*. Boston: South End Press, 1991.

Andersen, Margaret. *Thinking about Women: Sociological Perspectives on Sex and Gender*. New York: Macmillan, 1988.

Anthias, Floya, and Nira Yuval-Davis with Harriet Cain. *Racialized Boundaries: Race, Nation, Gender, Colour and Class and the Anti-Racist Struggle.* New York: Routledge, 1992.

Anzaldua, Gloria, ed. *Making Faces, Making Soul, Hacienda Caras: Creative and Critical Perspectives by Women of Color.* San Francisco: Aunt Lute Foundation Books, 1990.

Aptheker, Herbert, ed. *A Documentary History of the Negro People in the United States.* New York: Citadel Press, 1964.

Arendt, Hannah. *Antisemitism: Part One of The Origins of Totalitarianism.* New York: Harcourt, Brace and World, 1968.

Arnett, Ronald C. *Applying Nonviolence to Everyday Relationships.* Elgin, Ill.: Brethren Press, 1980.

Balbus, Isaac. *Marxism and Domination.* Princeton, N.J.: Princeton Univ. Press, 1982.

Barkan, Elazar. *The Retreat of Scientific Racism: Changing Concepts of Race in Britain and the United States Between the World Wars.* New York: Cambridge Univ. Press, 1992.

Barlett, Donald L. and James B. Steele. *America: Who Really Pays the Taxes?* New York: Simon & Schuster, 1994.

Barndt, Joseph. *Dismantling Racism: The Continuing Challenge to White America.* Minneapolis: Augsburg, 1991

Barrera, Mario. *Race and Class in the Southwest.* North Bend, Ind.: Univ. of Notre Dame Press, 1979.

Beam, Joseph, ed. *In the Life: A Black Gay Anthology.* Boston: Alyson Publications, 1986.

Beck, Evelyn Torton, ed. *Nice Jewish Girls: A Lesbian Anthology.* Watertown, Mass.: Persephone Press, 1982.

Bell, Derrick. *Faces at the Bottom of the Well: The Permanence of Racism.* New York: HarperCollins, 1992.

Bennett, Lerone Jr. *Before the Mayflower: A History of Black America.* Chicago: Johnson Publishing, 1986.

Bernal, Martin. *Black Athena: The Afroasiatic Roots of Classical Civilization.* New Brunswick, N.J.: Rutgers Univ. Press, 1987.

Biale, David. *Power and Powerlessness in Jewish History.* New York: Schocken Books, 1987.

Black Scholar, ed. *Court of Appeal: The Black Community Speaks Out on the Racial and Sexual Politics of Thomas vs. Hill.* New York: Ballantine, 1992.

Blauner, Bob. *Black Lives, White Lives: Three Decades of Race Relations in America.* Berkeley, Calif.: Univ. of California Press, 1989.

Blee, Kathleen. *Women of the Klan: Racism and Gender in the 1920s.* Berkeley, Calif.: Univ. of California Press, 1991.

Boxill, Bernard R. *Blacks and Social Justice.* Lanham, Md.: Rowman and Littlefield, 1984.

Brant, Beth, ed. *A Gathering of Spirit: Writing and Art by North American Indian Women.* Rockland, Maine: Sinister Wisdom Books, 1984.

Brod, Harry, ed. *A Mensch Among Men: Explorations in Jewish Masculinity.* Freedom, Calif.: Crossing Press, 1988.

Brown, Dee. *Bury My Heart at Wounded Knee: An Indian History of the American West.* New York: Bantam, 1970.

Bulkin, Elly, Minnie Bruce Pratt, and Barbara Smith. *Yours in Struggle: Three Feminist Perspectives on Anti-Semitism and Racism.* Ithaca, N.Y.: Firebrand, 1984/1988.

Butler, Judith. *Gender Trouble: Feminism and the Subversion of Identity.* New York: Routledge, 1990.

Camper, Carol, ed. *Miscegenation Blues: Voices of Mixed Race Women.* Toronto: Sister Vision, 1994.

Caraway, Nancie. *Segregated Sisterhood: Racism and the Politics of American Feminism.* Knoxville, Tenn.: Univ. of Tennessee Press, 1991.

Carlsson Paige, Nancy and Diane E. Levin. *Helping Young Children Understand Peace, War, and the Nuclear Threat.* Washington, D.C.: National Association for the Education of Young Children, 1985.

Carlsson Paige, Nancy and Diane E. Levin. *Who's Calling the Shots: How to Respond Effectively to Children's Fascination with War Play and War Toys.* Philadelphia and Gabriola Island, B.C.: New Society Publishers, 1990.

Center for Contemporary Cultural Studies, ed. *The Empire Strikes Back: Race and Racism in 1970s Britain.* London: Hutchinson, 1982.

Chesler, Phyllis. *Mothers On Trial: The Battle for Children and Custody.* Seattle: Seal Press, 1987.

chideya, farai. *Don't Believe the Hype: Fighting Cultural Misinformation about African Americans.* New York: Plume, 1995.

Churchill, Ward. *Indians Are Us? Culture and Genocide in Native North America.* Monroe, Maine: Common Courage Press, 1994.

Churchill, Ward. *Fantasies of the Master Race: Literature, Cinema and the Colonization of American Indians.* Monroe, Maine: Common Couarge Press, 1992.

Churchill, Ward, ed. *Marxism and Native Americans.* Boston: South End Press, 1983.

Chutzpah Collective. *Chutzpah: A Jewish Liberation Anthology.* San Francisco: New Glide Publications, 1977.

Cleage, Pearl. *Deals with the Devil and Other Reasons to Riot.* New York: Ballantine, 1993.

Collins, Patricia Hill. *Black Feminist Thought: Knowledge, Consciousness, and the Politics of Empowerment.* Boston: Unwin Hyman, 1990.

Connell, R. W. *Gender and Power.* Stanford, Calif.: Stanford Univ. Press, 1987.

Cose, Ellis. *The Rage of a Privileged Class.* New York: HarperCollins, 1993.

Cottle, Thomas J. *Black Children, White Dreams.* New York: Delta Book, Dell Publishing, 1974.

Council on Interracial Books for Children Bulletin. *Children, Race and Racism: How Race Awareness Develops.* Vol. 11, nos. 3–4. New York: Council on Interracial Books for Children, 1980.

Council on Interracial Books for Children. *Guidelines for Selecting Bias Free Textbooks and Storybooks.* New York: Council on Interracial Books for Children.

Crary, Elizabeth. *Kids Can Cooperate: A Practical Guide to Teaching Problem Solving.* Seattle: Parenting Press, 1984.

Creative Teaching Press *Rainbow Activities: Fifty Multicultural/Human Relations Experiences.* South El Monte, Calif.: Creative Teaching Press, 1977.

Creighton, Allan and Paul Kivel. *Young Men's Work: Building Skills to Stop Violence.* Minneapolis: Hazelden, 1995.

Creighton, Allan with Paul Kivel. *Helping Teens Stop Violence: A Practical Guide for Counselors, Educators, and Parents.* Alameda, Calif: Hunter House, 1992.

D'Emilio, John and Estelle Freedman. *Intimate Matters: A History of Sexuality in American.* New York: Harper & Row, 1988.

Davis, Angela Y. *Women, Race & Class.* New York: Random House, 1981.

Davis, Angela Y. *Women, Culture, Politics.* New York: Vintage Books, 1989.

Day, Kathleen. *Savings and Loan Hell: The People and the Politics Behind the $1 Trillion Savings and Loan Scandel.* New York: W. W. Norton and Company, 1993.

Derman-Sparks, Louise and the A.B.C. Task Force. *Anti-Bias Curriculum: Tools for Empowering Young Children.* Washington, D.C.: National Association for the Education of Young Children, 1989.

Dinnerstein, Leonard. *Natives and Strangers: Blacks, Indians, and Immigrants in America.* New York: Oxford Univ. Press, 1979.

Dobash, R. Emerson and Russell Dobash. *Women, Violence and Social Change.* New York: Routledge, 1992.

Domhoff, G. William. *Who Rules America Now: How the "Power Elite" Dominates Business, Government, and Society.* New York: Touchstone Books, 1983.

Dorn, Lois. *Peace in the Family, A Workbook of Ideas and Actions.* New York: Pantheon Books, 1983.

Drew, Naomi. *Learning the Skills of Peacemaking.* Rolling Hills Estates, Calif.: Jalmar Press, 1987.

Drinnon, Richard. *The Metaphysics of Indian-Hating and Empire-Building.* Minneapolis: Univ. of Minnesota Press, 1980.

Du Bois, W.E.B. *Black Reconstruction in America: An Essay Toward a History of the Part Which Black Folk Played in the Attempt to Reconstruct Democracy in America, 1860–1880.* New York: Atheneum, 1977.

Dumas, Lynne S. *Talking with Your Child about a Troubled World.* New York: Fawcett Columbine, 1992.

Durning, Alan Thein. *How Much is Enough: The Consumer Society and the Future of the Earth.* New York: W.W. Norton, 1992.

Duvall, Lynn. *Respecting Our Differences: A Guide to Getting Along in a Changing World.* Minneapolis: Free Spirit Publishing, 1994.

Dyson, Michael Eric. *Reflecting Black: African American Cultural Criticism.* Minneapolis: Univ. of Minnesota, 1993.

Easlea, Brian. *Witch Hunting, Magic, and the New Philosophy.* Brighton, England: Harvester Press, 1980.

Edsall, Thomas Byrne with Mary Edsall. *Chain Reaction: The Impact of Race, Rights and Taxes on American Politics.* New York: Norton, 1992.

Ehrenreich, Barbara. *Fear of Falling: The Inner Life of the Middle Class.* New York: HarperCollins, 1990.

Enloe, Cynthia. *Bananas, Beaches and Bases: Making Feminist Sense of International Politics.* Berkeley, Calif.: Univ. of California Press, 1990.

Enloe, Cynthia. *The Morning After: Sexual Politics at the End of the Cold War.* Berkeley, Calif.: Univ. of California Press, 1993.

Espiritu, Yen Le. *Asian American Panethnicity: Bridging Institutions and Identities.* Philadelphia: Temple Univ. Press, 1992.

Essed, Philomena. *Everyday Racism.* Alameda, Calif.: Hunter House, 1991.

Essed, Philomena. *Understanding Everyday Racism: An Interdisciplinary Theory.* Newbury Park, Calif.: Sage Publications, 1991.

Evans, Sara. *Personal Politics: The Origins of the Women's Liberation Movement in the Civil Rights Movement and the New Left.* New York: Vintage, 1980.

Ezorsky, Gertrude. *Racism and Justice: The Case for Affirmative Action.* Ithaca, N.Y.: Cornell Univ. Press, 1991.

Fanon, Frantz. *The Wretched of the Earth.* (trans. Constance Farrington). New York: Grove, 1963.

Fanon, Frantz. *Black Skin, White Masks.* (trans. Charles Markmann). New York: Grove, 1967.

Fausto-Sterling, Augusta. *Myths of Gender: Biological Theories about Women and Men.* New York: Basic Books, 1985.

Feagin, Joe R. and Vera Hernan. *White Racism: The Basics.* New York: Routledge, 1995.

Featherston, Elena, ed. *Skin Deep: Women Writing on Color, Culture and Identity.* Freedom, Calif.: Crossing Press, 1994.

Fleugelman, Andrew, ed. *The New Games Book.* Garden City, N.J.: Doubleday, 1976.

Fluegelman, Andrew, ed. *More New Games and Playful Ideas.* Garden City, N.J.: Doubleday, 1981.

Ford, Clyde W. *We Can All Get Along: 50 Steps You Can Take to Help End Racism.* New York: Dell, 1994.

Frankenberg, Ruth. *The Social Construction of Whiteness: White Women, Race Matters.* Minneapolis: Univ. of Minnesota, 1993.

Franklin, Raymond S. *Shadows of Race and Class.* Minneapolis: Univ. of Minnesota Press, 1991.

Fraser, Steven, ed. *The Bell Curve Wars: Race, Intelligence and the Future of America.* New York: Basic Books, 1995.

Freire, Paulo. *Pedagogy of the Oppressed.* New York: Continuum, 1970.

Friesel, Evyatar. *Atlas of Modern Jewish History.* Oxford: Oxford Univ. Press, 1990.

Frye, Marilyn. *Willful Virgin: Essays in Feminism.* Freedom, Calif.: Crossing Press, 1992.

Frye, Marilyn. *The Politics of Reality: Essays in Feminist Theory.* Freedom, Calif.: Crossing Press, 1983.

Fulani, Lenora, ed. *The Psychopathology of Everyday Racism and Sexism.* New York: Harrington Park Press, 1988.

Fussell, Paul. *Class: A Guide Through the American Status System.* New York: Summit Books, 1983.

Gabelko, Nina Hersch and John U. Michaelis. *Reducing Adolescent Prejudice: A Handbook.* New York: Teachers College Press, 1981.

Garcia, Richard A., ed. *The Chicanos in America, 1540–1974.* Dobbs Ferry, N.Y.: Oceana Press, 1977.

Garry, Ann and Marilyn Pearsall, eds. *Women, Knowledge, and Reality: Explorations in Feminist Philosophy.* Boston: Unwin Hyman, 1989.

Gates, Henry Louis Jr., ed. *"Race," Writing, and Difference.* Chicago: Univ. of Chicago Press, 1986.

Gerber, David A., ed. *Anti-Semitism in American History.* Urbana, Ill.: Univ. of Illinois Press, 1987.

Gibbs, Jewelle Taylor, ed. *Young, Black and Male in America: An Endangered Species.* New York: Auburn House, 1988.

Giddings, Paula. *When and Where I Enter: The Impact of Black Women on Race and Sex in America.* New York: Bantam Books, 1985.

Gilbert, Martin. *Atlas of Jewish History.* New York: William Morrow and Company, 1992.

Gilman, Sander. *Difference and Pathology: Stereotypes of Sexuality, Race, and Madness.* Ithaca, N.Y.: Cornell Univ. Press, 1985.

Gilroy, Paul. *There Ain't No Black in the Union Jack: The Cultural Politics of Race and Nation.* Chicago: Univ. of Chicago Press, 1987.

Giovanni, Nikki. *Racism 101.* New York: William Morrow and Company, 1994.

Gitlin, Todd, ed. *Watching Television.* New York: Pantheon, 1986.

Glassman, Bernard. *Anti-Semitic Stereotypes Without Jews: Images of the Jews in England 1290–1700.* Detroit: Wayne State Univ. Press, 1975.

Goldberg, David Theo, ed. *Anatomy of Racism.* Minneapolis: Univ. of Minnesota, 1990.

Goldberg, David Theo and Michael Krausz, eds. *Jewish Identity.* Philadelphia: Temple Univ. Press, 1993.

Gooding-Williams, Robert, ed. *Reading Rodney King, Reading Urban Uprising.* New York: Routledge, 1993.

Goodman, Mary Ellen. *Race Awareness in Young Children.* New York: Collier Books, 1964.

Goonatilake, Susantha. *Aborted Discovery: Science and Creativity in the Third World.* London: Zed Books, 1984.

Gould, Carol C., ed. *Beyond Domination: New Perspectives on Women and Philosophy.* Totowa, N.J.: Littlefield, Adams, 1983.

Gould, Stephen J. *Ever Since Darwin: Reflections in Natural History.* New York: W.W. Norton and Company, 1977.

Gould, Stephen J. *The Mismeasure of Man.* New York: W.W. Norton, 1981.

Grahn, Judy. *Another Mother Tongue: Gay Words, Gay Worlds.* Boston: Beacon Press, 1984.

Gramsci, Antonio. *Selections from the Prison Notebooks.* New York: International Publishers, 1971.

Greenberg, Selma. *Right From the Start: A Guide to Non-sexist Child Rearing.* Boston: Houghton Mifflin, 1979.

Gross, Beatrice and Ronald Gross, eds. *The Children's Rights Movement: Overcoming the Oppression of Young People.* Garden City, N.Y.: Doubleday, 1977.

Guha, Ranajit and Gayatri Chakravorty Spivak, eds. *Selected Subaltern Studies.* New York: Oxford Univ. Press, 1988.

Guinier, Lani. *The Tyranny of the Majority: Fundamental Fairness and Representative Democracy.* New York: Free Press, 1994.

Guthrie, Robert V. *Even the Rat Was White: A Historical View of Psychology.* New York: Harper & Row, 1976.

Gwaltney, John Langston. *Drylongso: A Self-Portrait of Black America.* New York: Vintage Book, 1980.

Hacker, Andrew. *Two Nations: Black and White, Separate, Hostile, Unequal.* New York: Ballantine, 1992.

Haessly, Jacqueline. *Peacemaking: Family Activities for Justice and Peace.* New York: Paulist Press, 1980.

Hansen, Karen V. and Ilene J. Philipson, eds. *Women, Class, and the Feminist Imagination: A Socialist-Feminist Reader.* Philadelphia: Temple Univ. Press, 1990.

Haraway, Donna. *Primate Visions: Gender, Race and Nature in the World of Modern Science.* New York: Routledge, 1989.

Harding, Sandra, ed. *The "Racial" Economy of Science: Toward a Democratic Future.* Bloomington, Ind.: Indiana Univ. Press, 1993.

Harding, Sandra and Merrill Hintikka, eds. *Discovering Reality: Feminist Perspectives on Epistemology, Metaphysics, Methodology, and Philosophy of Science.* Dordrecht: Reidel, 1983.

Harding, Vincent. *There is a River: The Black Struggle for Freedom in America.* New York: Vintage, 1981.

Hay, Malcolm. *The Roots of Christian Anti-Semitism.* New York: Freedom Library Press, 1981.

Heyck, Denis Lynn Daly. *Barrios and Borderlands: Cultures of Latinos and Latinas in the United States.* New York: Routledge, 1994.

Holt, John. *Freedom and Beyond.* New York: Dell Publishing, 1972.

Holt, John. *Escape From Childhood: The Needs and Rights of Children.* New York: Ballantine Books, 1974.

hooks, bell. *Ain't I a Women: Black Women and Feminism.* Boston: South End Press, 1981.

hooks, bell. *Feminist Theory from Margin to Center.* Boston: South End Press, 1984.

hooks, bell. *Talking Back: Thinking Feminism, Thinking Black.* Boston: South End Press, 1989.

hooks, bell. *Yearning: Race, Gender, and Cultural Politics.* Boston: South End Press, 1990.

Horne, Gerald. *Reversing Discrimination: The Case for Affirmative Action.* New York: International Publishers, 1992.

Horton, Robin. *African Traditional Thought and Western Science pts. 1–2.* Africa 37. 1967.

Hountondji, Paulin. *African Philosophy: Myth and Reality*. Bloomington, Ind: Indiana Univ. Press, 1983.

Hoxie, Frederick E., ed. *Indians in American History*. Arlington Heights, Ill.: Harlan Davidson, 1988.

Jacob, Margaret. *The Cultural Meanings of the Scientific Revolution*. New York: Knopf, 1988.

Jaimes, M. Annette, ed. *The State of Native America: Genocide, Colonization, and Resistance*. Boston: South End Press, 1992.

Jay, Karla and Allen Young, eds. *Out of the Closets: Voices of Gay Liberation*. New York: Jove/HBJ, 1972.

Jennings, Francis. *The Invasion of America: Indians, Colonialism, and the Cant of Conquest*. New York: Norton, 1975.

Jewell, K. Sue. *From Mammy to Miss America and Beyond: Cultural Images and the Shaping of U.S. Social Policy*. New York: Routledge, 1993.

Jordan, June. *Technical Difficulties*. New York: Vintage Books, 1992.

Jordan, Winthrop. *White Over Black: American Attitudes Toward the Negro, 1550–1912*. Chapel Hill, N.C.: Univ. of North Carolina Press, 1968.

Judson, Stephanie, ed. *A Manual on Nonviolence and Children*. Philadelphia and Gabriola Island, B.C.: New Society Publishers, 1977.

Kamin, Leon, Richard Lewontin and Stephen Rose. *Not in Our Genes*. New York: Pantheon, 1984.

Katz, Judith H. *White Awareness: Handbook for Anti-Racism Training*. Norman, O.K.: Univ. of Oklahoma Press, 1978.

Katz, Phyllis A. and Dalmas A. Taylor, eds. *Eliminating Racism*. New York: Plenum, 1988.

Kaye/Kantrowitz, Melanie. *The Issue is Power: Essays on Women, Jews, Violence and Resistance*. San Francisco: Aunt Lute Books, 1992.

Kaye/Kantrowitz, Melanie and Irena Klepfisz, eds. *The Tribe of Dina: A Jewish Women's Anthology*. Montpelier, Vt.: Sinister Wisdom Books, 1986.

Kitzinger, Sheila and Celia Kitzinger. *Tough Questions: Talking Straight with Your Kids about the Real World*. Boston: Harvard Common Press, 1991.

Kivel, Paul. *Men's Work: How to Stop the Violence that Tears Our Lives Apart*. New York: Hazelden/Ballantine, 1992.

Knowles, Louis L. and Kenneth Prewitt, eds. *Institutionalized Racism in America*. Englewood Cliffs, N.J.: PrenticeHall, 1969.

Kohn, Alfie. *No Contest: The Case Against Competition*. Boston: Houghton Mifflin Company, 1986.

Kozol, Jonathan. *Savage Inequalities: Children in America's Schools*. New York: HarperCollins, 1991.

Ladner, Joyce, ed. *The Death of White Sociology*. New York: Random House, 1973.

Lapham, Lewis. *Money and Class in America*. New York: Weidenfeld and Nicolson, 1988.

Lerner, Gerda, ed. *Black Women in White America*. New York: Pantheon Books, 1972.

Lerner, Michael. *Surplus Powerlessness: The Psychodynamics of Everyday Life*. Oakland, Calif.: Institute for Labor and Mental Health, 1986.

Lerner, Michael. *The Socialism of Fools: Anti-Semitism on the Left.* Oakland, Calif.: Tikkun Books, 1992.

Lerner, Michael and Cornel West. *Jews and Blacks: Let the Healing Begin.* New York.: G.P. Putnam's Sons, 1995.

Lester, Joan Steinau. *The Future of White Men & other Diversity Dilemmas.* Berkeley, Calif.: Conari Press, 1994.

Levins, Richard and Richard Lewontin. *The Dialectical Biologist.* Cambridge, Mass.: Harvard Univ. Press, 1987.

Lloyd, Genevieve. *The Man of Reason: "Male" and "Female" in Western Philosophy.* Minneapolis: Univ. of Minnesota Press, 1984.

Lorde, Audre. *Sister Outsider: Essays and Speeches.* Freedom, Calif.: Crossing Press, 1984.

Lowe, Marian and Ruth Hubbard, eds. *Woman's Nature: Rationalizations of Inequality.* New York: Pergamon Press, 1983.

Madhubuti, Haki R. *Black Men, Obsolete, Single, Dangerous? The Afrikan American Family in Transition.* Chicago: Third World Press, 1990.

Majors, Richard and Janet Mancini Billson. *Cool Pose: The Dilemmas of Black Manhood in America.* New York: Touchstone, 1992.

Mallon, Gerald L., ed. *Resisting Racism: An Action Guide.* San Francisco: National Association of Black and White Men Together, 1991.

Manmer, Jalna and Mary Maynard, eds. *Women, Violence and Social Control.* Atlantic Highlands, N.J.: Humanities Press International, 1987.

Marable, Manning. *The Crisis of Color and Democracy: Essays on Race, Class and Power.* Monroe, Maine: Common Courage Press, 1992.

Martin, Emily. *The Women in the Body.* Boston: Beacon Press, 1987.

Mason-John, Valerie and Ann Khambatta. *Making Black Waves: Lesbians Talk.* London: Scarlet Press, 1993.

McCarthy, Cameron and Warren Crichlow, eds. *Race Identity and Representation in Education.* New York: Routledge, 1993.

McGinnis, Kathleen and Barbara Oehlberg. *Starting Out Right: Nurturing Young Children as Peacemakers.* New York: Crossroad Publishing, 1988.

McIntosh, Peggy. *White Privilege and Male Privilege: A Personal Account of Coming to See Correspondences Through Work in Women's Studies.* Wellesley College, Wellesley, Mass.: Center for Research on Women, 1988.

McLaurin, Melton A. *Separate Pasts: Growing Up White in the Segregated South.* Athens, Ga.: Univ. of Georgia Press, 1987.

Meier, Matt and Feliciano Rivera. *The Chicanos: A History of Mexican Americans.* New York: Hill and Wang, 1972.

Memmi, Albert (trans. by Howard Greenfield). *The Colonizer and the Colonized.* Boston: Beacon Press, 1965.

Miedzian, Myriam. *Boys Will be Boys: Breaking the Link Between Masculinity and Violence.* New York: Doubleday, 1991.

Mies, Maria. *Patriarchy and Accumulation on a World Scale: Women in the International Division of Labour.* London: Zed Books, 1986.

Mies, Maria, Veronika BennholdtThomsen and Claudia von Werlhof. *Women: The Last Colony*. London: Zed Books, 1988.

Mohawk, John. *Exiled in the Land of the Free: Democracy, the Indian Nations, and the U.S. Constitution*. Santa Fe, N.M.: Clear Light Publishers, 1992.

Moraga, Cherrie and Gloria Anzaldua, eds. *This Bridge Called My Back: Writings by Radical Women of Color*. New York: Kitchen Table—Women of Color Press, 1981.

Morrison, Toni, ed. *Race-ing Justice, En-gendering Power: Essays on Anita Hill, Clarence Thomas, and the Construction of Social Reality*. New York: Pantheon, 1992.

Morrison, Toni. *Playing in the Dark: Whiteness and the Literary Imagination*. Cambridge, Mass.: Harvard Univ. Press, 1992.

Mosse, George L. *Toward the Final Solution: A History of European Racism*. New York: Howard Fertig, 1978.

Mudimbe, V. Y. *The Invention of Africa: Gnosis, Philosophy, and the Order of Knowledge*. Bloomington, Ind.: Indiana Univ. Press, 1988.

Nasr, Seyyed Hossein. *Islamic Science: An Illustrated Study*. London: World of Islam Festival Publishing, 1976.

Nicholson, Linda J., ed. *Feminism/Postmodernism*. New York: Routledge, 1989.

Nowotny, Helga and Rose Hilary, eds. *Counter-Movements in the Sciences: The Sociology of the Alternatives to Big Science*. Dordrecht: Reidel, 1979.

Ogawa, Brian. *Color of Justice: Culturally Sensitive Treatment of Minority Crime Victims*. Sacramento, Calif.: Office of the Governor, State of California, 1990.

Okihiro, Gary Y. *Margins and Mainstreams: Asians in American History and Culture*. Seattle: Univ. of Washington Press, 1994.

Omi, Michael and Howard Winant. *Racial Formation in the United States: From the 1960s to the 1990s*. New York: Routledge, 1986.

Orfalea, Gregory. *Before the Flames: A Quest for the History of Arab Americans*. Austin, Tex.: Univ. of Texas Press, 1988.

Orlick, Terry. *The Cooperative Sports and Games Book: Challenge Without Competition*. New York: Pantheon, 1978.

Paley, V. *Bad Guys Don't Have Birthdays: Fantasy Play at Four*. Chicago: Univ. of Chicago Press, 1984.

Peachey, J. Lorne. *How to Teach Peace to Children*. Scottdale, Penna.: Herald Press, 1981.

Piven, Frances Fox and Richard A. Cloward. *Poor People's Movements: How They Succeed, Why They Fail*. New York: Vintage, 1979.

Piven, Frances Fox and Richard A. Cloward. *Regulating the Poor: The Functions of Public Welfare*. New York: Vintage Books, 1971.

Platt, Tony and Suzie Dod Thomas, eds. "Rethinking Race." *Social Justice*, Vol. 20, Nos. 1–2. 1993.

Pleck, Elizabeth. "Rape and the Politics of Race, 1865–1910." Center for Research on Women, Working Paper No. 213, Wellesley, Mass.: Wellesley College, 1990.

Pogrebin, Letty Cottin. *Growing Up Free: Raising Your Child in the 1980s*. San Francisco: McGraw Hill, 1980.

Pratt, Minnie Bruce. *Rebellion: Essays 1980–1991*. Ithaca, N.Y.: Firebrand Books, 1991.

Prutzman, Priscilla, Lee Stern, M. Leonard Burger and Gretchen Bodenhamer. *The Friendly Classroom for a Small Planet: A Handbook on Creative Approaches to Living and Problem Solving for Children.* Philadelphia and Gabriola Island, B.C.: New Society Publishers, 1988.

Rank, Mark R. *Living on the Edge: The Realities of Welfare in America.* New York: Columbia Univ. Press, 1994.

Reiter, Rayna Rapp, ed. *Toward an Anthropology of Women.* New York: Monthly Review Press, 1975.

Rich, Adrienne. *On Lies, Secrets and Silence: Selected Prose, 1966–1978.* New York: W.W. Norton, 1979.

Ridgeway, James. *Blood in the Face: The Ku Klux Klan, Aryan Nations, Nazi Skinheads, and the Rise of a New White Culture.* New York: Thunder's Mouth Press, 1990.

Riley, Sue Spayth. *How to Generate Values in Young Children.* Washington, D.C.: National Association for the Education of Young Children, 1984.

Rodney, Walter. *How Europe Underdeveloped Africa.* Washington, D.C.: Howard Univ. Press, 1982.

Roediger, David R. *Towards the Abolition of Whiteness.* London: Verso, 1994.

Roediger, David R. *The Wages of Whiteness: Race and the Making of the American Working Class.* London: Verso, 1991.

Root, Maria P., ed. *Racially Mixed People in America.* Newbury Park, Calif.: Sage Publications, 1992.

Rossides, Daniel. *The American Class System.* Boston: Houghton Mifflin, 1976.

Rothenberg, Paula S. *Racism and Sexism: An Integrated Study.* New York: St. Martin's Press, 1988.

Rubin, Lillian B. *Families on the Fault Line.* New York: HarperCollins, 1994.

Rubin, Lilian B. *Worlds of Pain: Life in the Working Class.* New York: Basic Books, 1976.

Ruether, Rosemary Radford. *Faith and Fratricide: The Theological Roots of Anti-Semitism.* New York: Seabury Press, 1974.

Ryan, William. *Blaming the Victim.* New York: Pantheon Books, 1971.

Said, Edward. *Orientalism.* New York: Random House, 1978.

Santoli, Al. *New Americans: An Oral History.* New York: Ballantine, 1988.

Saracho, Olivia N. and Bernard Spodek, eds. *Understanding the Multicultural Experience in Early Childhood Education.* Washington, D.C.: National Association for the Education of Young Children, 1983.

Schetcher, Susan. *Women and Male Violence: The Visions and Struggles of the Battered Women's Movement.* Boston: South End Press, 1982.

Schniedewind, Nancy and Ellen Davidson. *Open Minds to Equality: A Sourcebook of Learning Activities to Promote Race, Sex, Class and Age Equity.* Englewood Cliffs, N.J.: PrenticeHall, 1983.

Schoem, David, ed. *Inside Separate Worlds: Life Stories of Young Blacks, Jews and Latinos.* Ann Arbor, Mich.: Univ. of Michigan, 1991.

Segal, Lynne. *Slow Motion: Changing Masculinities, Changing Men.* New Brunswick, N.J.: Rutgers Univ. Press, 1990.

Segrest, Mab. *Memoirs of a Race Traitor.* Boston: South End Press, 1994.

Sennett, Richard and Jonathan Cobb. *The Hidden Injuries of Class*. New York: Vintage Books, 1972.

Shapiro, Joseph P. *No Pity: People with Disabilities Forging a New Civil Rights Movement*. New York: Random House, 1993.

Shor, Ira. *Critical Teaching and Everyday Life*. Boston: South End Press, 1980.

Sivanandan A. *Communities of Resistance: Writing on Black Struggles for Socialism*. London: Verso, 1990.

Sklar, Holly. *Chaos or Community? Seeking Solutions, Not Scapegoats for Bad Economics*. Boston: South End Press, 1995.

Smith, Barbara, ed. *Home Girls: A Black Feminist Anthology*. New York: Kitchen Table—Women of Color Press, 1983.

Smith, Lillian. *Killers of the Dream*. New York: W.W. Norton, 1961.

Sojourners. *America's Original Sin: A Study Guide on White Racism*. Washington, D.C.: Sojourners, 1992.

Spelman, Elizabeth V. *Inessential Woman: Problems of Exclusion in Feminist Thought*. Boston: Beacon Press, 1988.

Spivak, Gayatri Chakravorty. *In Other Worlds: Essays in Cultural Politics*. New York: Methuen, 1987.

Steiner, Stan. *The New Indians*. San Francisco: Harper Colophon, 1968.

Stalvey, Lois. *The Education of a Wasp*. New York: Bantam Books, 1971.

Stalvey, Lois Mark. *Getting Ready*. New York: Bantam Books, 1974.

Staples, Robert. *Black Masculinity: The Black Male's Role in American Society*. San Francisco: Black Scholar Press, 1982.

Stepan, Nancy. *Race and Gender: The Role of Analogy in Science*. Isis 77. 1986.

Stoltenberg, John. *The End of Manhood: A Book for Men of Conscience*. New York: Dutton, 1993.

Sway, Marlene. *Familiar Strangers: Gypsy Life in America*. Urbana, Ill.: Univ. of Illinois, 1988.

Swerdlow, Amy and Hanna Lessingler, eds. *Class, Race, and Sex*. Boston: G. K. Hall, 1983.

Takagi, Dana Y. *The Retreat from Race: Asian Admissions and Racial Politics*. New Brunswick, N.J.: Rutgers Univ. Press, 1993.

Takaki, Ronald. *Strangers From a Different Shore: A History of Asian Americans*. New York: Penguin, 1989.

Takaki, Ronald. *A Different Mirror: A History of Multicultural America*. Boston: Little, Brown and Company, 1993.

Takaki, Ronald, ed. *From Different Shores: Perspectives on Race and Ethnicity in America*. New York: Oxford Univ. Press, 1987.

Terkel, Studs. *Race: How Blacks and Whites Think and Feel About the American Obsession*. New York: New Press, 1992.

Terry, Robert W. *For Whites Only*. Grand Rapids, Mich.: William B. Eerdmans, 1970.

Tolley, Howard Jr. *Children and War: Political Socialization to International Conflict*. New York: Teachers College Press, 1973.

Turner, Margery Austin, Michael Fix and Raymond J. Struyk. *Opportunities Denied: Discrimination in Hiring*. Washington, D.C.: Urban Institute, 1991.

Van Sertima, Ivan. *They Came Before Columbus*. New York: Random House, 1976.

Van Sertima, Ivan, ed. *Blacks in Science: Ancient and Modern*. New Brunswick, N.J.: Transaction Books, 1986.

Vanneman, Reeve and Lynn Weber Cannon. *The American Perception of Class*. Philadelphia: Temple Univ. Press, 1987.

Vasquez, Hugh and Isoke Femi. *No Boundaries: A Manual for Unlearning Oppression and Building Multicultural Alliances*. Oakland, Calif.: TODOS Institute, 1993.

Ware, Vron. *Beyond the Pale: White Women, Racism and History*. London: Verso, 1992.

Waters, Mary. *Ethnic Options*. Berkeley, Calif.: Univ. of California Press, 1990.

Weatherford, Jack. *Indian Givers: How the Indians of the Americas Transformed the World*. New York: Fawcett/Columbine, 1988.

Weatherford, Jack. *Native Roots: How the Indians Enriched America*. New York: Crown Books, 1991.

Weiler, Kathleen. *Women Teaching for Change: Gender, Class & Power*. South Hadley, Mass.: Bergin and Garvey Publishers, 1988.

Wellman, David, ed. *Portraits of White Racism*. New York: Cambridge Univ. Press, 1977.

West, Cornel. *Prophetic Reflections: Notes on Race and Power in America*. Monroe, Maine: Common Courage Press, 1993.

West, Cornel. *Race Matters*. New York: Vintage, 1993.

Wilkinson, Doris Y. and Ronald L. Taylor, eds. *The Black Male in America*. Chicago: NelsonHall, 1977.

Winant, Howard. *Racial Conditions: Politics Theory Comparisons*. Minneapolis: Univ. of Minnesota Press, 1994.

Women's Action Coalition. *Stats: The Facts About Women*. New York: New Press, 1993.

Wright, Richard A., ed. *African Philosophy: An Introduction*. Washington, D.C.: University Press of America, 1979.

Zinn, Howard *A People's History of the United States*. New York: Harper Colophon, 1980.